American Indians
in World War I

American Indians in World War I

At Home and at War

THOMAS A. BRITTEN

UNIVERSITY OF NEW MEXICO PRESS
Albuquerque

© 1997 by the University of New Mexico Press
All rights reserved.
First paperbound printing, 1999

Library of Congress Cataloging-in-Publication Data

Britten, Thomas A. (Thomas Anthony), 1964–
American Indians in World War I at home and at war /
Thomas A. Britten.—1st ed.
p. cm.
Includes bibliographical references and index.
ISBN 0-8263-1804-5   ISBN 0-8263-2090-2 (pbk.)
1. World War, 1914–1918—Participation, Indian. 2. United States—Armed
Forces—Indians. 3. Indians of North America—History—20th century.
4. Indian veterans—United States. I. Title.
D570.8.I6B75   1997
940.4'03—dc21   97-4685
                                    CIP

To Connie,

Zachary,

and Reuben

Contents

Acknowledgments

I gratefully acknowledge my indebtedness to the faculty and staff at Texas Tech University in Lubbock, Texas, for their assistance in the early phases of this book's preparation. In particular, Dr. Paul H. Carlson, Professor of History, guided and supported the formation and development of the early drafts, as well as providing expert editing and sharing his keen insights into Native American history. The staff at the Texas Tech University Library was always glad to help, as were the archivists at the school's Southwest Collection.

I also extend my thanks to the staff at the Oklahoma State Historical Society in Oklahoma City and to the various libraries around the country that house sections of the Doris Duke Indian Oral History Collections (University of Oklahoma and University of South Dakota in particular)—sources that were indispensable in helping to gain a better understanding of Indian perspectives on the war. The folks at the National Archives in Washington, D.C., and at the Federal Records Center in Suitland, Maryland, were also very helpful. Ann Cummings, who works at the National Archives was my conduit to various record groups and her aid was much appreciated.

Dr. Tom Kavanaugh and the staff at the William Hammond Mathers Museum in Bloomington, Indiana, were a great help—particularly in allowing easy access to the Joseph K. Dixon Collection and to the photographs of the various Wanamaker Expeditions.

I also wish to thank the faculty and staff at Briar Cliff College in Sioux City, Iowa. Beth Heck and Sr. Mary Jane Koenigs in the interlibrary loan department were always willing to offer assistance and to go the extra mile to acquire needed materials. Phil Hey, Professor of English, helped edit the manuscript and his expert critique—both on form and content—was most useful.

Finally, I extend my gratitude to David Holtby and the editorial staff at the University of New Mexico Press, and to Dr. Donald Parman, Professor of

History at Purdue University, who served as an outside reviewer of the book. His critiques and advice were outstanding.

As is the case with most books, this one was a "community effort." However, every author must, in the end, exercise his/her own best judgment concerning matters of style and interpretation. Consequently, I bear full responsibility for any omissions, errors, or shortcomings.

American Indians
in World War I

Introduction

LATE ONE EVENING DURING THE SUMMER OF 1918, A PARTY OF twenty men from Company I, Fourth Artillery Regiment, made its way quietly across No Man's Land toward enemy lines near the Champagne sector in northern France. Night patrols are a dangerous duty in any war but were especially so during World War I, a conflict that one contemporary politician described as the "maddest orgy of blood, rapine, and murder which history records."[1] Initially each side employed nineteenth-century tactics that allowed for massive frontal assaults across open fields, but the development and use of high-powered rifles and machine guns by both the Central and Entente Powers soon forced opposing armies underground into vast networks of trenches. Nonetheless, the threat of death remained constant—from artillery barrages, poison-gas attacks, snipers, and disease.

Before stepping outside the relative security of their trench into No Man's Land, members of the patrol party must have experienced conflicting emotions—fear, foreboding, anxiety, perhaps even excitement. By all accounts, patrol duty was a nerve-wracking experience and every rattle of a tin can or loose piece of wire that littered the battlefield sent soldiers sprawling for cover.[2] A common mistake and thus an immediate source of concern was the possibility that the patrol might lose its way in the dark and stumble blindly into an enemy position. Consequently, each member of the patrol placed great faith in the man sent out front to guide them. On this particular mission, a Blackfoot Indian named Johnson, a former student at the Carlisle Indian Industrial School in Pennsylvania, received orders to lead the patrol. Johnson probably was not surprised. He had been out on an earlier patrol and was already familiar with the terrain ahead.

It was not uncommon for the men of Company I to rely upon Private Johnson to guide them back and forth through No Man's Land, on all-night marches and through the forests of north-central France. After all, he was an American Indian, and many of his comrades and officers believed that Indians had a natural aptitude for scouting, tracking, and the art of concealment. Johnson consequently seemed the logical choice to lead dangerous patrols and reconnaissance missions—to be his unit's "eyes and ears" on the Western Front.

On July 18, 1918, however, Private Johnson exceeded expectations and distinguished himself by performing several extraordinary acts of valor. Although wounded himself, he went out into No Man's Land to rescue a fallen comrade, hoisted the injured soldier up on his shoulders, and carried the man back to safety. Throughout the remainder of the night, Johnson continued to aid his colleagues by carrying blankets and other supplies to those who were lying wounded in the field.[3]

Private Johnson was only one of thousands of American Indians who served in the American Expeditionary Force during World War I. Unfortunately, Native American contributions have been largely ignored or discarded as too peripheral and insignificant to warrant serious attention. Even military studies of World War I neglect the participation of American Indians. Historians who have written on twentieth-century Native American topics have, instead, concentrated their studies on the long-term impact of the Dawes Act of 1887, the Indian Reorganization Act of 1934, or the Indian reform movements of the 1960s and 1970s. Less well known are the activities of American Indians during the first three decades after 1900, a period in Native American history that Francis Paul Prucha has described as "singularly devoid of serious historical studies."[4]

An examination of Native American roles in World War I is essential if one hopes to understand the evolution of Indian societies, cultures, and federal Indian policy in the early decades of the twentieth century. Providing a broad survey of Indian contributions during World War I, both at home and in Western Europe, is the major aim of this study. A second but related objective is to demonstrate the diversity and complexity of Indian responses to the war—both at home and abroad. A final aim is to show how Indian military service acted as a catalyst for change. The war years witnessed important modifications in Indian policy that affected thousands of Native Americans. Wartime service also had the ironic effect of altering public perceptions of Indian peoples on the one hand, while reinforcing popular racial stereotypes on the other. Military service provided thousands of Indian men with new educational opportunities and allowed them to escape, at least for a while, the confines of reservations and boarding schools. Military life also presented Native American soldiers with a chance to witness different lifestyles and cultures. Activities such as these exerted a considerable influence on many Indian soldiers and their families.

The book is arranged both topically and chronologically. The first chapter, "Indian Soldiers Prior to World War I," lays the historical foundation for Native American service in the United States Army from the colonial era up to the twentieth century. Particular attention is given to Native American activities in the 1890s, when army officials experimented with segregated Indian units. The army's assessment of the experiment later proved to be decisive in deliberations during World War I about segregated units for Native Americans.

The second chapter, "Indian Soldiers and the Issue of Segregated Troops," introduces the debate between assimilationists and preservationists over the direction of Indian policy and reform; it places the issue of segregating Indian soldiers within the context of that discussion. The activities of Dr. Joseph Kossuth Dixon, the eccentric, vain, and often Janus-faced reformer who championed the idea of creating all Indian units during and after World War I, are particularly important and receive a good deal of scrutiny. Finally, the chapter discusses Dixon's subsequent activities as a member of the American Indian Defense Association and his largely symbolic importance in the debate over the direction of Indian policy in the 1920s.

Chapter 3 discusses the responses of various Indian peoples to draft registration and to conscription itself. Why did Indian men enlist for service in such large numbers? Were there cases of draft resistance among Native Americans? What motivated Indian men to take up arms in defense of a nation whose Anglo majority had failed to recognize all Native Americans as citizens and had disenfranchised many of those who were citizens?

Indian contributions on the Western Front—both in combat and support roles—provide the foci of the next two chapters. Chapter 4 presents a general chronology of Indian military activities on the Western Front. Chapter 5 gives an evaluation of the effectiveness of Indian soldiers, the prevalence of racial stereotypes, and the impact of popular misconceptions on the types of jobs and duties that Native Americans performed.

In order to get a better appreciation and understanding of how the treatment of American Indian soldiers compared with that of other racial minorities during World War I, Chapter 6, "American Indians and Other Minorities in World War I," describes the treatment that military officials and the general public accorded to African American and Mexican American soldiers in the American Expeditionary Force. To broaden the comparison further, the role and treatment of Native American soldiers is compared with that of their Indian brethren in Canada, with France's utilization of Senegalese soldiers from West Africa, and with England's deployment of Indian soldiers from south-central Asia.

Chapter 7, "The Indian Homefront and the BIA," examines, among other things, the contributions of Indian noncombatants during the war. Native American women, farmers, and students, for example, sacrificed much and went to great lengths to demonstrate their loyalty and support for their loved ones overseas. Meanwhile, the Bureau of Indian Affairs stepped up its campaign to promote Indian self-sufficiency and assimilation. Indian health care and education, seldom a major priority for government officials and policymakers, suffered substantial cuts in funding during the war. The results, not surprisingly, were devastating for many Native Americans.

Chapter 8, "Indian Veterans in the Postwar Era," attempts to determine what became of the Indian veterans of World War I. Unfortunately, few oral histories and no quantitative analyses or statistical records exist to trace their postwar careers and salaries or to demonstrate conclusively how wartime lessons affected their lives. So what happened to the Indian veterans of World War I? How did military service impact their lives and that of their families? Were veterans able to translate their wartime training and experiences into improved jobs and economic mobility or, perhaps, into tribal leadership roles? Did Native American contributions during World War I lead to the passage of Indian citizenship laws? By examining the postwar careers of several individual Native American veterans from different Indian nations, by referring to oral histories of veterans who survived the war, by consulting the annual reports of the commissioner of Indian affairs, and by studying how service in other wars affected Indian veterans, one can draw tentative conclusions about how service in the "war to end all wars" affected the lives of at least a small sample of Indian veterans and their families.

Seventy-five years have passed since the end of World War I. While hundreds of books detail the activities of Anglo American soldiers in the war and perhaps half a dozen describe the service of African Americans, the contributions of Native Americans have yet to receive adequate attention. One should keep in mind, however, that there was no monolithic "Indian experience" during World War I. The war affected individual Indian people in diverse ways. Some Indian nations sent hundreds of their men to war while others escaped the terrors of trench warfare altogether. Thus, one must be cautious in discussing the "Indian experience" or the "Indian role" and remember that Native Americans are not a homogenous people but hundred of separate nations with unique languages, customs, and traditions.

As Provost Marshal General Enoch H Crowder noted in 1919, the overwhelming majority of American Indian soldiers nobly showed their "zeal for the great cause," and he predicted that the story of their wartime contributions would "someday be told in full."[5] The story begins with American Indian soldiers before World War I.

1

Indian Soldiers
Prior to World War I

ONE OF THE PARADOXES IN NATIVE AMERICAN HISTORY IS THAT MANY
Indian peoples cooperated with Europeans in the latter's conquest of the con-
tinent. By trading with, scouting for, and at times fighting beside Euro-Ameri-
cans against other indigenous peoples, the American Indians hastened Anglo
expansion west and, eventually, their own confinement to reservations.
Viewed from an Indian perspective, however, such factionalism was natural
and advantageous, for, as Gary Nash has written, the word *Indian* is a term
invented by Europeans to describe "a great variety of peoples who did not
think of themselves as united in any racial, political, or even cultural sense."[1]
Viewed in this light, the Native Americans took advantage of the Europeans'
advanced weaponry and technology for use against their traditional Indian
enemies.

The Anglo use of Indian scouts or auxiliaries in North America dates
from the colonial era. In 1637 the Narragansetts allied with the British against
the Pequots, and during King Philip's War (1675–1676) the Wampanoags
suffered defeat at the hands of a combined British-Mohawk army. The French
and Indian War (1754–1763) witnessed the tribes of the Iroquois Confederation as well as the Hurons, Chippewas, Delawares, Cherokees, Chickasaws,
Ottawas, and Shawnees fighting alongside French and British troops. A decade and a half later, the Iroquois Confederation split over whether to support the American colonists' war for independence. Choctaws and Chickasaws
served with General Anthony Wayne at the Battle of Fallen Timbers in 1794,
and General Andrew Jackson employed Creek and Cherokee scouts and auxiliaries in the War of 1812 and later against the Seminoles in Florida.

With the outbreak of the Civil War in 1861, both Union and Confederate
governments sought to establish alliances with Native Americans in the Indian Territory. The Union War Department, under the guidance of Secretary
Simon Cameron, initially opposed the enlistment of Indians. Northern mili-

tary officials feared that, once in battle, Native Americans would revert to "savagery," an idea not at all appealing to officers who had close friends and relatives fighting for the Confederacy. In response to the efforts of Confederate emissary Albert Pike in gaining Indian allies for the South, however, President Abraham Lincoln gave his approval of a plan to create a "Home Guard" of Indian troops whose primary duty was to defend the Indian Territory for the North.

Consequently, most of the Civil War battles in which American Indians participated took place in the Indian Territory; the Battle of Wilson's Creek, Missouri, in August 1861, and the Battles of Pea Ridge, Arkansas, in March 1862, and Honey Springs, Arkansas, in July 1863 were notable exceptions. Ironically, in late June 1865 the last Confederate officer to surrender to Union officials was General Stand Watie, a Cherokee who had commanded the Confederate Indian Cavalry Brigade during the last months of the war.[2]

On the western frontier, meanwhile, Major General Samuel R. Curtis, commanding the Department of Kansas, conceived the idea of utilizing Pawnee scouts. During the Civil War he hoped to use the Pawnees with regular troops to subdue the Sioux as well as to protect the construction of the Union Pacific railroad from Indian attack. Since they were long-time enemies of the Sioux, General Curtis believed that the Pawnees would be useful and trustworthy allies. In pursuance of this plan, in 1864 Curtis commissioned Frank North to go to the Pawnee agency and organize a troop of scouts. Once among the Pawnees, North enjoyed great success and within a short time had recruited some one hundred men. North's men received the pay of cavalrymen (about thirteen dollars a month for a private) and maintained their headquarters at Fort Kearney, Nebraska.[3] For the next thirteen years, North's "Pawnee Battalion," as it was called, served with a loyalty and distinction that inspired other western commanders to experiment with Indian scouts.

Native American participation in the Civil War, the example of the Pawnee scouts, and the renewed threat of Indian uprisings in the West after 1865 encouraged military officials to regularize the use of Indian scouts and auxiliaries. The establishment of these special units gained official approval when, in 1866, Congress passed the Army Reorganization Act. The law increased the number of cavalry regiments from six to ten and the number of infantry regiments from nineteen to forty-five. It also allowed for the enlistment of up to one thousand Indian scouts for six-month periods. The official order for the enlistment came on August 1, 1866, in General Order Number Fifty-six. For the next twenty years Indian soldiers served the frontier army as scouts, trackers, interpreters, and advisers. Although Indian scout activity peaked by the mid-1880s, the army continued periodically to employ special detachments of scouts until the United States entry, in 1917, into World War I.[4]

Native Americans chose to enlist as scouts for several reasons. As in colonial times, weaker tribes saw alliances with whites as essential to their survival vis-à-vis stronger tribes. Thus the Pawnees could readily be recruited to fight the Sioux, their traditional tribal foe. Another reason was their understanding that more could be obtained through alliance with the Anglos than through resistance. Indian scouts not only earned the pay of cavalrymen but also received food rations, clothing, and ammunition. Combined with annuity payments, such earnings often allowed their families to enjoy a better standard of living than that of other tribal members.

Moreover, serving as an army scout provided warriors with a chance to adjust to a more restricted lifestyle on a reservation. Military operations among Sioux warriors, for example, had once ensured them opportunities to obtain security, honor, prestige, and wealth, and to enact revenge on enemies. Warfare, Royal B. Hassrick has noted, nurtured essential aspects of the Sioux psyche.[5] But the seclusion of American Indians on reservations restricted the warriors' opportunities to achieve security and status. After detention on reservations, according to Francis Paul Prucha, "large numbers of the formerly energetic and aggressive warriors became enervated and dispirited recipients of the dole."[6] Thus, service as army scouts provided many young men with opportunities to achieve prominence among their people as well as a temporary respite against the social and economic confines of reservations.

General George Crook was another early employer of Indian scouts. In 1871 Crook enlisted Apaches for six-month tours of duty and organized them into companies under the leadership of white officers. During the spring of 1883, Crook led 193 Apaches and 42 regular cavalrymen into Mexico in search of Chiricahua Apache leaders Geronimo, Nana, and Chato. Crook's use of Indian scouts reportedly demoralized his Apache adversaries to the extent that many surrendered when they realized that their own kinsmen were tracking them.[7]

When he took command of the U.S. Army in 1883, General Philip H. Sheridan questioned Crook's strategy of using large numbers of Indian scouts. Sheridan never fully trusted the employment of Native Americans and ordered Crook to make better use of traditional cavalry. When he refused to carry out Sheridan's orders, Crook lost command of the Department of Arizona and subsequently received a transfer to the northern plains. His replacement, General Nelson A. Miles, attempted to carry out Sheridan's ban on the extensive use of Apache scouts but soon reverted to the policies of his predecessor.[8]

Sheridan was not alone in his skepticism about the utility of Native American soldiers. Like "Little Phil," many officers, driven by ethnocentrism and a basic misunderstanding about Indian attitudes toward war, distrusted Indian scouts and questioned their capabilities as soldiers. Contrary to conventional army wisdom, Indians viewed war as a temporary exercise that offered individual warriors opportunities to humiliate enemies without suffering heavy casualties. Waged mostly for revenge and prestige, Indian battles were usually hit-and-run skirmishes and rarely involved large standing armies or protracted sieges. Misinterpreting Indian attitudes about warfare, traditional or "old school" officers complained that Indians made unreliable allies, lacked discipline, and, at times, exhibited cowardice.[9]

Officers stationed in the East opposed reliance on Indian auxiliaries for additional reasons. They maintained, for example, that the practice made the army appear weak and incapable of controlling a small but powerful minority. Many of the officers had never commanded Indian troops or tried to track the mobile Apaches through the mountains and deserts of New Mexico and Arizona.[10]

In the West, however, few experienced commanders expressed reluctance to make use of Native Americans. Many, in fact, complained that they could never get enough Indian scouts. To them, the scouts added strength to deficient units, and their psychological impact on the enemy was an important deterrent to Apaches who hoped to escape reservation life. Because of their knowledge of Native American languages and customs, Indian scouts were also instrumental in conducting parleys with the enemy.[11] Many Apache scouts had served formerly with such military leaders as Geronimo or Victorio and could, therefore, provide useful strategic advice to their army commanders.

Within a decade of the passage of the Army Reorganization Act of 1866, some military and civilian officials suggested that the government expand the military use of Native Americans. In an article published in the *North American Review* in April 1873, Commissioner of Indian Affairs Francis A. Walker (1871–1873) endorsed the enlistment of Indians as regular soldiers. Military duty, he maintained, would keep Indians loyal to the government and out of trouble. The employment of Indians as soldiers or scouts, therefore, was not only justifiable, but "highly expedient."[12] Walker argued further that unlike veterans of the Civil War to whom the federal government owed pensions, Indian veterans would be easy to discharge and unlikely to file for benefits. In the long run, he reasoned, Indian soldiers would be more practical and cheaper than outfitting and maintaining regular cavalry troops.[13]

Other important officials supported the idea. In 1876 General William T. Sherman suggested the establishment of an "Indian Guard" to help maintain order among the tribes, and two years later Commissioner of Indian Affairs Ezra Hayt (1877–1880) proposed the formation of an Indian auxiliary of three thousand men to supplement army strength west of the Mississippi River. Coinciding with these efforts was congressional authorization and an appropriation in May 1878 for the establishment of Indian police forces at several western agencies. However, humanitarian and religious reform groups feared that military employment would be counterproductive to their plans of transforming nomadic Indians into sedentary farmers. Their opposition and the reluctance of the War Department kept the role of Indians in the army from expanding.

The failure of President Ulysses S. Grant's controversial "Peace Policy," however, led to important personnel changes in the Indian bureau. Grant had hoped to improve the sordid reputation of the Indian office by appointing prominent religious and humanitarian reformers as officials in the Bureau of Indian Affairs (BIA) and as agents on reservations. Efficient and honest administration, moreover, would encourage assimilation. But an insufficient number of qualified applicants, dissension within the various Christian denominations over appointments, and a new administration in the White House led to the policy's demise. Consequently, in the 1880s control of Indian affairs returned to patronage-dispensing politicians with far less altruistic objectives in mind for Native Americans. The development removed one of the primary obstacles (that being humanitarian and religious reformers) to an expanded role for Indians in the army.[14]

Still committed to Indian assimilation and able to exercise an influential voice in formulating Indian policy despite their loss of official status, humanitarians during the 1880s geared their efforts toward the disintegration of tribal governments and the "individualization" of American Indians. Only through individual ownership of property, so their thinking went, could the Indians retain possession of their lands and become productive citizens. The culmination of humanitarian efforts came in 1887 with the passage of the Dawes Severalty Act (or General Allotment Act), which authorized federal authorities to divide tribal lands into individual allotments. The Indian allottees were granted immediate citizenship and the federal government held their lands in trust for twenty-five years. Despite being touted by overly optimistic reformers as the "Indian Emancipation Act," the Dawes Act proved to be the nemesis of Native American life, landholdings, and cultures for decades.

Complementing the Dawes Act's promise of "individualizing" Indians through allotment was the federal government's growing involvement in Indian education. Impressed with Captain Richard Henry Pratt's model for Indian education at the Carlisle Indian Industrial School in Pennsylvania—which combined academic and vocational education with strong military-style discipline—Congress appropriated funds in the 1880s and 1890s for the construction of several other off-reservation boarding schools. "Vast in scope, military in organization, fervent in zeal, and violent in method," as one author has described them, off-reservation boarding schools were an important part of the federal government's educational crusade to transform and assimilate young Indian people. Marching and drill, Indian school administrators believed, taught order, discipline, punctuality, and self-control—attributes that would be needed if young Indian men were to become assimilated farmers, wage earners, and property holders. Indian girls, meanwhile, received instruction in the "domestic sciences" (that is, cooking, sewing, housekeeping), and by their example, school officials hoped, they would transmit Anglo cultural values to their husbands and children.[15]

Meanwhile, several military officials concluded that enlisting Indian soldiers would both expedite assimilation and serve the interests of the army. Consequently, officers presented their arguments for Indian units by stressing both the humanitarians' assimilationist-oriented goals and their own strategic and tactical interests. They reasoned, for example, that military service would provide work for reservation Indians, including troublesome young warriors. Rations and pay for Indian recruits, army officials argued, would supplement government issues of food and clothing made on reservations and perhaps relieve some of the poverty and misery associated with reservation life. Advocates of Indian enlistment also maintained that military service would weaken tribal ties and foster individualism. Indian recruits would live on military posts and receive their own monthly salaries, thereby aiding in the "individualization" of Native American soldiers. Army officials further suggested that enlisting Indians would give the military (rather than the Department of the Interior) greater control over the administration of Indian affairs, something the War Department believed was long overdue. Finally, military officials believed that the enlistment of Native Americans might improve Anglo–Indian relations by conveying the army's trust and respect for Indians. By the 1880s, therefore, many assimilationists had become convinced that the triad of allotment, education, and military service would provide a solution to the "Indian problem" that had stumped government bureaucrats and other "friends of the Indians" for decades.[16]

The movement for Indian military service continued to evolve during the 1880s. In an article published in *The United Service* (a military-service magazine) in the fall of 1880, Captain H. C. Cushing, Fourth Artillery, advocated the "military colonization" of Native Americans, whereby Indians would be organized into military settlements under the supervision of white officers. Military discipline and training would be encouraged and result in "the destruction of the tribal idea and the cultivation of individuality" among American Indians.[17]

Three years later, the United States Senate passed a resolution calling on its committee on Indian affairs to investigate the possibility of establishing a military academy west of the Mississippi River to train Indian youths for military service. Not surprisingly, army commander Philip H. Sheridan, who had previously chastised General George Crook for his excessive use of Apache scouts, blocked the plan. As long as he commanded the army, there was little chance that Native Americans would be anything more than short-term scouts.[18]

In a letter to army headquarters in February 1884, Sheridan enumerated several reasons for his opposition to Indian soldiers. He complained that Native Americans lacked discipline and did not possess "the tenacity of purpose" necessary to make good soldiers. He also maintained that Indians "cannot appreciate responsibility or the sacredness of an oath." Sheridan was convinced that no system could be devised that would "make the Indians other than what they are now—a race so distinctive from that governing this country that it would be neither wise nor expedient to recruit our Army from their ranks."[19]

Following General John M. Schofield's assumption of army command in 1888, however, the plan for enlisting Native Americans as regular soldiers gained momentum. Together with Secretary of War Redfield Proctor, Schofield lent his full support to the idea of enlisting Indian units. In keeping with Commissioner of Indian Affairs Thomas Jefferson Morgan's (1889–1893) policy of individualization, Christianization, and acculturation of the Indians, Schofield believed that military service might hasten the socialization of American Indians as well as their integration into the majority society. Well aware of the debilitating aspects of reservation life, Schofield postulated that military service would provide an outlet for the Indians' pent-up aggression and frustration. Such a development, he hoped, would ensure more tranquil conditions among the tribes and encourage peaceful relations between Native Americans and the army.[20]

The architect of the plan to enlist Native Americans as regular soldiers remains uncertain. Michael L. Tate has suggested that Schofield and Proctor spearheaded the scheme; Don Rickey maintained that the instigator may have been Indian Department Inspector Frank C. Armstrong. In a letter to

Secretary of War Proctor in January 1890, Armstrong proposed that the army enlist special units of Indian soldiers. A former brigadier general in the Confederate army, Armstrong as an Indian inspector in 1885 had enlisted 120 Cheyenne Dog Soldiers to help restore order on the Cheyenne-Arapaho reservation in western Indian Territory.[21]

Major William H. Powell, Twenty-second Infantry, and Lieutenant Edward Wanton (Ned) Casey also were early proponents of a greater Indian presence in the army. Writing in *The United Service* magazine in March 1890, Powell, the commanding officer at Fort Abraham Lincoln in Dakota Territory, argued that if Native Americans were absolutely necessary as scouts in Indian warfare (as some officers insisted), then why not use them as regular soldiers where their skills could be used perhaps with even greater effectiveness? Regiments of Indian troops could also be enlisted in the infantry, Powell maintained, and be stationed at posts in the East to learn the habits of civilization. After all, he intimated, American Indians were "keen observers and excellent imitators."[22]

Lieutenant Ned Casey, Twenty-second Infantry, an 1873 graduate of the United States Military Academy and veteran of General Nelson A. Miles's punitive expedition against the Northern Cheyennes and Sioux in 1876, also supported the establishment of Indian units. In June 1888 the Twenty-second Infantry received orders to head north to Fort Keogh in southeastern Montana to replace the Fifth Infantry. Distressed with the miserable living conditions of many Northern Cheyennes, Casey in the winter of 1889 and in March 1890 wrote to Colonel Peter T. Swaine (the commanding officer of the Twenty-second Infantry) and to General Schofield requesting permission to organize a troop of Cheyenne scouts, both to alleviate unemployment among the Indians and to ensure order. Casey suggested that recent graduates from government-administered Indian schools be recruited, presumably because they were already familiar with military-style discipline and the English language.[23]

By stressing the civilizing effects of military service for Indians, Powell's and Casey's arguments eased the doubts of skeptics who expressed concern that military service would only exacerbate the Indian question by lending government sanction to the Native Americans' "instinctive" warlike tendencies. In his March 1890 article in *The United Service*, Powell prophesied idyllically that after a few years' service, Indian soldiers and their families would establish small communities and towns on their reservations. Some would set up small shops and businesses. Others, having seen the good of the vegetables they learned to cook and eat as soldiers and were taught to raise as company gardeners, would take up the plow and become farmers. Thus, military service, Powell maintained, would encourage the development of Native American industry and agriculture that would "forever preclude the possibility of their returning to filth and squalor."[24]

Regardless of who was initially responsible for originating the idea to enlist Native Americans as regular soldiers, the support of General Schofield and Secretary Proctor was essential for the plan's implementation and success. In the spring of 1890 Schofield authorized the establishment of two experimental Indian companies of one hundred men each, one based on the northern plains under the guidance of Lieutenant Ned Casey and one on the southern plains under the command of Lieutenant Homer W. Wheeler.[25]

By August 1890 Lieutenant Casey (or "Big Red Nose," as the Cheyennes called him) had succeeded in enlisting forty-eight men in "Troop A." Emulating Casey's success, Lieutenant Samuel C. Robertson from nearby Fort Custer organized "Troop B" comprised of Crow scouts. In December the Cheyenne Indian Commission, headed by General Nelson A. Miles, arrived at Lame Deer, Montana, to investigate the possibility of removing all the Northern Cheyennes to Fort Keogh. Frederick Remington, the famed western artist who accompanied the commission, described Casey's men as "fine-looking, tall young men, with long hair" who "fill the eye of a military man until nothing is lacking."[26]

Homer W. Wheeler, meanwhile, had worked with Native American soldiers in the late 1880s, while serving at Fort Elliot, Texas. His outfit, Troop C, Indian scouts, was comprised of fifty Cheyennes and Arapahoes. They endured a tough and thankless job. Each day they patrolled the Indian Territory to maintain the peace and keep Anglo-owned cattle off reservation lands. In May 1890, however, Wheeler received orders to proceed to Fort Reno, Indian Territory, to form an experimental company of one hundred men to test whether or not American Indians would make good soldiers. On May 17, 1890, Wheeler, with forty scouts and their families, traveled to his new post where his men patrolled the Indian Territory for "Sooners" and other trespassers. In November, Major J. P. Sanger inspected Wheeler's unit and remarked that the Native Americans had a "peculiar aptitude" for military service and had performed their duties admirably. One of the primary reasons for Wheeler's success can be attributed to his sincere desire to help the men under his command. When his Indian first sergeant reported that his young daughter was ill, for example, Wheeler ordered him to move into his backyard and had his personal cook prepare nourishing meals for the youngster until she regained her health.[27] The personal qualities and character of the men commanding Indian troops proved to be a decisive factor in the success or failure in enlisting Indians as regular soldiers.

Despite its initial success, the army's highest ranking and most experienced officials remained divided over whether to support the plan. General Oliver Otis Howard supported enlisting Indians as soldiers, provided their number would not come at the expense of white troops. Generals George Crook and Nelson A. Miles did not believe that Indians could be fashioned into well- disciplined "spit and polish" soldiers and preferred that they continue to be enlisted as short-term scouts. Generals John R. Brooke, Wesley Merrit, and John Gibbon, as well as Benjamin H. Grierson, the former commander of the all-black Tenth Cavalry Regiment, all opposed the idea. Only Generals David S. Stanley, T. R. Ruger, and O. O. Howard favored the scheme. Thus, in the spring of 1890 six of the nine highest-ranking army officers expressed varying degrees of opposition to the plan to enlist Indians as regular soldiers.[28]

Even with the lukewarm reception accorded by top army brass, the success of Casey and Wheeler prompted General Schofield and Secretary Proctor to act on the matter of enlisting Indians as regulars. In November 1890 Schofield authorized General Nelson Miles to enlist up to five hundred Indian scouts and suggested that Miles recruit several companies and troops of Indian soldiers for a three-year enlistment period.[29] The massacre of nearly two hundred Sioux men, women, and children in December 1890, at Wounded Knee on the Pine Ridge reservation, served to strengthen Schofield's resolve to enlist Native Americans. By giving young warriors employment and an opportunity to achieve status, the chances for a recurrence of such a tragedy, he believed, would be diminished.

Consequently, on March 9, 1891, army officials issued General Order Number Twenty-eight. It provided that "Troop L of each Cavalry Regiment and Company I of each Infantry Regiment [would] be recruited by enlistment of Indian soldiers to the number of fifty-five for each troop and company."[30] Enlistment would be restricted to units west of the Mississippi River, where two years earlier army officials had skeletonized Troop L and Company I of each regiment to reduce the size of the army. Notable exemptions from the experiment were the all-black Ninth and Tenth Cavalry Regiments and Twenty-fourth and Twenty-fifth Infantry Regiments, presumably because military officials questioned the ability of African American troops to set the "proper example" for Indian soldiers.[31] In keeping with the precedent set by the army's segregation of the four black regiments, however, Indian soldiers were not integrated into white units—an irony considering that assimilation was a primary purpose of the experiment.

The task of overseeing the implementation of General Order Number Twenty-eight fell to Captain Jesse Lee, a career army officer and Indian expert. He expressed concern that the Bureau of Indian Affairs would oppose and possibly try to undermine the enlistment of Native Americans for fear that the military, if successful in its efforts to ameliorate Euro–Indian relations, would demonstrate the overall ineffectiveness of civilian control over Indian administration; however, Lee accepted the task with the conviction and enthusiasm of a crusader. For if the experiment of enlisting Native Americans proved successful, the army might at last prove to the nation that the War Department, rather than the BIA, could best administer Indian affairs. With this goal in mind, Lee set out in late March 1891 to organize recruiting efforts on western reservations.[32]

Recruiters enjoyed mixed results. Successful ones often had experience in dealing with Native Americans and, therefore, had some knowledge of tribal histories and cultures. Not surprisingly, the more productive recruiters spent a great deal of time with tribes from the northern and southern plains who possessed strong warrior traditions. Differences in tribal cultures remains one of the key factors in understanding the diversity of Native American responses to the government's call for Indian enlistments—both in the 1890s and afterward.

Lieutenant Edward Dravo was familiar with several aspects of Plains Indian cultures that aided his recruiting efforts among the Brule Sioux at the Rosebud agency in South Dakota. He attended tribal dances to gain support for the project and held councils with distinguished warriors and chiefs. As Byron Price has noted, recruiters recognized that the two keys to successful recruiting of Indians were the support of tribal elders and the enlistment of influential warriors and the sons and relatives of chiefs and other tribal leaders.[33]

By April 23, 1891, Dravo had succeeded in enlisting fifty-four Brules who subsequently formed "Troop L, 6th U.S. Cavalry." Less than one year later, recruiters had succeeded in enlisting seven troops of cavalry and five troops of infantry. Military officials reorganized Ned Casey's "Cheyenne Scouts" into Troop L, Eighth Cavalry, following Casey's death after the Wounded Knee crisis. Homer Wheeler's Southern Cheyenne and Arapaho scouts became Troop L, Fifth Cavalry, and were headquarted at Fort Reno, Oklahoma Territory. Members of the Crow and Sioux tribes, long recognized as expert horsemen, dominated the cavalry troops stationed on the northern plains, while Kiowas, Comanches, and Southern Cheyennes filled the ranks of the cavalry on the southern plains. Navajos, meanwhile, predominated in Troop L, Second Cavalry, at Fort Wingate, New Mexico. Large numbers of Sioux and Apaches and a few Mojave and Yuma men also joined the various infantry companies. Oglala and Brule Sioux enlisted in Company I of the Second and Sixteenth Infantry Regiments. Apache recruits from Arizona and New Mexico joined Company I in the Ninth, Eleventh, and Twelfth Infantry Regiments. Company I, Twelfth Infantry, commanded by Lieutenant William Wotherspoon, was the largest Indian unit in the nation and included Apache prisoners from Mount Vernon Barracks, Alabama, as well as men from the San Carlos reservation in Arizona. When given the choice of enlisting or remaining in jail, the Apache inmates opted for military service. Among the young officers assigned to Indian companies was future Army Chief of Staff Hugh L. Scott, who commanded Kiowas and Comanches in Troop L, Seventh Cavalry, at Fort Sill, Oklahoma. In March 1891, thirty-year-old John J. Pershing, the future commander of the American Expeditionary Force in World War I, arrived at the Pine Ridge reservation to take charge of a company of Oglala Sioux. In April he led them on what must have been an extremely delicate—and potentially volatile—mission to police the Wounded Knee battlefield. Pershing was greatly impressed with the men under his care and when the assignment ended five months later, he commented favorably on the enlistment of Native Americans as regular soldiers.[34]

Among the incentives to enlist was thirteen dollars a month for the first year of military service, a clothing allowance, comfortable quarters, three meals a day, medical care, and permission to recreate at the post canteen. While not the sole impetus for Indian enlistment, an economic crisis that gripped several western reservations in the early 1890s promoted very successful recruiting. Hence, many eager recruits came from the more destitute reservations. On the eve of the massacre at Wounded Knee, the Sioux, one author has noted, suffered from "the passing of the buffalo and the growing scarcity of the deer and other game which deprived them of food and clothing, and except for what the poor land of their reservation would produce, put them at the mercy of government annuities."[35] Thus, when economic hardship hit Indian peoples possessing strong warrior traditions, conditions were optimum for Indian enlistment.

While military service appealed to some Indian groups, others rejected the call to army life altogether. First Lieutenant William H. Johnston tried without success, in July 1891, to recruit Bannocks and Shoshones at the Fort Hall agency in southern Idaho. He organized a huge feast of beef and potatoes to attract perspective recruits and their families. Although he fed two hundred people, not one Indian signed up. Comanches and Kiowas were initially uninterested in the army because they were receiving about seventy-five thousand dollars annually from leasing their lands. Plains tribes residing in the Indian Territory expressed apathy about military service as well. Young men did not want to leave family and friends to go live with the whites, some loved their horses and did not want to join the infantry, while others feared that enlistment might jeopardize their claims to tribal rights and annuities. If that were not enough, many harbored an understandably deep suspicion of the federal government and did not trust the recruiters' promises. One tribal leader cautioned his people that the army secretly intended to gather up all the young recruits and send them far away, never to be heard from again. Bannocks and Utes in Utah, Hopis in Arizona, Paiutes and Klamaths in Nevada and Oregon, and Shoshones from Idaho also expressed disinterest in military service.[36]

A relatively small yet influential group of recruits were Indian policemen, many of whom were uniformed and drilled like soldiers. Although the establishment of Indian police forces did not receive official government sanction until May 1878, government agents at work with several different tribes (Pawnees, Klamaths, Modocs, Navajos, Apaches, Blackfeet, Chippewas, and Sioux) organized small Indian police forces as early as the 1860s and 1870s. Not only did Indian policemen serve the practical function of keeping the peace on reservations, but reformers hoped that they might hasten the process of assimilation by undermining (and ultimately assuming) the authority of conservative tribal elders, many of whom rejected Anglo culture. But many Indian policemen complained about poor pay (only about five dollars a month for privates and eight dollars a month for officers), inadequate equipment, and having to provide their own mounts. Not surprisingly, many policemen were envious of their brethren serving in the army as scouts. Army scouts received nearly three times the pay of Indian policemen, better rations, and more leisure time. It seems only logical, therefore, that Indian policemen would have been likely candidates for enlistment in the U.S. Army during the 1890s.[37]

To most observers, the first year of the army's experiment in enlisting American Indians as regular soldiers was a success. By the end of June 1891 over four hundred Native Americans, the majority of whom came from the Department of Dakota and the Department of the Platte, had enlisted. Brule Sioux soldiers in Troop L, Sixth Cavalry, expressed their excitement about the prospect of military service by singing the entire way while en route to Fort Niobrara, Nebraska, where they began their training. In October 1892 military officials took advantage of the opportunity to show off their Indian soldiers by sending Troop L, Sixth Cavalry, to Chicago for the World's Columbian Exposition. It was a promising start.

Despite its good beginning, acute problems undermined the experiment's success. By the end of 1893, less than three years into the program, the adjutant general's office declared the use of Indians as soldiers a complete failure, and within five years military officials scrapped the plan altogether.[38]

What went wrong so quickly? Reasons cited for the experiment's lack of success fall within three broad categories: cultural dissimilarities, racism, and bureaucratic indifference. The most common complaint among white officers commanding Indian troops was the problem of communication. Few Native Americans had an adequate grasp of English and even fewer white officers understood the various Indian languages. Some army posts offered Indian troops routine instruction in the English language, but a few hours of instruction per week proved inadequate. Many officers grew impatient when Indian soldiers failed to execute commands. Some accused the Native Americans of feigning misunderstanding so as to avoid performing tasks they found distasteful or unnecessary (such as saluting). When an Indian soldier failed to obey an order he found himself in the guardhouse, pulling kitchen patrol, or perhaps cleaning out the post stables. At times, Indian infantrymen or cavalrymen shared quarters with Indian scouts and came to resent the latter's comparative freedom from army restrictions and shorter period of enlistment.[39]

There were other culture-based problems. Native Americans were reluctant to adopt military-style haircuts, live in frame dwellings, or undergo routine physical examinations, which some found to be uncomfortable and humiliating. Several Indian soldiers refused to be vaccinated, while others found frequent bathing to be a waste of time. According to William Bruce White, Native American soldiers disliked wearing uniforms because they missed the contact of their leg muscles against the horse. Indian troops (as well as their Anglo counterparts) complained about the poor quality of army food and the boredom of barracks life. The greatest problem for Indian soldiers, however, was the long periods of separation from family and loved ones. Army officials allowed only ten men per unit to bring along their wives (only one wife per man) and families. Many Native Americans feared being stationed a long distance from their reservation and losing their share of tribal annuities and privileges. In March 1891, for example, Sioux warriors at Pine Ridge refused to enlist for service with Colonel William R. Shafter's First Infantry Regiment because it was headed for duty in California.[40]

Despite notices that Indian troops would not be stationed far from home, the army could not always make good on its promises. In the winter of 1891–1892, Captain William H. Clapa recruited Company I, Sixteenth Infantry, from the Rosebud agency in South Dakota. In February, military officials ordered the unit to Fort Douglas, Utah. Meanwhile, Company I, Tenth Infantry, comprised of Apaches from the desert Southwest, received orders to transfer from Fort Bowie, Arizona, to Fort Barrancas, Florida. When word spread that Indian troops could not expect to remain close to their reservations, enlistment numbers plummeted. As one historian has suggested, the rock on which the experiment to enlist Indians as regular soldiers was ultimately dashed to pieces was the difficulty in reconciling Indian family life and military life.[41]

Another problem arose over alcohol. While military officials initially justified the enlistment of Indian troops as a means to expedite assimilation and to set a proper example for reservation Indians, some Native Americans on the reservation came to resent the fact that Indian soldiers received canteen privileges while reservations remained dry. Post commanders, for their part, were reluctant to rescind the Indian soldiers' right to purchase alcohol for fear of setting a double standard and provoking a crisis. Indian soldiers might justifiably express outrage if white soldiers enjoyed canteen privileges after theirs had been revoked. Consequently, humanitarian reformers came to criticize the experiment as corrupting rather than civilizing Indian soldiers and setting a bad example for Native Americans on the reservation. Some local businesses, meanwhile, discriminated against Indian customers and some refused to sell them supplies at all.[42]

In addition to cultural dissimilarities, racism also contributed to the failure. Writing for *The Illustrated American* in 1895, Thomas H. Wilson, who had commanded a company of Sioux infantry, remarked that "making a United States soldier out of a recalcitrant redskin is almost certain in the end to result in failure."[43] He cited the Indians' lack of discipline, ignorance, and marrying at a young age as the primary reasons for the experiment's failure. Echoing the sentiments of Generals George Crook and Nelson Miles, Wilson advised that military officials use Indian troops as light cavalry or for scouting, but not as regular soldiers.[44] Hugh L. Scott attributed the failure of enlisting units of Native American soldiers to high-ranking military officials who were angry with General Schofield for mustering out white men and replacing them with Indians. In wake of the depression of 1893 and subsequent high unemployment, white enlisted men were bitter about losing their jobs to Native Americans. Some officers resented having to serve with their former enemies and proved unwilling to give the experiment a chance. White enlisted men expressed reluctance about taking orders from Indian noncommissioned officers.[45]

Bureaucratic indifference and inefficiency also undermined the experiment's success. In November 1891 Stephen Benton Elkins succeeded Redfield Proctor as secretary of war. Elkins did not possess the same optimism and enthusiasm for Indian soldiers as did his predecessor. During his term, Indian troops received inadequate equipment and provisions, thus curtailing their training and efficiency. Some cavalry units, for example, did not receive their mounts until nearly a year and a half after their enlistment. David Scott Lamont, Elkins's successor in March 1893, demonstrated even less interest in the plan. Finally, the number of qualified white officers was negligible. Officers selected to command Indian troops were supposed to be familiar with Indian languages, of high character, and possess a "missionary spirit," but the requirements were seldom met. The constant shuffling and reassignment of white officers prevented many Native American soldiers from developing an affinity for their commanders, which left Indian units in a constant state of laxity and confusion.[46]

On May 31, 1897, Hugh L. Scott watched as fifty-three members of his Troop L, Seventh Cavalry, received their discharges and left army service. They were the last of the Indian troops enlisted under the 1891 General Order Number 28. After only six years, the experiment of enlisting units of Indian soldiers came to a disappointing end. In fact, military officials mustered out the majority of Indian units well before the Native Americans completed their enlistments (three years for cavalry and five years for infantry). By the middle of 1894 there were only 547 men registered in the Indian units, and the army suspended enlistment of new Indian recruits. In 1895 the only unit in service was Scott's Troop L, Seventh Cavalry, which served as a quiet reminder of the experiment's failure.[47]

Despite its short duration, the venture of using all-Indian units in the regular army was not a complete disappointment, and an estimated 1,071 Native Americans had participated and gained useful knowledge and experiences. In his examination of the Brules in Troop L, Sixth Cavalry, Don Rickey has maintained that the Sioux veterans returned to their reservations with pride and many became leading men on the Rosebud reservation. Crow soldiers who had served in Troop L, First Cavalry, reportedly donned their old uniforms during special occasions and "carried themselves aloof and appeared haughty." A few veterans later joined the Crow police force. In addition, Indian units served the army faithfully and performed a variety of important tasks. Army officials dispatched Troop L, Sixth Cavalry, for example, to Wyoming to help maintain peace during the Johnson County range war; Northern Cheyennes in Troop L, Eighth Cavalry, protected property belonging to the Northern Pacific Railroad Company during periods of labor unrest, and Navajo soldiers assigned to Troop L, Second Cavalry, served as couriers and scouts in campaigns against off-reservation Apaches; Hugh L. Scott's Troop L, Seventh Cavalry, protected the Cheyenne-Arapaho reservation against cattle rustlers and trespassers.[48]

More important were the long-term results of enlisting Indians as regular soldiers. Military service provided hundreds of Native American men with an opportunity to gain a better understanding of the Anglo society and culture that had done so much to destroy their own. In Thomas Dunlay's words, "the army gave many Indian men their first real introduction to the culture that would soon dominate their lives."[49] Thus, military service equipped Indian veterans with certain advantages over other reservation Indians. Through their newly acquired knowledge and experience of the "white man's world," Native American veterans could more effectively resist further Anglo encroachments on their lands, cultures, and liberties.

The experiment also allowed Native Americans to escape restrictive legislation on later military service. An August 1894 law prohibited from enlistment aliens and persons who could not read, write, or speak English. Implemented in response to the burgeoning number of European and Asian immigrants arriving in the United States each year, the law could have affected significant numbers of American Indians. Because Native Americans were serving in the army at the time, however, military officials excluded Indians from the law's restrictions. In the future, therefore, Indians who might otherwise have been disqualified would have the opportunity to serve in the military.[50]

Finally, the failure in using American Indians in segregated units ensured that such an experiment would not be repeated. Consequently, after 1897 military officials treated Native American soldiers as individuals rather than as a racial group and integrated them into white units, where they served beside Anglo soldiers—a practice that continued through World War I and that exerted (as will be seen) a strong influence on men of both races.[51]

Nevertheless, the outbreak of the Spanish-American War in 1898 brought renewed efforts to enlist Native Americans into segregated units. The volunteer army bill of 1898 provided authorization for the secretary of war to organize companies, troops, battalions or regiments, possessing "special qualifications and regulations," and some people took the order to mean special units of Indian soldiers. The argument for establishing a special unit of cowboys and Indians received a boost when Colonel Henry Inman predicted confidently that three thousand well-armed Indian warriors, under the leadership of such a "strategist, diplomat, and statesman as was Sitting Bull" and allied with the "cowboys of the range," could clear Cuba of all the Spanish regulars. William "Buffalo Bill" Cody volunteered to raise such a force of cowboys and Indians for service in Cuba, but military officials politely declined his offer.[52]

On April 25, 1898, however, President William McKinley authorized Captain Leonard Wood to raise a regiment of cowboys and mounted riflemen and named Theodore Roosevelt to serve as Wood's second-in-command. In the weeks that followed, Wood and Roosevelt organized the First Volunteer Cavalry Regiment and sent recruiters to all four territories—Arizona, New Mexico, Indian, and Oklahoma—to round up volunteers.[53]

During the first two weeks of May 1898, the First Volunteer Cavalry rendezvoused at Camp Wood in San Antonio, Texas, where it participated in brief but vigorous training exercises. After the training had ended in Texas, the regiment went by railroad to Tampa Bay, Florida. From there, it departed to the coast of Cuba. Among the volunteers were a substantial number of American Indians, particularly from Indian and Oklahoma territories, while units from New Mexico and Arizona had many men of Mexican as well as Indian blood. Among the Indian Territory volunteers to enlist for army service during the Spanish-American War was Choctaw Victor M. Locke, who later served in World War I and rose to the rank of major.[54]

Although Indian participation in the Spanish-American War is not well chronicled, the scant evidence suggests that Native Americans performed with distinction. Many served as advance guards and scouts. Other Indian "Rough Riders" (as many Americans called members of the First Volunteer Cavalry Regiment) served in noncombat roles. Bert Holderman, a Cherokee farmer from Artkopa, Kansas, served as Roosevelt's cook. After a long day of fighting the Spanish, a very tired Roosevelt slumped into camp. Holderman responded by wrapping his commander in dry blankets and putting him to sleep on a nearby table.[55]

With the war's conclusion in August 1898, the Rough Riders enjoyed a final evening of revelry before the government mustered them out of service. After receiving the gratitude and best wishes of Roosevelt, the Rough Riders sat around campfires musing about the glories of the recent past and what lay in the future. The Native American members, meanwhile, conducted a going-away party, singing and dancing throughout the night and into the early morning hours, no doubt recounting brave deeds, mourning dead comrades, and expressing thanks for their own survival.[56]

During the first decade of the twentieth century, the War Department continued its policy of conscious assimilation of Indians into white units. In the aftermath of the Spanish-American War, Native American troops, fighting in integrated units, saw action in the western Pacific during the Filipino Revolution (1898–1902) and on the Asian mainland during the Boxer Rebellion (1900).

The arguments for enlisting Indians into segregated units did not go away. As new foreign policy crises developed between the United States and Mexico after 1910 and later with Germany, the demand for special Indian regiments gained renewed intensity. Supporters and opponents of segregated units aired their opinions via congressional hearings, the press, and public addresses. Their debates demonstrated an Hegelianlike struggle between the supporters of Indian assimilation into white society and the advocates for preservation of Indian cultures and traditions, a debate that led eventually to a "reorganization" or "new deal" in federal Indian policy and an end to forced assimilation as the BIA's dominant goal.

Along with the Dawes Act and increasing government involvement in Indian education in the late nineteenth century, the idea that military service would hasten assimilation and, thus, end the "Indian problem" was a good example of the "quick fix" mentality of many reformers, government bureaucrats, and military officials. The assimilationists rejected the theories of a growing number of anthropologists and ethnologists who argued that Indian acculturation and assimilation would be a lengthy, evolutionary process. Although the experiment with segregated Indian units failed to achieve its purpose, assimilationists continued to tinker with Indian education and the Dawes Act, hoping to "fine-tune" the allotment process so that Native Americans could enjoy the "benefits" of citizenship and Anglo civilization—albeit without much of their lands. The approach of World War I, however, provided reformers and policymakers with another opportunity to experiment with Indian military service as a means of expediting assimilation—which is the subject of Chapter 2.

2

Indian Soldiers and the Issue
of Segregated Troops

THE ARGUMENT FOR ESTABLISHING SEGREGATED UNITS FOR NATIVE AMERICAN soldiers surfaced again in the second decade of the twentieth century. But the rationale had changed. Earlier efforts to create all-Indian units stressed assimilation as the primary goal of military service. During World War I, however, many advocates of segregated Indian units hoped that military service would aid in the preservation of a "pure" Indian identity in the United States and give momentum to the campaign to gain citizenship for all Native Americans.

The change reflected an emerging reform movement, with roots going back over a century, to preserve particular aspects of Indian cultures and lifestyles before they—or the Native Americans themselves—became extinct. Convinced that Indians were a "Vanishing Race" due to alcohol use, disease, interracial and intraracial warfare, and land loss, a small cadre of politicians, scientists, and reformers demanded that native cultures and traditions be studied and recorded. If the task was not completed soon, they believed, it would be too late.[1]

The popular notion that Native Americans were a "Vanishing Race" and must, like the wilderness frontier, recede before the onslaught of Anglo civilization, had manifested itself during the nineteenth century in several ways. Influenced by the demise of the various indigenous peoples of Virginia, President Thomas Jefferson, for example, instructed Meriwether Lewis in 1803 to gather notes and materials on the Indian peoples that he encountered on his survey of the newly acquired Louisiana Territory. In the 1820s linguistic ethnologists set to work recording Indian vocabularies and grammars, and the ensuing decades witnessed the establishment of numerous anthropological societies and museums to collect and preserve native materials. Philadelphia artist George Catlin visited over forty western tribes during the 1830s to paint Native Americans in their "uncorrupted state." A decade later, Lewis

Henry Morgan, the "father of American anthropology," set to work study-ing the social organization of the Iroquois and Mary Eastman worked on the northern plains recording the tribal folklore and traditions of the Sioux.[2]

The notion that Indians were a "Vanishing Race" became the dominant influence on federal Indian policy in the latter half of the nineteenth century. Convinced that the only way to "save" Native Americans was to assimilate them into Anglo society, a dedicated and well-intentioned combination of politicians, Indian bureau officials, and reform groups employed various means to has-ten Indian acculturation and entry into the majority society. Secretary of the Interior Carl Schurz summed up the perceived state of emergency that ex-isted in Indian country when, in 1881, he declared that Native Americans must choose between two alternatives: "extermination or civilization." Op-timistic about the prospects for Indian survival, Schurz went on to suggest that it would be easy to introduce civilized habits and occupations among Indians, if only the "proper means" were employed.[3]

For Schurz and other assimilationist-minded officials, the "proper means" included citizenship, education, and the "individualization" of Indians through the allotment of their lands. The establishment of several off-reservation boarding schools and the passage in 1887 of the General Allotment Act (Dawes Act), therefore, were seen by many reformers as panaceas. Allotment prom-ised quick assimilation and citizenship, it furnished white settlers with new opportunities to acquire Indian lands, and it provided Native Americans with an alternative to the "Vanishing Race" scenario by offering Anglo civiliza-tion and individual property ownership as a means of avoiding extinction.

Yet support for allotment and other assimilationist measures was by no means unanimous. Indian leaders and spokespersons from around the na-tion held councils, adopted tribal resolutions, wrote petitions, and gave speeches in opposition to allotment. The Five Civilized Tribes maintained permanent delegations in Washington, D.C., to lobby lawmakers against passage of the Dawes Act. Commissioner of Indian Affairs J. D. C. Atkins became so concerned about the spread of tribal protests that he directed agency officials to forbid Indians to leave their reservations and to arrest and detain troublemakers.[4]

In 1885 Thomas A. Bland, editor of the *Council Fire*, a journal devoted to Indian rights, founded the National Indian Defense Association (NIDA), which fought for Indian self-determination and opposed unilateral govern-ment interference in Indian affairs. A lone voice in support of the notion that Indians should be consulted regarding their futures, the NIDA helped pioneer the way for subsequent efforts to preserve Indian cultures and allow Native Americans greater control over their lives.[5]

Criticisms also emanated from the ranks of government and academia. In the late 1870s Selden N. Clark, an employee with the Bureau of Education, and Garrick Mallery, an officer in the United States Geological Survey, concluded that the "Vanishing Race" theory was wrong, that Indians were not on the verge of extinction, and that new policies were needed to address the serious problems in Indian country. Meanwhile, anthropologists such as Lewis Henry Morgan and James Mooney criticized the government's attempts to assimilate Native Americans overnight and stressed, instead, the essential evolutionary processes of acculturation and assimilation. They urged government officials, consequently, to adopt a more gradualistic and realistic approach to assimilation that would allow Indians to hold on to aspects of their cultures for a longer period of time.[6] The federal government, however, impatient for a quick solution and under growing pressure from humanitarian and religious reformers who supported allotment as the only practical means of saving Indians from extinction and white settlers and land speculators who understood that allotment would open Indian lands, ignored the advice and backed the Dawes Act.

Contradicting Clark and Mallery's arguments that Native Americans were not a "Vanishing Race," alarming evidence of Indian decline appeared everywhere just a decade later. The U.S. Seventh Cavalry's massacre in 1890 of over two hundred Sioux from the Pine Ridge agency at Wounded Knee, South Dakota, along with Frederick Jackson Turner's announcement in 1893 that the frontier experience in the United States was essentially over, fueled the myth of a "Vanishing Race." Even more startling, perhaps, was the 1890 census, which estimated that the Indian population in the United States had plummeted to an all-time low.[7]

The popular media fueled the notion of a "Vanishing Race" as well by warning that "pure-blooded" Indians (who were presumably the only "real" Indians) were in immediate danger of losing their racial identities. In January 1902 William R. Draper composed an article for *Cosmopolitan*, entitled "The Last of the Red Race," in which he suggested that "full-blooded" American Indians were disappearing due to intermarriage with non-Indians. In addition, Draper noted with smug satisfaction, Indians were becoming "absorbed and amalgamated" rather than exterminated, but the Native Americans' loss of racial entity would be more than offset by the "advantages" gained by their assimilation into the majority culture.[8] Articles published in 1903 issues of *Current Literature* and *The Forum* warned that Native Americans were rapidly finding themselves face to face with the always inevitable, but long deferred, absorption by the white race. The hour of their elimination, the articles predicted, was at hand.[9] A piece in *The Word Carrier*, a newsletter published by the Santee Normal Training School in Santee, Nebraska, echoed a similar viewpoint. It stated that the American Museum of Natural History was working to preserve Indian cultures by collecting pictures and artifacts because Native Americans were merging with non-Indians. It was high time that museums were gathering in all they could find appertaining to aboriginal Americans, the article stated, for the prospects were that Indians would soon be living as ordinarily as "civilized people." Ella Higginson's poem "The Vanishing Race," which was published in 1911, likened Indians to spirits that were "mutely" and "uncomplainingly" drifting into oblivion to seek a place to rest. "How shall it be with us when they are gone," she queried, "when they are but a memory and a name?"[10] One recent author has gone so far as to place an exact date on the "Vanishing American." John Upton Terrell wrote in the *American Indian Almanac* that with the death on March 25, 1916, of a Yahi Indian named Ishi, "the last wild Indian in America was gone."[11]

Ironically, while many Americans accepted Indian extinction as inevitable, they simultaneously praised certain "manly" aspects of Indian cultures. The national glorification of "virile virtues," such as courage, energy and daring, peaked during the presidency of Theodore Roosevelt and provided the impetus for numerous efforts to capture the essence of Indian "manhood" for posterity. Fearing the loss of a unique Indian identity in the United States and hoping to preserve romanticized "native virtues," several photographic expeditions set out between the 1890s and 1920s to preserve the "Vanishing Race" on film. For some photographers, the task before them was a race against time. Frederick Monsen, for example, lamented the fact that entire tribes had been destroyed by disease, while others had been scattered by "encroaching civilization." He wrote that traditional Indian cultures and tribal characteristics were rapidly disappearing, and that Native Americans were giving up their "deeply significant nature-lore," as well as their religions, ceremonies, and ancestral manners and customs.[12]

In response to the apparent crisis in Indian country, photographer Sumner W. Matteson, Jr., traveled over twenty-five thousand miles between 1898 and 1908, taking pictures primarily of Hopis in the Southwest, but also of Gros Ventres and Assiniboines at Fort Belknap in northern Montana. John Alvin Anderson, a Swedish-born immigrant, served as a civilian photographer for the U.S. Army. From the 1880s to the 1920s he took thousands of pictures depicting Indian life and cultures. The most famous photographer, however, was Edward Sheriff Curtis, who between 1896 and 1930 recorded Indian folklore, myths, and legends and took over forty thousand pictures filling dozens of volumes.[13]

Less well known were the photographic expeditions financed by a Princeton-educated, department-store magnate named Rodman Wanamaker and led by Joseph Kossuth Dixon, a graduate of William Jewell College in Liberty, Missouri, and Rochester Seminary in New York. After a lengthy—if at times tumultuous—career as a Baptist minister (he allegedly lost one preaching assignment due to charges of adultery), Dixon gained employment in 1904 as a spokesman for Eastman Kodak Company in Europe. Two years later he moved to Philadelphia after being named director of the Wanamaker Department Store's "Educational Bureau." Dixon, who combined his talents as a preacher with his knowledge of photography and visual display, gave daily lectures and presentations on a variety of topics including music, poetry, art, and history. Eccentric, pompous, and possessing little practical knowledge or experience in dealing with Native Americans, the fifty-two-year-old Dixon seemed an odd choice to lead the Wanamaker "expeditions" to Indian country.[14]

Between 1908 and 1913, Rodman Wanamaker, who had inherited his father's interest in Native Americans, financed three photographic expeditions. The first two expeditions traversed the valley of the Little Big Horn River. In July 1908 Dixon's team arrived at the Crow Reservation in southern Montana and shot more than thirty thousand feet of motion-picture film including a version of Henry Wadsworth Longfellow's *The Song of Hiawatha*, a reenactment of the Battle of Little Bighorn (using Crow Indians instead of Sioux and Cheyennes), and about four thousand still pictures, much of which were "highly romanticized scenes of Indian life and reenactments of battles." Dixon, who personally supervised all the photography, posed his Indian subjects and staged action scenes in order to portray his own romanticized vision of the "Vanishing Race." To Dixon, Indians represented a race of strong, noble, virile, and courageous people. With good reason, therefore, he has been described as "an idealist and enthusiast" who wanted to "uplift the exploited Indian and restore him to a primitive Edenic state." Louis Pfaller, for example, has written that Dixon hoped to "preserve, especially through photography, the idyllic memory of the untainted 'noble savage,' who was supposedly an unspoiled 'child of nature.'"[15]

According to Rodman Wanamaker, the sole motive for the expeditions was "to perpetuate the life story of the first Americans and to strengthen in their hearts the feelings of allegiance and friendship for their country." Charles R. Reynolds, Jr., who studied the Wanamaker expeditions, gave a different rationale for the project. The pictures and movies, he suggested, were an expression of "national guilt and private sentiment of a time when the nation began to realize that it was responsible for the vanishing race and perhaps felt subconsciously that if you romanticize your victim you somehow hurt him less." Russel L. Barsh, meanwhile, placed the Wanamaker expeditions within the context of the post–Spanish-American War era, when the United States "witnessed a great outpouring of national smugness and sentimentality" but many Americans "worried lest some blot be found on their escutcheon, some flaw in their genealogy." Like Reynolds, he pointed to a national "guilt complex" as one of the driving forces behind the Wanamaker expeditions. Others have argued that Dixon's expedition to Montana was simply his "last farewell" to the "Vanishing Race."[16]

In the spring of 1909, Dixon and Wanamaker suggested that a memorial be constructed to honor Native Americans and to serve as a constant reminder of the "Vanishing Race" and "American ideals" of liberty, loyalty, and devotion to country. The memorial they envisioned was a towering bronze statue of a Plains Indian mounted atop a seventy-foot pedestal with a bow and arrow in his left hand and with his right hand "extended toward the open sea." Designed by sculptor Daniel Chester French and architect Thomas Hastings, the memorial, if built, would stand at the entrance of New York Harbor and surpass the Statue of Liberty in height by fifteen feet. After gaining final government approval for the project in December 1911, the newly organized National American Indian Memorial Association held a ground-breaking ceremony on February 22, 1913, at the Fort Wadsworth military reservation on the tip of Staten Island. Although the day was marked by "dismal skies and drizzling rain," President William Howard Taft, with thirty-two eminent Indian leaders, was on hand for the elaborate ceremony that included a twenty-one-gun salute, the signing of an Indian "declaration of allegiance," and the raising of a huge American flag. The president himself broke ground with a shovel while Northern Cheyenne Chief Wooden Leg did likewise with the thigh bone of a buffalo.[17]

A third and final Wanamaker-financed expedition set out by train from Philadelphia on June 7, 1913, and traveled over twenty thousand miles visiting 169 tribes and 89 reservations. Appropriately entitled the "Wanamaker Expedition of Citizenship," its members hoped to recreate the moving groundbreaking ritual held the previous February and to instill among the Indian participants a sense of patriotism, loyalty, and friendship for their country. With that goal in mind, Dixon brought along the flag used at the Fort Wadsworth ceremony as well as a portable phonograph donated by Thomas Alva Edison. On May 23, 1913, newly inaugurated President Woodrow Wilson had recorded a message for the occasion that Dixon played at each reservation visited. After a flag-raising ceremony, Indian leaders were encouraged to sign a declaration of allegiance to the United States. Thus, as some historians have pointed out, the Wanamaker expeditions were designed to foster the impression that Indians, by attending the flag-raising ceremony and declaring their allegiance to the United States, had "died into a new identity," or, in other words, they had "vanished as Indians and reappeared as Americans"—albeit with certain aspects of their cultures intact.[18]

Joseph Dixon never relinquished totally his belief that American Indians were a "Vanishing Race," and he mourned the nation's loss of a unique and "untainted" Indian identity. As he noted in his book *The Vanishing Race,* the study of Native American cultures and traditions was a "moral obligation" for whites. "So rapidly are the remaining Western tribes putting aside their native customs and costumes, their modes of life and ceremonies," Dixon wrote, "we belong to the last generation that will be granted the supreme privilege of studying the Indian in anything like his native state."[19] Thus, he welcomed Native American citizenship as a means by which Indians could better protect themselves and he accepted the inevitability of assimilation, but Dixon hoped that through his photographs and the proposed Indian memorial, the American public would remember its Indian heritage and retain some of the "man values" that he attributed to the "noble savage." Viewed in this light, Dixon's attitudes reflected the prevailing notions of Indians as a "Vanishing Race," of citizenship and assimilation as the only viable alternative for Indian survival, and the anthropologists' desire to preserve native cultures and traditions for posterity.

Just as the "Vanishing Race" belief influenced government policy in the late nineteenth century, the emerging desire to uphold Indian traditions and cultures exerted considerable influence on the formulation of federal Indian policy during the Progressive era. Arrell Morgan Gibson has pointed out that in the early twentieth century, the BIA was moving away from its nineteenth-century position of eradicating all signs of Indian cultures—although assimlation remained its ultimate goal.[20]

The policies of President Theodore Roosevelt's commissioner of Indian affairs, Francis Ellington Leupp (1905-1909), seem to demonstrate the trend. While he supported Indian assimilation and the eventual abolition of the Indian bureau, Leupp adopted the anthropologists' conviction that the assimilation process must be a gradual one; however, political exigencies prevented him, at times, from acting more forcefully on this point. Leupp apparently understood that cultural disparities existed between whites and Indians and that the differences should be considered in determining policy.[21] Consequently, while he continued to push for the eventual absorption of Native Americans into Anglo society, Leupp questioned many aspects of the Dawes Act and did not "believe it necessary to carry assimilation to the point of remaking the Indian in the white man's mold." He opposed sending Indian children to off-reservation boarding schools, hair-cut regulations, and blanket bans on Indian ceremonies and dances.[22] In 1905, Leupp commented that "I like the Indian for what is Indian in him. . . . Let us not make the mistake, in the process of absorbing him, of washing out whatever is distinctly Indian."[23]

One should be careful, however, not to exaggerate the extent of Leupp's "preservationist" tendencies. While the commissioner supported a more gradual approach to assimilation—one that allowed Native Americans to cling to fragments of their cultures—Leupp did so to ease their absorption into Anglo society, not to prevent it. In 1906 Leupp reflected on why previous efforts had failed to transform Native Americans into educated, English-speaking, Christian farmers. He criticized reformers for having "left wholly out of account the child-like strand in the Indian's composition," and for proceeding with assimilation as if Indians would rejoice at the chance of being transformed into "civilized" people. The comparatively few successes in assimilating Native Americans, Leupp continued, had been achieved by those reformers and teachers who recognized that American Indians would more readily accept European-based cultures if allowed to do so gradually and with a degree of flexibility.[24]

Leupp's gradualistic approach to assimilation brought him significant criticism from traditional Indian reform groups (the Women's National Indian Association and the Indian Rights Association) that continued to press for immediate assimilation. Between 1883 and 1916 these advocates of assimilation held annual meetings at Lake Mohonk, New York, to lament the problems in Indian administration and discuss strategies for reform. According to John Berens, participants in the Lake Mohonk conferences urged policies and practices that were little more than continuations of the Indian policy of the 1880s and 1890s. Their two main goals were the assimilation of Native Americans into Anglo society and the termination of federal control over Indian affairs. Like their late nineteenth-century counterparts, therefore, most Progressive era Indian reformers sought to "individualize" and "uplift" American Indians through allotment in severalty, education, and farming or other vocational trades.[25]

Leupp caused reformers consternation. He suggested that Indian cultures need not be completely eradicated, he opposed off-reservation boarding schools, and he supported the Burke Act of 1906 (which amended the Dawes Act by delaying the bestowal of citizenship until after the twenty-five-year trust period had expired). The traditional reform groups argued that any delay in the assimilation process only retarded the entry of Native Americans into Anglo society. Assimilationists and many preservationists also shared the belief that Native American entry into the mainstream was inevitable. Nevertheless, preservationists were intent on countering the hopelessness of allotted reservation life, upholding native cultures that they believed were an integral part of the American heritage, and maintaining an Indian identity in the United States.[26]

Amid such developments, the issue of enlisting Indians into segregated units emerged once again. Arizona newspaper editor C. C. Cole suggested, in 1911, that the army enlist a special regiment of Apaches to relieve unemployment on the various reservations in that state. The War Department, however, clung to its policy of integrating Indian soldiers into white units. The failed experiment of the 1890s apparently exerted a strong influence over military policy. Two years later, Representative Carl Hayden of Arizona, with a similar lack of success, recommended the creation of Native American regiments from graduates of Indian boarding schools. His familiarity with the Phoenix Indian School, whose graduates (like those of many other Indian boarding schools in the country) received a daily regimen of military-style discipline, may have influenced his recommendation.[27]

The Mexican Revolution in 1910 further stimulated discussion concerning the use of Indian soldiers. Following the abdication of Mexican President Porfirio Díaz, American President William Howard Taft mobilized United States troops along the border for fear that the violence and unrest in Mexico might spread north of the Rio Grande. In the fall of 1913, continued fighting in Mexico prompted President Woodrow Wilson to send additional forces to the border. The next year, Richard H. Pratt, superintendent of the Carlisle Indian Industrial School, volunteered to organize a brigade of Indian cavalry for duty along the border, and the Board of Indian Commissioners (a nonpartisan advisory committee of ten prominent citizens founded in 1869) supported similar plans to enlist Indian units. The War Department, nonetheless, continued its policy of opposing segregated units for Native Americans.[28]

Then, suddenly on March 9, 1916, the Mexican revolutionary hero Pancho Villa conducted a daring raid on Columbus, New Mexico, leaving several American casualties. President Wilson responded by ordering a forty-eight hundred-man punitive expedition into northern Mexico under the command of General John J. Pershing. Pershing's men had a difficult time trying to locate Villa's band. The harsh environment, inadequate maps, and an uncooperative Mexican population exacerbated their problems. American officials went so far as to offer a fifty-thousand-dollar reward for information leading to the capture of Pancho Villa.

In late March, Pershing requested a detachment of Indian scouts to aid in tracking down the Villistas. Because of Apache familiarity with Sonora, Chihuahua, Coahuila, and other northern states in Mexico, the War Department authorized Pershing to enlist Company A, Apache Scouts, from Fort Apache, Arizona, a detachment whose ancestors had served in the army as early as 1866. Shortly afterward, Pershing gave command of the twenty-man-scout detachment to Lieutenant James A. Shannon, a young West Point graduate and veteran of the Filipino Revolution, but who had no previous experience in working with Indian troops.

When he first met his scouts, Shannon had expected to find "tall, lean, eagle-eyed and eagle-beaked redskins, with little or nothing on except moccasins and a rifle belt, with probably a knife or tomahawk fastened somewhere." Instead, he found "twenty short, stocky, pleasant mannered individuals fully equipped in cavalry uniform." For the next several months Shannon's scouts, or "Pershing's Pets" as they were sometimes called, conducted scouts, led patrols, hunted game, and tracked down American deserters. Although deeply impressed with the scouts' attentiveness to an orderly camp, their devotion to traditional Apache religious rites (the scouts took daily sweats, for example), and their amazing abilities as scouts and trackers, Shannon remarked that the "Indians' military value is and always will be as guides, scouts, or trailers. . . . I don't believe that they could be made into soldiers—reliable, disciplined, fighters[—]in a hundred years."[29]

"Pershing's Pets" were not the only Native Americans to serve along the Rio Grande. Like other young Americans, Indian men rushed to enlist. They wanted to serve their country, to escape the restrictions of home and Indian boarding schools, and to seek adventure. Shelby Perkin, for example, was a young Choctaw student at the Chilocco Indian Agricultural School in Oklahoma. Upon hearing of the troubles along the Mexican border, he enlisted in the U.S. Cavalry and later served during World War I. In addition, President Wilson activated units of the Oklahoma National Guard, many of which contained Native American soldiers, and dispatched them for duty along the Texas–Mexico border.[30]

As early as 1912 Arizona officials had organized an all-Indian unit, Company F, of the Arizona National Guard, comprised of Phoenix Indian School graduates. Following Villa's raid, Company F received orders to proceed to the Arizona–Mexico border, where for nearly a year it guarded the town of Naco. While there, Company F engaged in numerous skirmishes with Mexican guerrillas. Phoenix Indian School Superintendent John B. Brown later recommended that in return for their service, the federal government grant citizenship to members of Company F.[31]

The question of segregated units surfaced again in 1917. Edward E. Ayer, a member of the Board of Indian Commissioners, convinced fellow board members to endorse a plan to raise ten to fifteen regiments of Indian cavalry commanded by white officers. Ayer's scheme received valuable support when fellow commissioner Frank Knox and U.S. Army Chief of Staff Hugh L. Scott gave their endorsements to the idea. Speaking from his own experience in the 1890s, Scott rebuffed criticism that Indians could not be made into soldiers. As evidence that American Indians would make good soldiers, he cited Britain's use of Egyptian auxiliaries.[32]

Nonetheless, the Bureau of Indian Affairs and Indian reform groups continued to oppose designs for segregated units. They argued that such plans would undermine assimilation and prevent Indian soldiers from gaining the valuable experience that would come from working side by side with Anglos. Moreover, they scorned the emerging preservationist movement as an attempt to keep Native Americans in a state of perpetual backwardness and inferiority.

An editorial in *The Indian School Journal* criticized Ayer and the Board of Indian Commissioners for attempting to "quarantine" Indian soldiers in segregated units. The piece chastised the board for its preservationist tendencies. "We have been trying assiduously for years to break up reservation conditions and banish the reservation idea," the editor asserted. "Now comes along a body of patriotic, dignified men" who "make the proposal that fifteen thousand Indian young men, the finest we have, be mobilized and put into the field carefully labeled 'Indian' for fear their race might be forgotten and they become known only as Americans."[33]

President Wilson's call on April 2, 1917, for a declaration of war on Germany and the United States' official entry into World War I four days later gave further impetus to enlisting Indian units. On April 30, 1917, Representative Julius Kahn of California, a member of the House committee on military affairs, introduced H.R. 3970. It called for the immediate organization of "ten or more regiments of Indian cavalry as part of the military forces of the United States, to be known as the North American Indian Cavalry." The bill indicated that Indian cavalrymen would receive citizenship upon enlistment without jeopardizing their rights to tribal identification, land, or annuities. Within two weeks, Representative Charles Carter of Oklahoma and Senator Boies Penrose of Pennsylvania introduced similar bills.[34]

Approximately three months following the introduction of the Kahn and Penrose bills, the House committee on military affairs met to discuss the merits of H.R. 3970. The most vocal advocate of the measure (and the bill's author) was Dr. Joseph Kossuth Dixon. As has been noted, Dixon had long been convinced that Indians were a "Vanishing Race," and through his efforts in the three Wanamaker photographic expeditions he had hoped to preserve a romantic vision of Indian masculinity, strength, and courage. Establishing segregated units and promising citizenship, therefore, were very much in keeping with Dixon's earlier efforts. After the placement of American troops along the Rio Grande border in 1916, Dixon had urged War Department officials to establish several regiments of Indian soldiers and dispatch them for duty near the border.

Following the United States' entry into World War I, Dixon stepped up his campaign, and he authored several bills dealing with the creation of special Indian units. His preservationist sympathies were key to his thinking: what better way was there to preserve one of the most prominent and glorified aspects of Indian culture, the "cult of the warrior," than by organizing several segregated regiments of Indian soldiers? Set apart from Anglo and African American troops, pure-Indian units presumably would enable Native Americans to retain their "warrior traditions" and other "noble" traits. With the preservation of these romantic aspects of Native American cultures and traditions in mind, therefore, Dixon led the fight for segregated Indian units.

On July 25, 1917, Dixon testified before the House committee on military affairs. Prone to grandiloquent rhetoric and a questionable rendition of the facts (Major James McLaughlin, who accompanied Dixon on the Wanamaker Expedition of 1913, characterized him as a "hot air artist"), Dixon made an impassioned appeal in support of segregated Indian units. In his description of Native American character, Dixon complimented Indians for their "spirit of intrepidity, their unwearying fidelity, their unswerving integrity, their unstained honor, their unimpeachable veracity, their undaunted bravery, their loyal friendship," and "their glad spirit of service."[35] In hopes of appealing to the committee members' patriotism and devotion to American ideals, Dixon cited the Declaration of Independence and its call that "all men are created equal." He reminded his audience that President Wilson supported self-determination for minorities and that the present war was "to make the world safe for democracy."[36]

How these latter sentiments related to the establishment of segregated Indian regiments is unclear. Perhaps Dixon was trying to lay a broad foundation for the plan by using long-cherished, though irrelevant, American themes. More likely, he was engaging in a bit of "sandbagging" in hopes of adding greater emotional weight to his arguments.

Dixon cited a number of specific reasons why the Kahn bill should be enacted. In a manner reminiscent of General Schofield and Secretary of War Proctor in the 1890s, he argued that enlistment would improve the deplorable state of reservation Indians brought about by unemployment, disease, and alcohol consumption. Dixon suggested that a majority of Indian people supported the establishment of segregated units, as did the majority of officers in the United States Army. He challenged the committee members to make efficient use of every resource that the country had to offer, and he insisted that the Indians were willing and ready to enlist in large numbers. After all, Dixon argued, an Indian man had all the qualities of a natural soldier: "strength, courage, intelligence, loyalty, power of endurance, stoicism, sagacity, persistence and relentlessness of purpose. He is a good hater and a staunch friend, a valorous ally and a fearless foe."[37]

Taking liberties with the facts, Dixon reminded the committee members of the "successful" experiment in the 1890s and announced that U.S. Army Chief of Staff Hugh L. Scott supported the Kahn bill. Hoping to appeal to his listeners' pragmatism, Dixon cited the Europeans' use of segregated colonial troops, Canada's utilization of Indian soldiers, and the United States' own policy of segregating black troops. He also suggested that the deployment of Indian troops along the Mexican border would relieve white troops for duty in Europe, an ironic suggestion considering how he had commended Indians so highly on their fighting abilities. Dixon may have recognized that committee members had political exigencies to consider and probably could not have countenanced allowing Indian troops the honor and recognition that would accompany those Americans first deployed in Europe. By suggesting that Indian troops take over border duty while white troops sailed to Europe, he may have been trying to tone down the controversial notion that the United States would be deploying an army of American Indians overseas while the non-Indian majority remained safely at home. By restricting Indian soldiers to border duty, Dixon's plan also may have demonstrated his own racist proclivities. Finally, Dixon reminded committee members that the federal government had invested millions of dollars in educating Native Americans and it would, therefore, be a tremendous waste not to use this great Indian resource.[38]

The influence of Dixon's preservationist sympathies became even more evident in his appeal that the "Indian spirit would be crushed if we insist that he take his stand beside the white man." He added that when Indians are banded together there is "an *esprit de corps*, a unity of feeling, an enthusiasm and an expression of daring purpose, not to be encompassed in any other possible fashion."[39] Ten years earlier Dixon had bidden farewell to a "Vanishing Race." Indian military participation in World War I, he hoped, would resurrect some of the Indians' romantic martial qualities that he so admired—provided that Native Americans were kept segregated from the powerful influences of Anglo culture.

Despite his preservationist leanings and renewed hope that the "Indian spirit" might rise anew, Dixon enumerated several reasons why Native Americans should be given citizenship, a classic assimilationist goal. He apparently saw no inconsistency. Faced with what he believed to be a rapidly declining Indian population, Dixon viewed citizenship as a means by which Native Americans could protect themselves from an often hostile non-Indian population. Thus, citizenship served to further Dixon's ultimate goal of maintaining a discernible Indian presence in the country. He also pointed out to committee members the basic contradiction in the government's policy, which allowed Native Americans to fight in World War I but, at the same time, refrained from giving them citizenship. In a secondary argument, Dixon illustrated the then-prevailing national obsession with eugenics and craniology with his report that Indians had the capacity for citizenship as evidenced by the size of their skulls.[40]

Two witnesses who followed Dixon also supported the Kahn bill. Victor J. Evans, a BIA agent on the northern plains, testified that the Northern Cheyennes wanted segregated units, as did the Sioux, Blackfeet, and Crows. Francis La Flesche, of Omaha descent and an employee of the Bureau of American Ethnology, maintained lamely that Indians easily became homesick and would serve better in segregated units.[41]

In addition to Dixon, Evans, and La Flesche, supporters of segregated Indian units had powerful and influential backers. Secretary of the Interior Franklin K. Lane, for example, endorsed the Kahn bill, as did General John J. Pershing, commander of the American Expeditionary Force. Army Chief of Staff Hugh L. Scott initially supported segregated Indian units but later changed his mind, perhaps influenced by Secretary of War Newton D. Baker's opposition to the plan. The Board of Indian Commissioners, under the direction of Edward Ayer, also came out for segregated Indian units.[42]

The opinion of the general Indian population on the subject is difficult to ascertain, although substantial numbers of Native Americans apparently supported the establishment of segregated units. In a letter to the adjutant general of North Carolina, W. F. Love, the chief clerk of the local registration board, reported that the Cherokees in Robeson County preferred segregated units "as they do not like to associate with either white or colored people."[43] In May 1920 Private Thomas L. Slow wrote to Commissioner of Indian Affairs Cato Sells, asking that he be transferred to an all-Indian unit if the War Department created one. Slow, a Sioux stationed at Fort George Wright, Washington, expressed resentment that "Uncle Sam let the colored boys have their own regiment. Why not let the Indians too?"[44] The nations of the

Iroquois Confederation endorsed the establishment of segregated Indian units, as did some of the Native Americans who enlisted in the Oklahoma National Guard. According to an article in *The Indian School Journal,* published in December 1917, the Blackfeet leader Three Bears made "an eloquent appeal to the president that an Indian army be conscripted to patrol the Mexican border."[45]

It is hardly surprising that young men stationed far from home, family, and friends would have desired to live and fight beside comrades with similar cultural ideas and experiences. On the other hand, some Indian soldiers probably viewed segregated units as relegating them to an inferior social status—akin to that of blacks. The Lumbee Indians of North Carolina, for example, objected strenuously when army officials classified them as blacks and demanded that, in the future, they be classified appropriately—as Indians. Indian men may have also viewed segregated units as an insult—that non-Indians did not trust them or their abilities as soldiers. Inclusion in white units, conversely, may have been interpreted by some Native Americans as a sign of acceptance and respect. In that case, some Indian soldiers, in hopes of protecting their social status and position, desired to be integrated into white units.

Despite the backing of Dixon, Secretary Lane, General Pershing, and some Native Americans, the army would not budge, reasoning that its experiment in the 1890s had ended in failure and that new efforts to do so would likely meet the same fate. The majority of its top officials refused to countenance the establishment of segregated Indian units and did not support the Kahn and Penrose measures. Criticism from the Bureau of Indian Affairs and traditional Indian reform organizations that supported assimilation provided further impetus for the military's decision.

Secretary of War Newton D. Baker and U.S. Army Chief of Staff Peyton C. March were among the military leaders who opposed segregated Indian units. Secretary Baker opposed the scheme for a variety of reasons. The failure of segregated Indian units in the 1890s was the dominant cause for his dissent, although other factors contributed as well. Joseph Dixon suggested that Baker disapproved of the plan because "he did not believe in the segregation of troops according to race" and because Commissioner of Indian Affairs Cato Sells opposed the idea.[46]

Another factor in understanding Secretary Baker's opposition to segregated Indian units was the status of black troops during the period. Just months after the United States entered the war, a series of race riots erupted in East St. Louis and in Houston, Texas, in response to government indifference to lynchings, floggings, and other assaults that became increasingly common during the Wilson administration. Army officials expressed concern when intelligence reports indicated more unrest among black soldiers than ever before. In light of such events, critics could not expect the federal government to initiate another controversial policy designed to segregate one race from another, particularly with the country already embroiled in a world war. In response to increasing discontent among African American soldiers, Secretary Baker warned President Wilson that as commander in chief he could no longer continue his policy of silence in the face of racial violence and lynchings. However, as Henry Blumenthal characterized them, "political expediency and political exigencies" were the primary determinants of Wilson's race policy.[47]

Army Chief of Staff Peyton C. March opposed the enlistment of Indian units on different grounds. While testifying before the House committee on military affairs shortly after the war had ended, March stated that "the organization of Indian regiments is impracticable. You cannot get those men." The heart of March's opposition was that the number of Indian enlistees would never be adequate to fill the ranks of several cavalry regiments.[48] The problem of keeping all-Indian units up to full strength in the face of potentially high casualty rates also undercut the plan's appeal. Thus, March based his opposition on logistics rather than on Baker's historic and social reasons.

The drive to establish segregated units of Indian soldiers also had critics within the Bureau of Indian Affairs. A lawyer from Iowa, Commissioner of Indian Affairs Cato Sells had served as a U.S. district attorney during the Grover Cleveland administration. After moving to Texas in 1907, Sells became president of Texas State Bank and Trust Company. As a reward for his active support during the election of 1912, Woodrow Wilson awarded Sells the commissionership of the Bureau of Indian Affairs, a post that he occupied until 1921. Because Sells was a strong advocate of assimilation, he opposed segregating Indians from whites. In his 1918 annual report, Sells stated that the Indians' logical place was shoulder to shoulder with the white men, where they would receive discipline and the same respect and consideration given to other soldiers. Sells concluded that "the military segregation of the Indian is altogether objectionable. It does not afford the associational contact he needs and is unfavorable to his preparation for citizenship."[49]

Contrary to preservationists, Commissioner Sells labored for the speedy "individualization" and acculturation of Native Americans as the necessary prerequisites toward assimilation. Sells summed up this view with his assessment that the "mingling of the Indian with the white soldier ought to have, as I believe it will, a large influence in moving him away from tribal relations and toward civilization."[50] In February 1918, J. W. Dady, the superintendent of the Red Cliff School and Agency in Bayfield, Wisconsin, wrote a letter commending Sells's policy of opposition to segregated units. In his description of Chippewa recruits within his jurisdiction, Dady wrote that fourteen young men had enlisted, and one had been drafted. They were doing well, he continued, but particularly the boys who were separated from those who enlisted in the local (predominantly Indian) company.[51]

In addition to opposition from Baker, March, and Sells, resistance to the establishment of segregated troops emanated from the ranks of Indian reform organizations. The Society of American Indians (SAI), an Indian-led reform organization dominated by well-educated "Red Progressives," advocated self-help and education as the key to Indian advancement. Although its policies often reflected the attitudes and ideals of the Indian elite rather than common folk, the SAI, under the leadership of Arthur C. Parker, opposed segregated units because, as Parker stated, "segregation has done more than bullets to conquer the red man."[52] The SAI argued further that segregated units encouraged the maintenance of racial stereotypes, undermined Indian progress, and gave Native Americans an inferior social status. Through speeches and editorials in *The American Indian Magazine*, the SAI worked to defeat measures designed to segregate Indians in the army. An editorial in the fall 1917 issue likened segregated units to "walking reservations" that denied Native Americans the advantages of understanding such important American ideals as "universal Americanism and equal citizenship."[53]

The Philadelphia-based Indian Rights Association (IRA) also opposed segregating Indian soldiers. Founded in 1882 by Herbert Welsh and Henry B. Pancoast, the IRA supported allotment and citizenship as the best means of securing the "civilization" of Indians. Welsh, the executive secretary of the IRA, opposed segregated units on grounds similar to those of Commissioner Sells. In April 1918, Welsh wrote that the federal government should strive to bring about the dismemberment of tribal relations among the Indians and their complete absorption into the majority society. Any measure that suggested "segregation and a perpetuation of the old order of things," he continued, was a "backward step."[54]

Commissioner Sells demonstrated his strong influence over government-sponsored Indian school publications by ensuring that both *The Indian School Journal* (published by the Chilico Indian School in Oklahoma) and *The Native American* (published by the Phoenix Indian School in Arizona) carried the sections of his annual addresses referring to segregated units and other official pronouncements on the topic.[55] An article in *The Native American*, for instance, quoted Sells as stating that "if the native goes into this conflict as the equal and comrade of every man who assails autocracy and ancient might, he will come home with a new light in his face and a clearer conception of the democracy in which he may participate and prosper."[56]

In the face of such overwhelming opposition, the Kahn and Penrose bills failed to gain passage, but Joseph Dixon nonetheless persisted. In January 1920 he again endorsed legislation that would establish one or more Indian divisions in the army. Appearing on January 28, 1920, before the House committee on military affairs, which was considering a bill to reorganize the army and increase its efficiency, Dixon reminded his audience about his earlier attempts to raise ten or more regiments of Indian cavalry. Venting his anger against Secretary of War Newton Baker and Commissioner of Indian Affairs Cato Sells (the spoilers of the Kahn bill), Dixon testified that Baker "did not believe in the segregation of troops according to race, although he segregated the Negro." According to Dixon, Sells opposed the plan because he did not support citizenship for Indians. Granting Indians citizenship, he accused Sells of thinking, would deprive BIA officials of seeking for their own benefit the "spoliation of Indian property and Indian rights."[57]

Dixon was certainly justified in pointing out the inconsistency in the army's position in segregating black troops but refusing to establish separate units for Indians. But his assessment of Cato Sells was flawed. The commissioner was a strong advocate of Indian citizenship and opposed segregated units as detrimental to the assimilation process. Moreover, granting Indians citizenship would hardly have deprived private interests or the federal government of opportunities to usurp Native American properties and rights. Hundreds of Indians who had received citizenship after the passage of the 1887 Dawes Act had lost their allotments, and the amount of tribally owned lands declined precipitously in ensuing decades. Furthermore, in 1916 the Supreme Court had ruled in *United States* v. *Nice* that Indian citizenship was not incompatible with continued federal guardianship. Thus, the government could (and did) maintain many of its restrictions and regulations over Indian life.

In order to bolster his contention that the majority of Native Americans supported segregated Indian units, Dixon testified that, in October 1917, he had sent copies of the Kahn bill to every reservation in the country. Each tribe, he indicated, was to read the plan and then sign a declaration of "patriotic sentiment." The declaration, which reveals much of the stereotypical image of American Indians, also demonstrated Dixon's preservationist sympathies. By signing the declaration, Native Americans attested to the notion that they had been trained to fight by "instinct and tradition" and that all Indians had grown up as warriors. Therefore, they preferred to fight in separate units so that they could preserve and prove their "old time Indian spirit" and show to the world that their "proud boast as warriors was not in vain."[58]

Dixon claimed to have received forty responses, but expressed regret that some reservation officials refused to distribute the declarations. The officials, apparently under orders from Commissioner Sells, risked losing their jobs, Dixon claimed, if they distributed the petitions. In response to their timidity, Dixon wrote those officials who refused to distribute the declarations and chastised them for such "violations of Indian rights." He compared Sells's censorship of the mail to a warden's censorship of a prisoner's mail.

Not surprisingly, Dixon received some heated responses. Robert E. L. Daniel, the superintendent of Cantonment Indian agency in Oklahoma, for instance, penned a response in which he described Dixon's latest plan as "a penny wise and pound foolish scheme to organize a big Wild West show under the camouflage of Indian military duty."[59]

After relating his experiences in trying to get reservation officials to distribute the declarations, Dixon repeated many of the arguments he had used in July 1917 in support of segregated Indian units, emphasizing the need to make efficient use of all available manpower. In addition, he denounced as a failure the BIA's long-held policy of forcing Indians to become farmers and argued, instead, that "the North American Indian is a natural soldier by inheritance," declaring that "the laziest lounger on a reservation can be transformed in a minute to undertake a ride or tramp of many miles in the hottest or coldest weather." The Indian soldier, Dixon continued, would perform as well in Alaska or in the Philippines as he would in the United States: "He is inured to cold and the blizzard as he is to the heat of the desert, or the tropics. In other words an all-around good soldier." Dixon concluded, therefore, that military service would provide promising careers for some fifty-thousand Indian men.[60]

Next, he launched into an explanation of how his new scheme would operate. The First Indian Division would consist of two brigades of infantry, he testified, while the Second Indian Division would contain two cavalry brigades. Desertions, Dixon predicted, would be rare and many soldiers would re-enlist. Keeping the two divisions up to strength would be easy, Dixon maintained, because a "healthy vigorous Indian of fifty years is as fit to make a campaign as a white man of thirty." To cut costs, the proposed divisions would use Indian ponies (broncos and cayuses, in particular) in lieu of regular cavalry horses. Indian ponies could go days with little or no water, Dixon testified, and could subsist by browsing cactus and other desert vegetation that a regular cavalry horse would not touch. Regimental or battalion headquarters, according to Dixon's plan, would be established close to important Indian reservations, and the army would create and maintain a system of vocational-military schools for the purpose of preparing Indian youths for a military career and citizenship.[61]

Attendance at these schools, Dixon continued, would be compulsory for all Native American children between the ages of eight and eighteen. Graduates would have the opportunity of attending an "Indian West Point" for noncommissioned officers. Qualified Indian sergeants and corporals were to be allowed entrance into regular officers' schools. All Native Americans of one-eighth or more Indian blood who were twenty-one years old and who enlisted in the army, furthermore, would be granted citizenship, as would those who had served in the past. After 1929, all Indian graduates of reservation or public schools would receive citizenship upon reaching the age of twenty-one, provided that they could read and write the English language.[62]

Finally, Dixon argued, for the first twenty-one years of the plan all Indian lands would be held inalienable. "If the Indian is to be a soldier he must be trained," Dixon argued, "and while being trained the inviolability of his lands must be maintained." Moreover, by declaring all Indian lands to be inalienable for twenty-one years, Native American children would have the opportunity to receive an education and citizenship before receiving fee patents.[63]

The committee on military affairs, not surprisingly, found several aspects of Dixon's plan unacceptable. Both Congressmen James W. Wise of Georgia and Frank L. Greene of Vermont pointed out that the committee on Indian affairs and the Department of the Interior had jurisdiction over Indian education and that the War Department should not involve itself with such matters. Greene nonetheless expressed reservations about the constitutionality of compulsory vocational and military training for Native American children. He also questioned the prudence and ethics of relegating Indians to a military career while letting non-Indians sit at home and follow "trades of peace."[64]

Much like his previous attempts to gain passage for the Kahn-Penrose bills, Dixon's new efforts to establish segregated units of Indian soldiers met with defeat. The failure of his second attempt to segregate Indian troops also ended the belief that the War Department held the answer to the Indian question.[65] Dixon had hoped to revamp the entire administration of Indian affairs by bypassing the BIA and appealing directly to the War Department. In 1920, however, the War Department evidently no longer desired to acquire jurisdiction over Indian affairs. That being the case, control over Indian administration remained firmly in the grip of BIA bureaucrats.

Despite his failure to preserve the "old time Indian spirit" through the establishment of segregated Indian units and the Indian memorial project (which was shelved with the beginning of World War I), Dixon's career as an

Indian enthusiast and advocate is important for several reasons. First, by working tirelessly for segregated Indian units during World War I, he helped focus attention on federal Indian policy and its assimilationist agenda. Perhaps more important, he brought national attention to Indian contributions during the war and helped educate the majority society about the loyalty and honorable character of American Indians—many of whom did not possess United States citizenship or the right to vote.

Dixon is also important for his work with the American Indian Defense Association (AIDA), a nonpartisan, nonsectarian reform organization that sought "to secure to the American Indian just treatment from the government and people of the United States and to promote his welfare." After receiving an invitation, in June 1923, to accept membership to AIDA's national advisory council, Dixon and Rodman Wanamaker joined the organization. Coincidentally, they also accepted Secretary of the Interior Hubert Work's appointment, in May 1923, to the short-lived Committee of One Hundred, an eclectic group of civic leaders, reformers, politicians, anthropologists, and "Red Progressives," who were to review and advise the federal government on Indian policy.[66] Though not a leading voice, Dixon was clearly at the heart of the Indian reform movement.

The extent of Dixon's participation in AIDA was probably minimal, although he corresponded regularly with John Collier, the executive secretary of AIDA, and he represented the ailing Rodman Wanamaker's interests in matters relating to Indian policy. Dixon kept abreast of the Pueblo land issue and attended AIDA meetings when time permitted. On at least one occasion, Collier asked Dixon for money to support AIDA. In February 1924, Collier, who was with an AIDA delegation in Chicago, wired an urgent telegram to Dixon, stating that they had no money and needed seven hundred dollars.[67] Aware of Dixon's relationship with the millionaire Rodman Wanamaker, Collier may have expected that Dixon could easily arrange to get the needed funds. Whether or not Wanamaker helped bankroll AIDA is unknown, but if he did provide financial support it might help explain why Collier continued working closely with the eccentric and pompous Joseph Dixon.

On June 11, 1925, Dixon and Rodman Wanamaker resigned their positions on AIDA's national advisory board. In a letter to John Collier, Dixon cited the "unseemly and ribald features of the Aztec Ball at the Hotel Ambassador," held on February 6, 1925, in New York City, as the reason for the decision. The ball, which was an AIDA benefit event, included Indian dancing, music, and a collection of artifacts and paintings. At one point in the tableau, a group of young women in bright feathered costumes performed a "totem pole dance." Such a display, apparently, was too risqué for Dixon.

Although he had not personally attended the event, Dixon claimed to have reliable reports that the entertainment "contraven[ed] a wholesome respect for law and the amenities of life." Furthermore, Dixon argued, the fact that members of AIDA's executive committee were in attendance placed "the society and those who are named as its responsible patrons in the hands of its adversaries."[68]

Collier responded with surprise to Dixon's resignation. In a letter dated June 26, 1925, Collier wrote that he was unaware of any improprieties at the Aztec Ball. He acknowledged that the AIDA had several adversaries but that none of them had criticized the ball. Furthermore, Collier expressed astonishment that Dixon and Wanamaker, who "had an abiding interest in the cause" of Indian reform and who wanted the same kind of results that the AIDA was seeking, should summarily resign over such a trivial matter. Collier concluded the letter with the plea that Dixon reconsider his resignation. "The biggest work is still ahead," Collier entreated, "and we don't want to lose you or Mr. Wanamaker from the National Advisory Board."[69]

Disregarding Collier's request that he remain a member of AIDA, Joseph Dixon refused to return to the organization. Two months later, at the Wayland Memorial Baptist Church in Philadelphia, he married Edith Sloane Reid, a former social worker and teacher. His interest in Indian affairs remained strong, however, and he continued working on behalf of Native Americans by pushing for Indian citizenship and better living conditions on reservations. To educate and help raise the public's level of awareness regarding Native American cultures, Dixon arranged exhibitions of Indian photographs taken a decade earlier during the Wanamaker expeditions.[70]

Dixon's contributions to the Wanamaker expeditions, his persistent stand during and after World War I for segregated Indian units as a means of preserving the "cult of the warrior" and maintaining a strong Indian identity in the country, and his involvement with the American Indian Defense Association, provide convincing evidence that he possessed strong preservationist sympathies. Nonetheless, other scholars have stressed the fact that Dixon lacked any realistic understanding of Indian cultures, that he seemed more interested in photographing Indians than he did in the Indians themselves, that he unduly pressured Indians into taking part in his foolish ceremonies, and that he supported Indian citizenship and patriotism—and thus assimilation. As a result, they dismiss him as little more than a pompous eccentric and his activities during the Wanamaker expeditions as a "charade fossilized in rituals of patriotism."[71]

Dixon was a complex individual and his attitudes regarding the "Vanishing Race" were, at times, inconsistent and misguided. However, that flaw should not be grounds to dismiss him as insignificant. After all, federal Indian policy and the activities of the BIA and several different Indian reform organizations during the early decades of the twentieth century can also be described, in hindsight, as inconsistent and misguided. Unlike the majority of reformers, however, Dixon had (at least for a while) strong financial backing, he traveled thousands of miles visiting nearly all the major reservations, he had considerable access to officials serving in the highest levels of government and in the military, and he helped educate hundreds of thousands of non-Indians about Native American life and cultures.

Although his lack of professional training in anthropology and history manifested itself quite frequently, Dixon wrote several pieces of legislation that were ultimately introduced and debated in Congress, he testified before various congressional committees, he served on both governmental and private advisory boards dealing with Indian policy and reform, and he was consulted frequently by Native Americans for advice and help. Thus, while Dixon may have been both eccentric and vain, he was far from insignificant. From 1908 until his death in 1926, Dixon was a controversial but important contributor to the debate over the direction of Indian policy in the United States.

Dixon's efforts can be said to symbolize the evolution of Indian policy during his time. Going from "Vanishing American" to involvement in AIDA, Dixon's changes of mind reflected the motion from assimilation to self-determination and cultural pluralism. By the mid-1930s this evolutionary process brought John Collier to the forefront of Indian policy reform, and the Indian Reorganization Act of 1934 (or "Indian New Deal") ended officially the harmful allotment provisions of the infamous Dawes Act of 1887. Interestingly, in June 1940, in the midst of a second world war, Commissioner Collier, in an attempt to find a wartime role for the BIA, proposed without success the formation of an all-Indian division. Segregated Indian units, he maintained, would allow Native Americans to retain their own identities, would ensure that their wartime contributions would be recognized fully, and would help preserve Indian cultures.[72] Joseph K. Dixon couldn't have argued the case any better!

It is likely that Collier, at one time or another, discussed the issue of segregated troops with Dixon or, having failed to do so, that he at least studied Dixon's efforts during World War I. Had he done so, Collier would have discovered that even in integrated units, Indian soldiers performed with distinction. He would have also learned that most Indian draftees and enlisted men served faithfully and without protest—which provides the focus for Chapter 3.

3

The Draft and Enlistment of American Indians

THE DRAFT AND ENLISTMENT OF NATIVE AMERICAN MEN FOR DUTY IN World War I signaled an important point in the evolution of Anglo–Indian relations during the early twentieth century. Through service in the war, Indian soldiers demonstrated a degree of patriotism and loyalty that surprised many non-Indians. The war years witnessed a resurgence of racial pride among Native Americans and provided thousands of Indian soldiers with opportunities to learn new skills, a chance to escape the restrictions of Indian schools and reservation life, and a reason to be proud of their accomplishments. Consequently, service in the war, although brief, fostered a dual pride among Native Americans: pride of Indian heritage and race, and pride of being American.

The United States maintained a position of neutrality during the first two and a half years of World War I. After Germany's resumption on February 1, 1917, of unrestricted submarine warfare, President Woodrow Wilson severed diplomatic relations with Germany and the regime of Kaiser Wilhelm II. Two months later the United States entered the war.

Shortly after diplomatic ties had been cut, Judge Advocate General Enoch Herbert Crowder, a West Point graduate and former Indian fighter, began work on legislation designed to secure eligible men for military service. His efforts were rewarded on May 18, 1917, when Congress passed the Selective Service Act. A few days later, Wilson appointed Crowder as provost marshal general to direct the formulation of Selective Service policies and to supervise the registration and mobilization of American manpower.[1]

The first call to register for the draft came on June 5, 1917, when the federal government required that all men between the ages of twenty-one and thirty-one report to their local boards.[2] Native Americans also had to enroll, but only those possessing citizenship were liable for the draft. During the period between May 18, 1917, when the Selective Service Act became law, and the first registration day on June 5, Provost Marshal General Crowder and Commissioner of Indian Affairs Cato Sells conferred on the draft status of American Indians. They concluded that registering Native Americans would require special arrangements, for in 1917 over one-third of all Indians in the country were not citizens. Crowder and Sells reasoned further that provisions needed to be made to determine the citizenship status of Indian registrants.

There were related problems. Many Native Americans lived on remote reservations, where contact with the dominant Anglo culture and law was infrequent. Crowder and Sells were uncertain how those Indians would be notified in time to enroll. Compounding difficulties further were communication problems. Many Native Americans had trouble speaking English while others could not speak the language at all, and few draft officials had command of Indian languages. Thus, administrators needed time to explain the Selective Service Act to Native Americans and convince them that the United States' entry into the war was justifiable and merited their assistance.

With these issues in mind, Crowder requested that Sells and the Bureau of Indian Affairs (BIA) supervise the registration of Native Americans living on remote reservations rather than forcing Indians to present themselves before the regular draft boards as whites did. According to Sells's 1917 annual report, "the peculiar conditions applicable to each separate band or tribe of Indians caused their registering for the [draft] . . . to be assigned to this bureau."[3] Although Sells did not specify the nature of the "peculiar conditions," a subsequent memorandum, circulated in June 1918, clarified the reason why the Indian bureau assumed responsibility for Indian enrollment. According to the memorandum, the BIA undertook the task at the request of the provost marshal general because it could handle the work more "expeditiously" than could the local registration boards. Due to the isolation of many reservations and considering the "temerity" of Indians, Sells reasoned, "it was considered advisable that our reservation officials who were familiar with the Indians should undertake this work."[4]

Acting on Crowder's recommendation that the enrollment of Native Americans be flexible, Sells called for the establishment of registration boards on several Indian reservations. The reservation draft boards consisted of the agency's superintendent, clerk, and physician. If for some reason they could not carry out their duties, Sells could appoint a person of his own choosing. To preclude the possibility of failing to register Native Americans in time, Crowder authorized Sells to begin the enrollment process early.[5]

The first major problems were educating the Indians as to what registering for the draft meant and instructing them that they were liable to register. Many noncitizen Indians believed that they were exempt from register-ing because they were not citizens. Why should Indians have to register for the draft, some asked, if they were exempt from compulsory service? Others feared that enrollment meant that they would be automatically called for military duty.

Confusion regarding the draft manifested itself at various levels. Tom Ration, a Cherokee, was laid up in an Oklahoma sanitarium during the war, suffering from a bout with pneumonia. His father had to register, however, and early on the morning of June 5, 1917 (the first registration day), he mounted his horse and rode off to enroll, hoping to get back quickly to his farm and family of eight. But when he arrived at the registration center, draft officials instructed him to tether his horse outside and to come in and help register others. The man returned home to his family late that evening, after finally getting a chance himself to enroll. Neither of the Ration men were called, however, believing that the elder Ration's work for the local board had, somehow, exempted him from the draft.[6]

Commissioner Sells, meanwhile, wrote to James Hildebrande, a Native American living in Oklahoma, to inform him that the registration applied to Indians as well as whites and that those within the prescribed age limits had to register or be subject to punishment. He added, "you should understand that registration does not mean drafting and you should explain this to your people."[7] In June 1918 Sells responded to a query from Congressman John E. Raker of California, regarding Indian registration and the application of the draft law to particular tribes. Sells responded that all Indians were subject to the Selective Service Act and had to register, regardless of their tribal affiliation.[8]

The Bureau of Indian Affairs continued to receive numerous inquiries pertaining to Indian enrollment over a year after the United States declared war. This continuing uncertainty suggests that Sells and his associates struggled to disseminate draft information to Native Americans, to res-ervation employees, and to government officials. Their difficulties resulted in needless worry and increased bitterness on the part of many American Indians.

A second major problem related to the government's determination of Indian-citizenship status. During his testimony before the House commit-tee on military affairs in July 1917, Joseph K. Dixon recounted a dramatic story that illustrated well the ambiguous legal status of thousands of Ameri-can Indians. Dixon testified that in the summer of 1917, a Sioux man pre-sented himself before a local board to register. A member of the board then asked him, "Are you an alien?" "No," he responded, "I was born in the United

States." "Then you are a citizen," they informed him. "No," he responded again, "I am not a citizen. I am not an alien." "What are you then?" the board inquired. "I am an Indian," he said. "I have neither the rights of an alien nor of a citizen, yet I was born in the United States. My father is a full blood Sioux Chieftain . . . and I must offer myself up for service."[9]

Because citizenship status determined whether or not Indian registerees could be drafted, the determination of Indian citizenship was literally a matter of life or death. Many Indians were unsure if they were citizens, however, and the task of determining their status was complex. The more sophisticated Native Americans demanded that if the federal government declared they were citizens and thus subject to the draft, they should also be enfranchised.

To extricate itself from the quagmire of determining Indian citizenship, the Bureau of Indian Affairs turned the entire matter over to the draft boards. Because they were designed to be flexible and to respond to local needs, the draft boards operated with considerable autonomy. Consequently, the application of the Selective Service Act on reservations was at times erratic. Not surprisingly, inconsistent rulings by registration officials only exacerbated the confusion and disillusionment of Native American registrants.

During the first enrollment in June 1917, draft officials on Indian reservations did their best to figure out the citizenship status of each enrollee. Without firm guidance or direction from the Bureau of Indian Affairs, the registration boards performed the daunting task of determining citizenship status on a case-by-case basis. Therefore, prior to the second enrollment on June 5, 1918 (for men who had reached the age of twenty-one after June 5, 1917), and the supplemental registration of August 24, 1918 (for men becoming twenty-one after June 5, 1918), Commissioner Sells sent general guidelines to aid in the determination of Indian citizenship. The guidelines, which enumerated four criteria, were technical: (1) Indians whose trust or restrictive fee patents were dated prior to May 8, 1906, were considered citizens as provided in the Dawes Act of 1887;[10] (2) Indians whose trust or restrictive fee patents were dated after May 8, 1906, and who had received patents in fee for their allotments were citizens by virtue of the competency clause in the Burke Act; (3) every Indian born within the territorial limits of the United States who had voluntarily lived apart from his people and had adopted the habits of "civilized life" was considered a citizen; (4) minor children of parents who had become citizens upon allotment, and children born to Indian citizens were also considered American citizens.[11]

If the reservation draft boards determined that a particular Indian registrant was a citizen, they forwarded his enrollment card to the regular local board. The Native American in question was then liable for the draft. In the case of noncitizen Indians, however, the board sent one copy of the registration card to the commissioner of Indian affairs and another to the superintendent of the agency where the Indian resided. Registration officials then informed the noncitizen Indian that he could claim exemption from the draft. Those Native Americans who claimed exemption due to citizenship status were given a deferred classification that prevented their induction. If a noncitizen Indian expressed a desire to waive his right to exemption from the draft, problems arose because, as yet, there were no official provisions that allowed for noncitizen Indians to enlist for military service.[12]

Occasionally, the registration boards were unable to determine the citizenship status of an Indian registrant. When such cases arose, the federal government instructed draft officials to declare the person a noncitizen. Policymakers within the Bureau of Indian Affairs apparently reasoned that it would be better for them to make mistakes—to declare Indians to be noncitizens and thus protect them from the draft—than to allow a true noncitizen Indian to be drafted for service when he should be exempt. Consequently, in a letter to agency superintendents in July 1917, Sells directed registration officials on reservations that "if there is any doubt whatever in your mind as to the status of the individual, or his clear liability to the draft, resolve it in favor of non-citizenship."[13]

Other difficulties arose concerning the federal government's application of the Selective Service law on Indian reservations. One such problem concerned the classification of noncitizen Indians. After the first draft, Crowder developed a system to classify every registrant according to his occupational and marital status. During subsequent enrollments, therefore, local boards classified registrants into one of five categories for exemption. Class I, for example, included registrants whose immediate induction into military service would least interfere with the industrial, economic, and agricultural life of the nation. Possessing few grounds for exemption, Class I registrants were the first called for duty. Classes II and III included men who were married and employed in war-related industries. Married men with children and those exempted by statute made up registrants in Class IV. Class V included those with special vocational exemptions (that is, ministers, pilots, armory employees) as well as "alien enemies" (noncitizens from nations allied with the Central Powers) and resident aliens (noncitizens from nations other than those allied with the Central Powers). Although Native Americans were not included within the government's definition of "alien" (any person not a native-born or naturalized citizen of the United States), the provost marshal general's policy was to assign noncitizen Indians to Class V. Some local boards erroneously (and at times intentionally) placed noncitizen Indians into Class I. As John Chambers has written, "the classification system was open to considerable partiality at the local level in the determination of particular cases." Thus, noncitizen Indians were at times misclassified into Class I.[14]

Such was the case with the local board at the Cheyenne River Indian Reservation in South Dakota. Although the local board correctly classified the noncitizen Sioux into Class V, the district board (which had the authority to overrule the decisions of local draft boards) reclassified them into Class I. The district board initiated the change because, it reasoned, the Indians were "not 'Alien Enemies' nor 'Resident Aliens,' in fact not aliens at all." But after receiving instructions from the provost marshal general's office, the district board rescinded its decision.[15]

On April 17, 1918, a committee of Sioux men from the Pine Ridge reservation petitioned the provost marshal general's office to investigate irregular draft proceedings in Bennett County, South Dakota. The committee alleged that the local board was intentionally misclassifying Native American registrants and "holding non-citizen Indians for military service under the draft, contrary to the expressed wishes of such Indians." It also reported that local authorities had arrested the chairman of the local board, Charles Milner, for failing to inform his fellow committee members that noncitizen Indians were exempt from compulsory military service. General Crowder promptly ordered W. A. Morris, adjutant general of South Dakota, to conduct an investigation of the charges. On April 29, the new local board chairman of Bennett County, Milton T. Benham, refuted the Sioux charges and asserted that "these Indians have the franchise here, vote at our elections, hold office in the county, and have adopted the ways of civilization. This Board is inducting no 'Non-Citizen' Indians."[16]

Implicit in Benham's remarks is the assumption that noncitizen Indians who exercised de facto citizenship rights should be treated as citizens relative to the draft. Adjutant General Morris summed up such sentiments in a May 1918 letter to General Crowder. Like Benham, Morris maintained that many Native Americans residing in South Dakota exercised the right of citizenship by taking part in elections. He failed to understand, therefore, why such people could claim exemption from service as noncitizen Indians. "If they have been allowed to vote and exercise the right of citizenship in the past," Morris wrote, "it occurs to me that they should be required to perform the duties of citizens at this time."[17]

Governor S. V. Stewart of Montana dispatched a letter to the provost marshal general's office with a different, but related, complaint. Stewart resented the government's exemption of noncitizen Indians because such an action resulted in the drafting of a larger percentage of whites to meet the state's quota of soldiers. In his letter to Crowder, Governor Stewart enclosed several letters from citizens and officers of Big Horn County showing the "injustice" worked in that county by counting the registered Crow Indians for quota purposes and then automatically exempting them.[18]

The racial classification of Native Americans posed an additional problem for local boards. During the first registration period, registration cards included a section providing a physical description of the registrant, but did not specifically ask for the registrant's race. In the case of African American registrants, however, local boards were instructed to tear off the lower left-hand corner of the card to indicate "if a person is of African descent." Native Americans, consequently, were classified as white.[19]

Because each county was required to induct a quota of white and black registrants based on the number of eligible men residing therein, the racial classification of Native American registrants was important. If Indians were classified as "white," for example, the actual number of whites inducted would decrease. In September 1917, Crowder ordered T. W. Bickett, the governor of North Carolina, to send 40 percent of his state's quota of men to Camp Jackson, South Carolina, to begin training. To maintain the segregation of black troops, Crowder ordered that "this increment should be made up entirely of white men." Because several of the counties in North Carolina had predominantly black populations, Bickett faced difficulties in finding enough white registrants to fill the quota. Consequently, the governor asked for authorization to classify fifty-seven Lumbee (Croatan) Indians as whites in order to fill his state's quota. Crowder responded in the affirmative on September 14, 1917, stating that "Indians must be classed as white men for the purpose of this movement. What we desire is to prevent numbers of the African race from moving with this white contingent."[20] Subsequent registrations provided cards that included four categories for racial identification (white, Negro, Oriental, Indian), a procedure that solved the problem of classifying Native Americans. Nevertheless, for quota purposes, American Indians (as well as Mexican Americans) continued to be counted with whites.

A fourth problem was the desire of noncitizen Indians to enlist for military service. Such a desire posed a unique dilemma for members of registration boards. Because noncitizen Indians were exempt from compulsory military service, some draft officials took the immunity to mean that Indians could not enlist—although some local boards invariably winked at the regulations and allowed noncitizen Indians to do so. When Assiniboine Clarkson Maine presented himself before the local board at Great Falls, Montana, in February 1918 and stated his intention to enlist, board members replied that noncitizen Indians were not eligible to do so. Consequently, C. D. Munro, the superintendent at the Fort Belknap reservation, took up Maine's petition to Commissioner Sells, who turned the matter over to the War Department. The adjutant general of the army skirted the issue and passed the matter on to the provost marshal general's office for a ruling. In April 1918, Crowder, after informing the War Department that a Native American could waive his claim for deferred classification on the ground of being a noncitizen Indian, declared that "it seems reasonable to say that a non-citizen Indian . . . should not be barred from enlistment" simply because he is a noncitizen Indian.[21]

In May 1918 the provost marshal general's office distributed formal guidelines for noncitizen Indians to enter military service. When such Native Americans expressed a desire to waive their exemptions and enlist for duty, the rules read, the reservation superintendent should forward the applicants' registration cards to the local board to be processed. When draft officials reached their order number, the Indians could then be inducted into the service.[22]

Reminiscent of the difficulties facing Indian soldiers in the 1890s, a final problem confronting draft officials was the understandable Native American preference for using Indian languages. Although the inability to speak English did not prevent their induction into the military, some Native American soldiers encountered problems when they reported to their designated army training camp. The local board of McIntosh County, Oklahoma, inducted several Creeks who were then rejected at training camp because of their inability to speak the English language.[23]

Eastern Cherokees from Graham County, North Carolina, encountered similar difficulties. During the summer of 1918 officials at Camp Jackson, South Carolina, rejected several Cherokee inductees because they could not speak English. Consequently, the Graham County local board requested that the Cherokees be allowed, instead, to work for the forestry service. It concluded that the Indians "feel themselves alien among the Whites and are absolutely worthless so far as soldiering is concerned." Board members suggested, moreover, that Native American men, serving under the direction of an Indian foreman who could speak English but would give them orders in their own language, be placed in the forestry service or "any branch of service where it requires work." The provost marshal general's office responded that it had no authority to draft Native Americans into the forestry service. "The fact that these Indians do not speak the English language," the office ruled, "is not a cause for their rejection at camp."[24]

Of the 11,803 Native Americans who registered for the draft prior to

September 1918, the federal government inducted 6,509 into the service, over 55 percent of Indian registrants and an estimated 13 percent of the adult male population.[25] Only 228 (less than 2 percent of the total registered) claimed deferment. Approximately 5,500 more Native American men registered after September 11, 1918, bringing the total registered to over 17,000. (The number of Indians inducted after the September call is unknown.) Jennings Wise, who has studied the draft, pointed out that the majority of Indians who claimed deferment did so because of age, and some of the claimants later tried to enlist. In his second annual report to the secretary of war, Provost Marshal General Crowder commented that "the ratio of Indian registrants inducted was twice as high as the average for all registrants," which demonstrated that the Native Americans supported "the great cause."[26]

Nevertheless, some Native Americans requested discharges from military service and a few went "absent without leave" (AWOL). George Lawrence, an Indian stationed at Camp Sherman, Ohio, requested a discharge because he was going to marry soon and hoped to take up farming in the spring. Mrs. Florence Gritts of Tahlequah, Oklahoma, requested that her husband, Burney Gritts, a Cherokee, be discharged because she was entirely dependent upon him for support. Private Alex Cadotta left Camp Grant base hospital in northern Illinois without permission. He claimed that while he was recuperating at the hospital from wounds received in France, two orderlies had physically abused him. Private John Red Bean, a Standing Rock Sioux, went AWOL from the Canadian army and requested that he be repatriated in the American Expeditionary Force.[27]

In addition to Indian draftees, thousands of Native Americans enlisted for service. Just how many Indians enlisted, however, is a matter of considerable dispute. Contemporary accounts varied widely. Joseph Dixon estimated that 17,000 Indians served, but he was probably citing the total number of Indians that registered for the draft. Commissioner of Indian Affairs Cato Sells estimated that as many as eight thousand American Indians eventually served in the armed forces of the United States during the war—80 percent by enlistment. A year after the conflict ended, the Bureau of Indian Affairs revised the estimate to over ten thousand Indian soldiers, nearly 20 percent of the adult male Indian population. Given the latter estimate, approximately thirty-five hundred Native Americans enlisted for service.[28] There may have been more enlistees. In his recent examination of Native Americans in World War I, Russel Barsh has estimated that as many as 30 percent of the adult male population may have served, bringing the total number of Indian soldiers to fifteen thousand (eighty-five hundred by enlistment). John Chambers, who studied the draft in World War I, has suggested that 6,000 Native Americans enlisted in addition to the 6,509 draftees, an estimate supported by the Board of Indian Commissioners. In addition, press reports indicated that hundreds of Native Americans from the United States enlisted in the Canadian army between 1915 and 1917.[29] Given the small number of Native Americans who claimed deferment and the disproportionately large number of Indian soldiers who entered the military via the draft or voluntary enlistment, widespread Native American support for the United States involvement in the war cannot be refuted.

American Indians supported the war effort for numerous reasons despite the fact, as Thomas Holm has pointed out, that many Native Americans "took the military oath to defend the constitution without possessing any rights under it."[30] More importantly, it should be remembered that Indian responses to the draft were diverse, and to suggest that there was a monolithic "Indian response" would be both inaccurate and stereotypical. Cultural differences, the level of acculturation, geography and demographics, education, and the relationship of a particular Native American community with the federal government all affected and helped shape Indian responses to the war effort.

An important impetus for Native American willingness to serve was BIA encouragement. Indian peoples with a strong BIA presence on their reservations and with children attending government-administered boarding schools (those living in the former "Indian Territory," for example) were probably influenced a good deal. Although Commissioner Sells opposed the establishment of segregated units of Indian soldiers, he supported Native American participation in World War I. In September 1918 he wrote that the BIA had "endeavored to give the Indians a clear understanding of their relation to the war and their part in its prosecution."[31] Sells also suggested that Indian schools teach and emphasize "the spirit of patriotism and loyalty" and that "all Indians acceptable under military regulations should be encouraged to enlist."[32] At the Santee Normal Training School's forty-eighth anniversary celebration held in May 1918, school administrators took Sells's suggestions to heart. They organized a program entitled "The Good Growing Out of the War," with eighth grade students reciting passages entitled "Deliverance from Menace" and "Science at the Front." Their tenth-grade colleagues, meanwhile, recited an editorial, "The Bright Side of the War." Each session was prefaced with a brief introduction in the Dakota language so that everyone in attendance could understand.[33]

Bureau of Indian Affairs officials may have had ulterior motives for encouraging Indian enlistment. After the passage of the Dawes Act in 1887, the bureau's policy of assimilating Native Americans into Anglo society enjoyed limited success. At a time when the assimilation policy was coming under increasing attack from preservationists, anthropologists, and reformers, the Indian office, as Russel Barsh has noted, sought to justify its continued existence and seized on Indian patriotism and enlistment for duty in the war as evidence that its assimilation programs had been successful.[34]

Several Indian reform organizations complemented the BIA's policy of encouraging Native American participation in the war, but once again, their influence would have been limited to the more acculturated elite and their families, Indian school students and graduates, and Native Americans employed by the federal government. Much of their literature and wartime propaganda, furthermore, was published in Indian school journals and newsletters with a limited readership. The National Indian Association, a reform organization founded in 1879 and whose expressed purpose was to "aid in the civilization and evangelization of Indians," expressed pride "that our Indians responded to their country's call so promptly," and through its organ, *The Indian's Friend*, it called upon Native Americans to continue their service to the country. The September 1918 issue praised the efforts of Simon Webster, a member of the Oneida tribe, who walked fifty miles from Shawano to Green Bay, Wisconsin, to enlist in the army.[35]

The Society of American Indians (SAI) also supported the war effort. Through editorials in its publication, *The American Indian Magazine*, the SAI advanced the goals of "Red Progressives" like Thomas L. Sloan, Arthur C. Parker, and Dr. Charles Eastman (Eastman's son, in fact, served during the war). Opposed to the bureaucratic paternalism of the Indian office, members of the SAI stressed race consciousness, self-help, self-reliance, and initiative as the "foundations for Indian betterment." The SAI, therefore, viewed the war as a means to gain respect and appreciation for Native Americans. In an editorial in *The American Indian Magazine* entitled "Reasons Why Indians Should Join the Regular Army," the writer exhorted Indians to serve their country to "win respect and high valuation in the estimation of the world." When the war was over, he continued, the "Indian will have proved himself a man as other men and able to cooperate in any activity America may demand."[36]

Not all members of the SAI, however, gave such unqualified support for the war effort. Dr. Carlos Montezuma, a Yavapai physician and reform activist, for example, felt that the United States had so mistreated the Indians, it should not be able to force Native Americans to fight on its behalf. Indians who wanted to serve, he believed, should be allowed to do so; Indians who did not want to serve should not have to. After all, Montezuma insisted, the

American war aims were for self-determination and democracy, but Indians at home received none. Montezuma expressed these concerns as well as his increasing criticisms of the SAI and the Bureau of Indian Affairs through his own publication, *Wassaja*.[37]

While encouragement from the BIA and Indian-reform agencies gave impetus to Indian enlistments, Native Americans had several motives of their own for serving in the war. In 1914 an agent for a Berlin circus employed sixteen Onondagas from New York to stage a miniature "Wild West" show for German audiences. The outbreak of World War I in August, however, left one group of Onondagas stranded in Trieste, Italy (at the time a part of the Austro-Hungarian empire), and another in Essen, Germany. As the latter group made its way out of the country, German mobs verbally and physically abused them. A few Onondagas were apparently mistaken for Russian or Serbian spies and arrested. In response to the maltreatment of their brethren (as well as to press their demands for federal recognition of Iroquois sovereignty), the Onondagas and Oneidas in America unilaterally declared war on Germany.[38]

Economic opportunity, a secure job, and the prospects of excitement and adventure lured Americans of all races to enlist for service in the war. The habitual unemployment and lack of opportunities that characterized many of the country's Indian reservations gave Native Americans an added incentive. According to Thomas Mails, Apache men enlisted for service in World War I to escape the confinement and poor economic conditions on their reservations. A comparison of salaries provides compelling evidence why many Native Americans selected military service over reservation employment. A Native American employed either privately or by the government in 1916 earned an annual average income of $91.66. A year later the average earnings increased slightly to $100.55. A first-year sailor in the United States Navy, meanwhile, could expect to earn at least $200.00 a year, and the average pay for enlisted men was $528.00 per year. Their counterparts in the army earned similar salaries. William Baldridge, a graduate of Chilocco Indian Agricultural School who was stationed at Fort Douglas, Utah, wrote that he was "making good in the army" and receiving $36.00 a month as a private first-class. In addition, after four years of military service, veterans had the opportunity of joining a reserve unit and receiving a retainer pay of $50.00 annually.[39] Thus, military service offered young Native American men a chance for economic mobility and a more stable financial future.

Military service also offered chances for travel and opportunities to engage the hated "Huns" in western Europe. According to an article in *The Indian School Journal*, "the call of the trenches and of a work more thrilling" inspired John C. Alexander, a Choctaw, to quit his job in Wichita, Kansas, and enlist in the army.[40] And while not all Native Americans who entered military service during World War I traveled to Europe, even domestic military service took Indian participants away from reservations and boarding schools and exposed them to outside influences at the numerous training camps scattered across the country.

During the experiment of the 1890s, when military officials organized segregated units of Indian soldiers, recruiters appealed to leading warriors and chiefs to gain support for the project. During World War I, some tribal leaders likewise encouraged their young men to serve in the military. The Crow chief Plenty Coups, who had fought for the United States Army during the Sioux Wars of the 1870s, encouraged his men to enlist for military service to prove their patriotism and to rescue them from the miseries of reservation life. Chief Strongheart, a Yakima from Washington state and a former army scout himself, visited over two hundred military posts and camps and entertained the troops with stories about Indian life and warfare. He later traveled and lectured throughout the East to encourage support for the war effort and to boost enlistments. Following his speech in front of the New York Public Library, a reported 233 men rushed to enlist. In Montana, meanwhile, Red Fox James, a member of the Blackfeet tribe, called on the War Department to give his people "a chance to fight," and in New Mexico, Chief Mexes, a Mescalero Apache, urged young men of his tribe to enlist.[41] Thus, encouragement from tribal leaders proved once again to be an important impetus for Indian enlistments.

But not all tribal elders counseled their young men to serve. Josephine Gwin Wadena, a Chippewa, lived in northern Wisconsin during the war. She recollected that the tribal elders in her community resented the draft and claimed that it violated past treaties. Consequently, they encouraged their children not to fight. Leaders representing the Pamunkey and Mattaponi tribes of Virginia voiced similar objections, stressing that the draft encroached on tribal rights. Indian peoples from across the nation, but particularly those from remote reservations with unacculturated and noncitizen populations, expressed a surprising degree of resentment in response to the Selective Service Act and the draft[42]—a topic that will be discussed in greater detail later in the chapter.

Important and compelling reasons for Indian service, however, were the same that led thousands of Anglos, Mexicans, and African Americans to fight: patriotism, the desire to defend their homeland, and devotion to American ideals of freedom and democracy—although such ideals motivated different Indian peoples in diverse ways. The acculturated and better-educated Indian men were certainly more influenced by the workings of the Wilson administration's propaganda organ—the Committee on Public Information—than were those Native Americans living on isolated reservations in California and in the Southwest. Established shortly after the United States entered the war, the Committee on Public Information published patriotic books and produced movies to encourage support for the war effort. A'wa Tseighe, a Pueblo from New Mexico, reportedly enlisted after seeing a government-sponsored "moving picture" about Germans and World War I.[43]

Other Indian veterans were also influenced by Wilson administration proclamations that the war would "make the world safe for democracy" and be the "war to end all wars." In November 1919, Carlisle Indian Industrial School graduate and war veteran Alex Cadotta wrote to Secretary Baker and explained why he had enlisted for duty in World War I: "Why did I enlist in the army? Because I wanted to hold up my flag which we and every one of us love so much! All that was in me was to save my Country for democracy, and I am a true American."[44] Arthur C. Parker, the noted Seneca anthropologist and leader of the SAI, wrote in the fall of 1917 that the "Indian fights because he loves his freedom" and because "his country, his liberties, his ideals, and his manhood are assailed by the brutal hypocrisy of Prussianism." Other Native Americans described their wartime service as a "religious sense of patriotism" and a "hot compound of militant Americanism."[45]

In February 1918, Francis Nelson, an Oglala Sioux from the Pine Ridge reservation, wrote to Secretary of War Baker requesting permission to enlist for service in the war. In an impassioned appeal, Nelson stated that he was willing to "fight for his country and willing to die. . . . I think lots of our country for I was born here in America and being a Real American I will fight and die for it." To illustrate his eagerness (and lend greater weight to his request), Nelson noted that "if I could only get out in those trenches and scalp a few of this [sic] dirty Germans, I would be one of the happiest Indians living."[46]

Young men like Francis Nelson may have had culturally based reasons for wanting to enlist as well. The Sioux, along with several other Plains tribes, have strong warrior traditions that date back centuries. According to custom, only men who proved themselves in battle could gain access to warrior societies, which were the elite associations among many Plains peoples. Members of the warrior societies enjoyed great respect and privileges, and at times, membership could lead to band and tribal leadership positions.

But young men in the twentieth century had little hope of gaining admittance into the exclusive warrior societies. Reservation and boarding-school life afforded few opportunities for them to demonstrate courageous deeds in battle—usually a prerequisite for admittance. World War I, therefore, provided young men with perhaps their last opportunity to prove their bravery and worthiness. John Thunder, a Sioux from Pipestone, Manitoba, challenged his brethren to demonstrate the courage and bravery of their warrior ancestors. "The bad-language people [Germans] are trying to destroy our government and rob us of our homes so all our men and youth have risen to defend ourselves," he wrote. "But woe to the young man who fears either wounds or death."[47] After the war, several Southern Cheyenne veterans organized a new "War Band" or joined existing warrior associations.[48] Thus, the desire to gain entrance into elite warrior societies may have influenced men from those tribes with strong martial traditions to support the war effort.

An important source of Indian recruits was the government-administered Indian boarding schools. Among the most prominent were the Hampton Institute in Virginia (a boarding school for both black and Native American students); Chilocco Indian Agricultural School, Oklahoma; Haskell Institute, Kansas; Carlisle Indian Industrial School, Pennsylvania; and the Phoenix Indian School in Arizona. Many Indian school administrators subjected their students to a regimented lifestyle complete with uniforms, military drill, and strict discipline. At the Oglala Indian Training School on the Pine Ridge reservation in South Dakota, students had to adhere to a strict disciplinary code based on a merit system. If a student earned fifteen demerits in one week, he lost all privileges for one month! Unbrushed uniforms and unpolished shoes earned one demerit, but more "serious" offenses like spitting, fighting, or using profanity could result in the accumulation of up to four demerits. At the Santa Fe Indian School in New Mexico, and at the Chilocco Indian Agricultural School in Oklahoma, administrators divided incoming students into military-style battalions and companies. Male students wore army uniforms and carried unloaded guns while they drilled. Students awoke each morning to roll call and a flag-raising ceremony. Afterward, they marched to breakfast accompanied by the school band. Because boarding-school students were already accustomed to military discipline, one editor pointed out, Indian schools soon became "automatic recruiting stations."[49]

Urged on by enthusiastic school administrators, Indian school students and alumni from certain tribes enlisted in large numbers. The superintendent of the Standing Rock Indian School at Fort Yates, North Dakota, reported that about 130 Indian boys served in the army during the war. Ten Pueblo and Apache alumni of the Santa Fe Indian School saw military service, and practically all seventy of the Indian soldiers from the Mission Indian agency in California were students or graduates of the Sherman Institute located in Riverside, California. Chilocco Indian Agricultural School sent over one hundred men to war,[50] while Hampton Institute reported that forty-four of its Indian students served.

The more isolated Indian schools in the desert Southwest, on the other hand, often had few students who served in the conflict. Officials at the Shivwits Indian School in Santa Clara, Utah, at the Western Shoshone Schools in Owyhee, Nevada, at the Fallon Indian School in Fallon, Nevada, and at the Goshute Indian School in Ibapah, Utah, reported that none of their students served during World War I. Only one student from the Fort McDermitt Indian School in Nevada, a Paiute named Thomas Wasson, saw duty.[51]

Superintendent John R. Brown of the Phoenix Indian School is an example of an administrator who was initially reluctant to encourage his students to enlist, but later became a strong advocate of military service. Prior to the United States entry into the war, Brown had forbidden his students to enlist, even in the Arizona National Guard, because fewer students translated into fewer funds, and Brown's primary concern had been to protect enrollment numbers. Some students ran away from the school, however, and enlisted without his permission. At an April 10, 1917, meeting, Brown reversed himself and encouraged his male students to enlist. He assured his students that they would no longer need to "go in the night nor escape down an alley in your overalls" to join the military. Brown warned the students that "war is not a picnic or a joy-ride. It is hard serious business" and required sacrifices. After the war, however, Brown reverted to his policy of forbidding his students to enlist in the military without his expressed consent.[52]

Indian school students and alumni also enlisted because many possessed vocational skills that allowed them to enter at a pay scale higher than what was possible for other soldiers or sailors. Although a majority of Indian soldiers entered the army as infantrymen, many graduates from the Phoenix Indian School entered the U.S. Navy as carpenters' mates, shipwrights, blacksmiths, and electricians, where they earned between thirty-three dollars and fifty-five dollars a month. In June 1918, Phoenix Indian School reported forty-five of its students in the army and twelve in the navy. Sixty-nine students from the Cushman Indian Trades School in Tacoma, Washington, served, and the Carlisle Indian Industrial School reported nearly sixty of its students in military service, about 15 percent of the total male enrollment.[53]

Editorials and articles in Indian school newsletters also encouraged Indian men to enlist, but once again, one should bear in mind the limited audience of such literature. Headlines such as "Hampton Indians Doing Their

Bit," "Six Carlisle Indians Join the Navy," "Chilocco Boys in the Army and Navy," and "Schools Have Furnished More Than 1,200 to Navy Alone" served during the war years as constant reminders to young men enrolled at Indian schools or who subscribed to the school's newsletters.[54] It would seem unlikely, however, that Indian school literature would have had much impact on Indian men who had never attended the schools and did not receive subscriptions.

By the end of 1917 Commissioner Sells commented that the patriotic attitude of Native Americans toward the war was "especially noticeable among the younger generation, largely the product of our Indian schools." He also noted that many of the schools reported twenty to thirty enlistments and some as many as fifty. An estimated 90 percent of Indian school students who fought in the war volunteered for duty.[55]

While the majority of eligible American men registered for the draft and either enlisted or accepted conscription as their patriotic duty, draft evasion was not uncommon. The provost marshal general's office placed draft resisters into three categories: those who failed to register (slackers), those who failed to submit themselves after registration to the jurisdiction of the local board (delinquents), and those who failed to obey the orders of the local board and report for military duty (deserters). Although less than 2 percent of all Indian registrants claimed deferment from the draft, convincing evidence of Native American loyalty and willingness to serve, incidents of Indian draft evasion occurred, the overwhelming majority of which fell under the category of "slacker."

In the isolated mountains of the Qualla Boundary reservation in North Carolina, some twenty-three hundred Eastern Cherokees expressed little interest in the war. Despite the fact that the Eastern Cherokees voted in local elections from time to time, their citizenship status remained ambiguous. Not until the United States entered the war in April 1917 did reservation officials concern themselves with the long deferred question of Cherokee citizenship. When Superintendent James Henderson attempted to coax his people to register for the draft or enlist for service, many Eastern Cherokees demonstrated reluctance. David Owl, for example, questioned the legality of Indian liability to the draft. Others claimed exemption because they could not speak English. After convincing the Cherokees that they were citizens, Henderson was able to get over one hundred to register. Nearly seventy served during the war, half of them as draftees.[56]

One of the more dramatic and publicized episodes of Indian draft resistance took place at the Goshute (Gosiute) reservation along the Nevada–Utah border. Inhabited by only 150 Goshutes and long neglected by the

Bureau of Indian Affairs, the Goshute reservation, in response to the corrupt administration of reservation superintendent Amos Frank, erupted in the summer of 1917. For months the Goshutes had sent letters of grievance to Commissioner Sells. They complained that Frank employed discriminatory hiring practices, that whites were trespassing on reservation lands with impunity, and that there was no justice on the reservation. Moreover, the Goshute men opposed military service and refused to register for the draft. Being noncitizens, they believed that they did not have to register as required by the Selective Service Act. As Richard Ellis pointed out, the trouble on the Goshute reservation grew from a "deep and pervasive disenchantment with bureau officials and a basic misunderstanding of the Selective Service Act."[57] To compound the problems, rumors circulated that foreign agents were inciting the Indians to defy registration, and newspapers, influenced by wartime hysteria, printed unsubstantiated stories about German operatives at work among the Goshutes.[58]

In June 1917 and again in January 1918, Sells dispatched Inspector L. A. Dorrington to investigate conditions on the reservation. Ignoring the Goshutes' complaints against Superintendent Frank, Dorrington expressed concern, instead, with the Indians' unwillingness to register for the draft, and he encouraged the tribe to adhere to the provisions of the Selective Service Act. Their refusal, Dorrington warned, could result in possible arrest, imprisonment, and a stint in the army.[59]

In response to reports in late January and early February 1918 of continued unrest at the Goshute reservation, Inspector Dorrington decided that matters were getting out of hand. Bureau of Indian Affairs officials had become increasingly alarmed after receiving reports that Western Shoshones at nearby Owyhee, Nevada, had raised funds to pay Jack Wilson (better known as Wovoka, the Paiute prophet and one-time practitioner of the Ghost Dance religion) to visit them. After obtaining authorization from both Interior and War Department officials and consulting the attorney general's office, Dorrington organized a strike force to capture Indian troublemakers and settle the nagging problems associated with the Goshutes. On February 19, 1918, Dorrington, accompanied by Captain Walter C. Gullion and Second Lieutenant W. E. Bergin of the Twentieth Infantry, and fifty enlisted men from Fort Douglas, Utah, staged an early dawn raid on the Goshute reservation. After a house-to-house search, Dorrington's force gathered all seventy-five Goshute men and placed them under guard at the agency's headquarters. It arrested seven Indians and charged four of them with inciting members of the tribe to evade the Selective Service Act. After three weeks confinement, the four Goshute "ring-leaders" were released after promising to behave and respect Superintendent Frank's authority.[60]

The federal government also experienced difficulty in registering the tribes of the Iroquois Confederacy in New York. The Iroquois, determined to press their claims of tribal sovereignty, in 1918 unilaterally declared war on Germany and then enlisted for service in United States armed forces as allies. Nevertheless, they had to register for the draft. In May 1918, Dr. Erl A. Bates, president of the Onondaga Indian Welfare Society, requested permission to create a special "Indian registration board" on the Onondaga reservation because, he claimed, New York officials had no authority on Onondaga-owned lands.[61] In a letter to Commissioner Sells, Bates maintained that by establishing a special registration board for the Onondagas, his people would be better protected against those who might incite them to resist registration and those who would swindle the Onondagas by selling them bogus deferments. Located just a few miles south of Syracuse, New York, however, the Onondaga reservation could hardly be considered a "remote" location and, therefore, did not qualify for a special reservation board. Thus, for the sake of "maintaining uniformity in all matters connected with the administration of the draft," General Crowder denied Bates's request, and he ordered that the appropriate local board continue to exercise jurisdiction over Onondaga registration.[62]

Following the second registration on June 5, 1918, Bates wrote again to Commissioner Sells, this time to complain about the local board's handling of Onondaga registration. He alleged that local board members had failed to consult with the tribal chiefs and had established the registration center nearly eleven miles from the reservation. Consequently, only one Onondaga had registered. In his letter, Bates warned that if the provost marshal general's office did not change the registration process, "this confusion will lead us into serious trouble or at least endless confusion" and New York reservations would become "places of discontent and pools where the germs of sedition can gain greater growth."[63]

As evidenced by the Goshute reservation crisis, two important factors that help explain why some Indians became "slackers" were poor communication on the part of the Bureau of Indian Affairs and Native American misunderstanding of the Selective Service Act. As late as September 1918, Chief Thunderwater (or Oghema Niagara) of the Council of Tribes wrote to the adjutant general on behalf of an Iroquois man who had failed to register. Thunderwater noted that "it has been a question for many months as to whether or not these Indians are subject to the draft and I wish you to decide the matter officially [so] that I may put an end to the confusion of these Indians."[64]

Other cases of draft resistance among Native Americans occurred. The Standing Rock Sioux in South Dakota had initial misgivings about service in the army, as did the Chippewas of Sucker Point in Tower, Minnesota. In January 1918 the Chippewas held a council and drew up a petition, wherein they protested against the drafting of Indians. When he heard of the petition, Minnesota Congressman Clarence B. Miller reproached the Chippewas for acting "like children." He asserted that they should be glad they had strong, young men, capable of serving their country in its time of need.[65]

Draft officials also experienced difficulties in registering Creeks in northeastern Oklahoma. Sammie Bear, a Creek from Mason, Oklahoma (and an American citizen), opposed registering for the draft for several reasons. Throughout the fall of 1917 Harry B. Seddicum, a BIA field clerk, attempted without success to persuade Bear to enroll. The Creek responded that former treaties with the federal government exempted his tribe from fighting and that he would have to "consult with the Higher Powers or Unseen Powers," and if they instructed him that it was his duty to register he would do so; otherwise he would "wait for a message from above." In response to these objections, Joe Strain, acting superintendent for the Five Civilized Tribes, requested that Bear be spared prosecution for failing to register because the young man was obviously "mentally unbalanced."[66]

Less than a year later, local and federal authorities became alarmed at what they initially believed was a widespread antidraft uprising among the Creeks that began at the Hickory Grounds, a popular Indian gathering place located near Henryetta, Oklahoma. At a Hickory Grounds meeting held on June 5, 1918, forty-year-old Ellen Perryman, whose father had fought for the Union during the Civil War, reportedly encouraged the thirty people in attendance (which apparently included a few blacks) to resist the draft, and according to witnesses she seemed to be "hostile" toward the U.S. government and spoke "disrespectfull [sic] towards the American Flag." Although the meeting broke up without incident, Jack Carter, a local reporter, exacerbated matters by writing an exaggerated account of the meeting, and before long newspapers from around the country were embellishing the story, further contributing to national wartime anxieties. The *Louisville Herald* reported, for instance, that "200 Indians of the Creek nation [had] armed themselves and taken refuge in the hills surrounding the old Hickory stamping grounds" and that they had murdered three farmers. The *Tulsa Times*, meanwhile, broke the news that only two farmers had been shot, but nearly two hundred soldiers and civilians had rushed to the Hickory Grounds to squelch the uprising. The *New York Times* reported that three farmers had been killed and that Ellen Perryman had recently arrived back from Washington, D.C., where she had consulted with German agents or other persons suspected of "pronounced anti-American sentiments." In December, authorities arrested Perryman and charged her with violating the Espionage Act, but released her a short time later after she promised to obey the law. Reminiscent of the Sammie Bear case, they dismissed the incident and its alleged inciter as the "product of a disordered mind."[67]

In September 1917, reservation officials at the San Xavier Indian reservation in Arizona declared that E. W. Spears, a white man residing on the reservation, and a Native American named Kahn-a-rone were advising Indians against registering for the draft. Three months later, Ray R. Parrett, the superintendent of the Bishop Indian School in California, reported the presence of a pro-German agitator, who was arousing the Indians against draft regulations and "causing ill-feelings" within the tribe. Reservation officials disclosed other minor cases of draft resistance among the Pitt River Indians, on the Malki Indian reservation in California, and among the Choctaws in Oklahoma, the Southern Utes in Colorado, and the Western Navajos in Arizona. The Navajos apparently mistook registration to mean that they would be drafted. Hilda Faunce, a trader's wife who lived near Black Mountain, Arizona, wrote that many of the Indians feared that they would be placed in the front lines to save the lives of white soldiers. Consequently, some Navajos reportedly armed themselves to prevent induction and plotted to massacre the white residents living near them.[68]

Despite occasional resentment about registering for the draft, the majority of Native Americans supported the war effort. Native Americans were no more likely to be "slackers" or deserters than their Anglo American, Mexican American, or African American countrymen. In fact, Provost Marshal General Crowder reported that only 2 percent of the total number of Americans who registered for the draft deserted, a testimony to the nation's overwhelming support for the war effort.[69] Many of the cases where Native Americans resisted registration can be linked to their misunderstanding of the Selective Service Act, although there were a few American Indians (as well as Anglo, Mexican, and African Americans) who resisted military service for different reasons.

The overwhelming majority of Indian participants, however, submitted to the draft without complaint, and thousands enlisted for duty. Some Native Americans, especially the more acculturated and educated, supported the war effort to demonstrate their patriotism and identification with the nation's principles, hoping perhaps that their service would translate into greater respect in the postwar era for Indian rights and freedoms. Indian peoples with strong warrior traditions, meanwhile, sent their sons off to war with the expectation that they might gain entrance into elite warrior societies upon their return. Many young men had fathers or grandfathers who had served as army scouts and as regular soldiers during the Spanish-American War, in the Philippines, or along the Mexican border. For them, military service was a "family tradition." Indian men living on economically stagnant reservations probably saw wartime service as an opportunity for mobility and a better life. In short, there was no monolithic "Indian response" to World War I. Instead, there were a multitude of Indian responses that were about as varied as those of non-Indians.

4
Indian Soldiers in the American Expeditionary Force

IN MANY RESPECTS, NATIVE AMERICAN SERVICE IN WORLD WAR I WAS similar to that of other Americans. The federal government drafted over sixty-five hundred Indian men for duty during the war, and thousands more enlisted. Like other soldiers, Native American inductees experienced the rigors and harsh discipline of military training camps and suffered from homesickness and initial discomfort in their new surroundings. The voyage to Europe was exciting for some, a misery for others. For virtually all the Indian "doughboys," World War I provided their first chance to visit Europe. For many it was their first opportunity to venture outside their home state.

Following their induction into the United States Army, Native American soldiers departed for one of the numerous training camps around the country. The Cherokees in North Carolina received their initial training at Camp Jackson, South Carolina, while Indians from Oklahoma often went to one of the four major training camps in Texas. Apaches, Navajos, and Pueblos trained at Camp Cody, New Mexico, and at Camp Arthur J. Jones in Arizona. Recruits from the northern plains traveled to Camp Funston, Kansas, and Camp Dodge, Iowa. Upon arrival at the military training facilities, soldiers received a series of vaccinations, a medical examination, and a revised version of the Stanford-Binet intelligence test.[1]

Shortly after the United States entered the war in 1917, the American Psychological Association appointed a committee to consider ways in which psychology might assist in the conduct of the war. Of immediate concern to psychologists was to develop an instrument to gauge each soldier's general intellectual level. Such information was relevant to many administrative decisions, including rejection or discharge from military service, assignment to particular jobs or specialties, or admission to officer-training camps. The instruments finally developed were based upon the relatively new Stanford-Binet test and came to be known as the Army Alpha and Army Beta tests.[2]

While the composition and validity of the tests have been the subjects of considerable scrutiny, the examinations revealed that a surprising number of American soldiers (some 20 to 30 percent) were illiterate. An important criticism of the intelligence tests was that they were developed with an educated, white, middle-class test group in mind—hardly a fair representation of the burgeoning U.S. Army in 1917. Consequently, racial and ethnic minorities, immigrants, and many Americans from rural and inner-city areas were at a disadvantage, as were Native Americans from remote reservations. Their comparatively poor performance on the tests might help explain why army officials placed a disproportionately large number of men from these groups in the infantry or in labor units.[3]

Within a week of their arrival at training camp, those new inductees who had completed the initial medical and psychiatric examinations received their equipment, began to learn military drill, and endured endless marches. Robert B. Huffman, a former student at the Santee Normal Training School in Nebraska, traveled to Omaha to enlist shortly after the war started. The army sent him to Fort Logan, Colorado, for training in field artillery. In a December 1917 letter to one of his old school administrators, Huffman reported that he had been issued a "mess kit, plate, cup, knife, fork, spoon, haversack, half-shelter, slicker, and two blankets." A month later, Huffman received a transfer to a training camp near San Antonio, Texas. It did not take him long to get acclimated. "There is nothing here but rocks, scrubby timber, and rough country," he wrote, "but somehow I like the place."[4]

Many soldiers found the daily military routine tiring and monotonous, but some reveled in the new environment. Lewis E. Sears, a former student at Chilocco Indian Agricultural School, stationed at Fort Logan, Colorado, reported that "I sure do like this place as we drill from 7:45 until 11:30" each day. Robert Starr, another Chilocco student, stated that he was "getting along fine" and liked Camp Bowie, Texas, "because it looks more like Oklahoma."[5]

In spite of its policy of integrating Native Americans into white regiments, the army inadvertently established a few all-Indian units. Robert Starr maintained that some companies at Camp Bowie, Texas, had Indian boys in their ranks and that one company at least was composed wholly of Indians.[6] One newspaper estimated that there were fifteen hundred Indian soldiers training in four of the Texas camps alone. Native Americans in the Arizona National Guard, meanwhile, received assignments to a predominantly Indian company in the 158th Infantry Regiment, Fortieth Division. Indian companies also existed in the 358th Infantry Regiment, Ninetieth Division, and in the Second and Third Battalions of the Forty-second "Rainbow" Division. Approximately six hundred Native Americans (mostly from the "Five

Civilized Tribes" of Oklahoma) served in the Thirty-sixth "Panther" Division, particularly in the 142d Infantry Regiment. The Canadian army also had several Indian units scattered throughout its forces.[7]

After completing their training, American soldiers boarded trains that took them to embarkation points at New York Harbor, Hoboken, New Jersey, or Newport News, Virginia. The trip across the Atlantic Ocean must have been a stressful experience for many soldiers, especially for those from provincial areas or for those with limited travel experience. The threat of German submarines compounded any mental discomfort.

During the late nineteenth and early twentieth centuries, Native Americans who had toured Europe in "Wild West" shows" reportedly suffered great anxiety during their boat rides across the ocean. Carolyn Foreman noted that some Indian performers had become "so sick that they sang their death songs," while others feared that their flesh would waste away if they went across the "Big Water." Native Americans had reportedly experienced terror in rough waters and suffered continuous seasickness. Luther Standing Bear, a Teton Sioux who toured with Buffalo Bill in England, wrote that during his voyage across the Atlantic, in 1902, some Native Americans never became ill, but he became so sick that he hated to hear the dishes rattle, and for nine days he suffered the "tortures of the damned."[8]

Whether or not Indian soldiers experienced similar anxieties and discomfort aboard transport ships during the war is unknown. Felix Renville, a Sioux veteran from Sisseton, South Dakota, remembered that his ship had to zigzag to avoid German submarines. Leo Shooter, a Standing Rock Sioux, recollected that he had been concerned that the trip across the Atlantic had taken nine days. "By golly there's I don't know how many miles of water, that ocean," he stated. "Quite a while to get there . . . I don't know . . . ship must be stuck some place."[9]

Native American troops were among the first to reach France, arriving the last week of June 1917. During the Bastille Day celebration on July 14, General John J. Pershing marched his men through the streets of Paris in a parade honoring the Allied powers. Among the American soldiers who marched that day were seven Indians representing seven different Indian nations. For the next six months members of the American Expeditionary Force (AEF) trained and prepared for deployment on the Western Front.[10]

American Indians fought in every major engagement from Chateau-Thierry, in May 1918, to the Meuse-Argonne offensive, four months later. Many won medals for meritorious service and received commendations from their commanders, but not all Indian soldiers lived up to the country's unrealistic expectations of them. The national media tended to over-glorify Native American exploits during the war, but most Indian soldiers served their country quietly and without fanfare. Nonetheless, Indian contributions to the Allied victory were substantial and worthy of examination.

In the spring of 1918 German Field Marshal Paul von Hindenburg and General Eric Ludendorff planned a major offensive to win the war before substantial numbers of American troops arrived. Code-named "Operation Michael," the offensive began on March 21, and within two months the Germans had broken through the French and British lines. Responding to French commander Ferdinand Foch's urgent appeals for reinforcements, Pershing dispatched two American divisions to help guard the bridges across the Marne at Chateau-Thierry.

Between May 31 and June 4, 1918, the Americans played a key role in stopping the German advance. Native Americans there included Private William Stoneburner, Company F, 166th Infantry Regiment, who carried messages during heavy combat. Corporal John Victor Adams, a Siletz Indian from Oregon and member of the Forty-second "Rainbow" Division commanded by Colonel Douglas MacArthur, received wounds in the leg and eye at Chateau-Thierry, and he suffered from a poison-gas attack. His injuries did not keep him down for long. "I felt that no American could be or should be better than the first American," Adams later stated. "Therefore, I did not linger in the hospital." The *New York Times* reported that "Indian scouts . . . played a prominent part in the scout work in the river region [of Chateau-Thierry]."[11]

The primary task facing the Allied forces in mid-July 1918 was to destroy the three German strongholds that threatened Allied positions in France: the Amiens salient north of Paris, in the British sector of operations; the Marne position, in the French sector; and the St. Mihiel salient about twenty-five miles south of Verdun, in the American sector. Although the AEF participated in operations in all three sectors, the majority of American troops fought in the Marne and St. Mihiel campaigns.

One of the first battles of the Aisne-Marne Offensive—the name given to the Allied attempt to force the Germans out of their Marne stronghold from July 18 to August 1918—occurred at Soissons. For four days, July 18 to July 21, American troops of the First and Second Divisions, along with the First Moroccan Division, attacked German trenches and fortifications south of the city before forcing the enemy to retreat.

Among the Native American participants at the Battle of Soissons was Sergeant Otis W. Leader, a Choctaw, who served as a machine gunner with the Sixteenth Infantry Regiment. Before the war, Leader had been the foreman of a cattle ranch in Oklahoma. After he was falsely accused of being a spy for the German empire, Leader quit his job and, to prove his loyalty, enlisted in the army. In addition to the Battle of Soissons, Leader saw action at Chateau-Thierry, at St. Mihiel, and in the Argonne Forest. During his tour of duty, Leader suffered two wounds and was twice gassed. The French government later selected him as a model Native American soldier, and the Frenchman De Warreux reportedly painted Leader's portrait for a display in the French War Museum.[12]

Sergeant Thomas E. Rogers (Charges Alone), an Arikara, who served in Company A, Eighteenth Infantry Regiment, and Joe Young Hawk, a Sioux army scout, also participated in the Battle of Soissons. Army officials cited Rogers for bravery and for "capturing at night barehanded and alone, many sentinels who were taken back to the American camp for questioning." The Germans captured and briefly detained Joe Young Hawk while he was on patrol duty at Soissons. Awaiting a favorable moment, however, Young Hawk "turned on his captors, slew three with his hands," and captured the other two. Although he was himself shot through both legs in the fight, Young Hawk endured the pain and marched his prisoners into camp.[13]

By the end of July, the German troops in the Aisne-Marne sector had retreated to the Ourcq River near the town of Sergy, about fifteen miles northeast of Chateau-Thierry. On July 26, in preparation for an imminent American offensive, Lieutenant Richard Bland Breeding's platoon conducted a patrol of the region around the Ourcq River. A detachment of German snipers opened fire, however, killing the young Creek officer, two corporals, and six privates. Breeding's company commander later wrote that "Breeding had the distinction of being the most capable, daring, and fearless platoon leader in the division. . . . His people have just cause to be proud of him." From July 28 to August 1, the American Fourth, Thirty-second, and Forty-second Divisions attempted to break the Germans' hold on the hills, woods, and small villages situated near the Ourcq River.[14]

Major Frederick Palmer characterized the fighting at the Battle of the Ourcq as "ugly" and "terrible." Poignantly describing the often primitive nature of the battle, Palmer remembered hearing the "hot panting shouts of the Americans" mixed with the "outcries of Germans and with the breaking of twigs and the straining breaths of struggle."[15] In a grisly recollection of the carnage at Ourcq, Sergeant John Northrup, a Chippewa, who lost a leg at the battle, stated that while he was lying on a stretcher awaiting evacuation, he witnessed another Indian soldier crawling in on his hands and knees under heavy German machine-gun fire. On the Indian's back was a badly wounded soldier. As the Native American passed by, Northrup noticed that both the Indian's feet had been shot off.[16]

By mid-August 1918 the Allies had successfully cleared the Germans from the Marne salient, but their advance stalled temporarily after the Germans dug in along the Vesle River near the town of Fismes. Although the river was only about thirty feet wide and six to eight feet deep, the Germans had laid barbed wire in the creek bed and established good defensive positions in the heights commanding the Vesle River Valley. Through the month of August and into September the Germans withstood attacks from units in the American Third, Fourth, Twenty-eighth, and Thirty-second Divisions. Casualties ran high enough that Americans dubbed the Vesle front "Death Valley." Private Arthur L. West, a Winnebago in Company C, Fifty-ninth Infantry Regiment, scouted along the Vesle River for nearly a week in August. While on patrol, West noticed a German sniper perched in a tree. After notifying his comrade and pinpointing the location of the sniper, the two men fired and brought the sniper down. Meanwhile, Private "Chief" Ross, a Cherokee from Oklahoma, along with three other men, drew the task of silencing an enemy machine-gun position as the AEF made its way across the Vesle. Ross led the patrol, armed with two hand grenades and a captured German Luger pistol. He reached the enemy position ahead of the others, destroyed the enemy machine-gun with a grenade, and killed one of the two German soldiers operating it. As the surviving German soldier attempted to escape, Ross shot him with the Luger.[17]

Meanwhile, as fighting continued along the Vesle sector, Pershing in mid-August began preparations for an offensive against the St. Mihiel stronghold. Early on September 12, 1918, nearly three thousand American artillery guns opened fire on German positions near St. Mihiel. Four hours after the artillery began its bombardment, the American ground assault began, and for the next five days American and French troops swarmed through the forests and villages near St. Mihiel. By September 16, the AEF had reported 7,000 casualties, taken nearly 15,000 German prisoners, captured 450 guns, and secured the German position.[18]

Major Frank Knox, recalling the St. Mihiel Offensive, noted that the Indians "made a splendid record for bravery and resoluteness under fire." Privates John Claymore, Company K, 355th Infantry Regiment, and Ernest Spencer, a Yakima from Company D, Sixth Machine-Gunners Battalion, received commendations for their service as scouts and messengers. Army officials later awarded Spencer the Distinguished Service Cross for extraordinary heroism near Thiercourt, a town on the southeastern edge of the St. Mihiel position.[19]

Other Indian soldiers received praise for their service during the St. Mihiel Offensive. Sam Lanier, a Cherokee with Company B, 315th Ammunition

Train, received praise for his performance as a truck driver. His commander reported that Lanier was "an expert wagoner and truck driver. He has operated habitually on roads exposed to severe shelling and has never abandoned his truck." In addition, the officer stated, for a stretch of six days during the St. Mihiel drive Lanier worked "frantically without any sleep. He is a faithful, obedient, and loyal soldier."[20]

Following the destruction of the St. Mihiel salient, the AEF participated in a final offensive against Germany, the Meuse-Argonne campaign. The American objective was to overwhelm the Germans and penetrate the formidable trench network known as the "Hindenburg Line" (which spanned the twenty miles separating the Meuse River from the Argonne Forest before continuing west). The terrain, marked by heavy growth and steep ravines, was ideal for German defensive purposes, but problematic for attackers.[21]

For most of the American soldiers who participated in World War I, the Meuse-Argonne Offensive provided their first taste of battle. After the attack began on September 26, Americans fought their way through the Argonne Forest. During the Meuse-Argonne campaign, Major Tom ("Fighting Tom") Reilley, commander of the Third Battalion, 165th Infantry Regiment, estimated that he started out with 876 men and returned from the battle with only 400. "The Indians in the front ranks were thoroughly swept away," he reported grimly. "When an Indian went down, another Indian stepped immediately to the front." Reilley also commended Native American soldiers for their bravery. "They were always at the front," he stated, "if a battle was on, and you wanted to find the Indians, you would always find them at the front."[22]

Captain Wendell Westover, Fourth Machine-Gunners Battalion, Second Division, echoed such sentiments. His unit, which included a squad of Native Americans, also participated in the Meuse-Argonne campaign. After the war, Westover wrote that his Indian soldiers "were courageous, steady, skillful, [and] reliable. They could be counted upon to do the thing required under any circumstances, only death bringing a cessation to their performance of duty. No finer group of Americans," he maintained, "served on the Western Front."[23]

On October 2, seven companies and two machine-gun sections of the Seventy-seventh Division (better known as "New York's Own") found themselves trapped in German-held territory in the Argonne Forest. For six days, the men of the "Lost Battalion" ate leaves and grass and endured constant enemy shell fire. Airplanes from the rear tried without success to drop supplies of food for the men, but were unable to do so with accuracy. One night nine men ventured into No Man's Land to search for some of the fallen parcels of food. Of the nine, the Germans killed five and captured the remaining four—one of whom was reportedly an Indian soldier. Although subjected to intense interrogation, the Indian soldier refused to give the enemy any information regarding the condition of his comrades. Robert Dodd, a Paiute from Nevada, suffered wounds in the ankle and shoulder during the six-day ordeal. Nevertheless, he "kept up his courage as well as the courage of the men" and "kept on shooting" until "his gun got too hot to shoot."[24]

A Native American physician, Lieutenant Josiah A. Powless, serving with the 308th Infantry Regiment, Seventy-seventh Division, died in October 1918 near the Argonne Forest. His death occurred during an engagement at the front after Captain James H. McKibben, another army physician, went to the aid of a soldier who had been wounded and was lying out under heavy machine-gun fire. While attempting to save the soldier, McKibben too fell wounded. Upon seeing the captain go down, Powless, disregarding the great danger from "Boche" machine-gun fire, went to the rescue and succeeded in treating his comrade's wounds. German soldiers also shot and killed him. Powless was awarded posthumously the Distinguished Service Cross.[25]

The fighting in the Argonne campaign was not without its lighter moments. James McCarthy, a Papago soldier in Company D, 109th Infantry Regiment, apparently suffered from dysentery. On one occasion he had diarrhea so bad that, in the midst of fierce fighting, he leapt outside his trench to relieve himself. Neither the earnest warnings of his comrades nor the bullets and shrapnel of the enemy deterred him from his mission. Although he escaped serious injury during the foolish (but understandable) stunt, McCarthy later received wounds from a grenade and was taken prisoner, sent to a camp near Rastatt, Germany, where he remained until the war's end.[26]

As American forces continued to fight their way through the Argonne Forest, units of the AEF were active in the Vosges sector, near St. Jean d'Ormont, and in the Champagne sector, at St. Etienne. On the morning of October 5, 1918, unit commanders dispatched Corporal Ammons Tramper, an Eastern Cherokee from Company I, 321st Infantry, Eighty-first ("Wildcat") Division, to patrol the perimeter and locate enemy machine-gun emplacements. In the course of the patrol, however, Tramper and four other soldiers became lost. Fearing capture, they decided to hold up in a shell crater until nightfall. Around eight o'clock that evening the five men started out. But instead of returning to American lines, they found themselves even deeper in German-held territory. At that point Tramper took charge and led the men safely back to American-held territory.[27]

At the same time, Sergeant George Allen Owl, an Eastern Cherokee in the same unit as Tramper (there were a reported seventeen Eastern Chero- kees in Company I), conducted extensive patrols and performed vital scout- ing work. His commander, Captain John Emerson, noted that Owl "is without fear and has proven himself a very capable leader of men. . . . I believe him to be the best scout in the battalion."[28]

Perhaps the most famous Native American hero in World War I was Pri- vate Joseph Oklahombi, a Choctaw from the Ouachita Mountains of south- eastern Oklahoma, who served with Company D, 141st Infantry Regiment, Thirty-sixth Division. While on duty in the St. Etienne sector, Oklahombi (whom the press treated as the Indian equivalent to Alvin York) won the French Croix de Guerre for extraordinary service. "Under a violent barrage, [Oklahombi] dashed to the attack of an enemy position, covering about 200 yards through barbed wire entanglements. He rushed on Machine Gun nests, capturing 171 prisoners." Oklahombi reportedly stormed a strongly held position containing more than fifty machine guns and a number of trench mortars, and turned the captured guns on the enemy, holding the position for four days. Perhaps he was only trying to live up to his name: in the Choctaw language Oklahombi means "man-killer" or "people killer."[29]

Oklahombi was not the only Native American soldier in the Thirty-sixth Division to win decorations for valor. Lonnie White, who has examined the contributions of Indian soldiers from the "Panther Division," reported that six other Choctaws from Company E, 142d Infantry Regiment, gained rec- ognition for their military exploits, while Bob Carr and Nicholas E. Brown received posthumously the French Croix de Guerre.[30]

By the middle of October the AEF had secured the Argonne Forest, and on November 5 American units crossed the Meuse River. During the move- ment Walter G. Sevalia, a Native American from Wisconsin serving near the town of Brieulles with Company F, Seventh Engineers, swam the Meuse under terrific fire with a cable for a pontoon bridge and later carried another cable over the Est Canal and across an open field covered by enemy machine guns. James M. Elson, a Snohomish Indian from the Tulalip reservation in Washington state, also received citations from his commanding officer for showing "exceptional skill, courage, and coolness under fire" while guiding sentry squads through No Man's Land and guiding patrols to the outskirts of Brieulles.[31]

The Allies captured 26,000 German prisoners, 874 cannon, and 3,000 machine-guns during the Meuse-Argonne campaign, but with a dreadful cost in lives lost. In this final offensive 26,277 Americans died (a total of 50,280 AEF were killed in World War I) and 95,786 men suffered wounds.[32]

Less than a week after the crossing of the Meuse, the government of Kaiser Wilhelm II fell, and the new republican regime signed an armistice. Herbert Whiteshield, an Indian soldier in Company E, 142d Infantry Regiment, wrote, while in the hospital recovering from his wounds, that "we are coming back with the great victories won for the allies and Uncle Sam's great armies. We have done our duty; we are not a bit sorry that we came over for the good cause. . . . We have given the Huns a good medicine and they got wise and quit."[33]

The number of Native American casualties in World War I was high. Russel Barsh has estimated that 5 percent of all Indian servicemen died in action, compared with 1 percent for the AEF as a whole. Some Indian people suffered even higher casualty rates. The Pawnees, for example, lost 14 percent of their soldiers, and the various Sioux people lost an average of 10 percent.[34]

Given their often perilous duties as scouts, snipers, and messengers, the high casualty rate among Native Americans is not surprising. Army officers, motivated in part by popular stereotypes of the legendary fighting prowess of American Indians, frequently assigned their Native American troops the most dangerous duties. A French officer, for example, suggested that Indian troops could serve to special advantage in dangerous No Man's Land enterprises. Ward Bowman, a Cherokee from Oklahoma, with a squad of men, received orders to conduct a scout in No Man's Land. The Germans located the scouting party, however, and shelled the Americans for several hours. The next morning, a member of Bowman's squad made the mistake of poking his head out from cover and received a fatal shot to the forehead. According to Bowman, the man "never even grunted just groaned and he was gone." Officers in the 167th Infantry Regiment, meanwhile, sent an Indian soldier out "twenty-one times in succession in patrols, night after night" until he was finally killed. Privates Bluesky and Jenkins, both Indian scouts with the Twenty-third Infantry Regiment, established reputations as fearless soldiers and expert reconnaissance personnel. Officers commended the two men frequently for their ability to cover ground at night. Later, while on patrol, both Indian soldiers received serious wounds.[35]

Native American soldiers also served with distinction in noncombat roles. Sergeant James M. Gordon, a Chippewa from Wisconsin, served as a driver for a sidecar motorcycle. He received the Croix de Guerre from the French government for rescuing, while under fire, a French officer who had been wounded while on an inspection tour of American troops. Lieutenant J. B. Hess, commanding Company A, Supply Train, 308th Infantry Regiment, commended Private Moses H. Smith, a Sioux, for keeping his "transport outfit in better shape than any other man in the Supply Company." He added that Smith often worked overtime without complaint, and "kept his equipment complete at all times." Officers characterized Corporal Benjamin Barnett, a clerk in Company D, 142d Infantry Regiment, as "one of the best clerks in the Regiment," and officials in Field Remount Squadron 302 commended Private "Chief" Beard for his expertise in handling horses. Sergeant John Shawnego, a Chilocco graduate and a member of the 316th Bakery Company, reported proudly that his commander had placed him "in charge of two large ovens that bake over 200 pounds [of bread] at a time."[36]

Native Americans also served as pilots and aviators. The first Indian aviator to join the Lafayette Escadrille may have been Oklahoma-born Floberth (or Philbert) W. Richester, who was later credited with seven "kills." An article appearing in the *Washington Sunday Star* explained the "fascination" that Indians apparently held for aviation by suggesting that the Native Americans' "kinship with nature" made the ability of human beings to rise and go skyward "doubly alluring."[37] Given the size of the American air force during the war, however, the number of Indian pilots was undoubtedly small.

Approximately one thousand Native Americans served in the United States Navy during World War I.[38] Although most served on escort or transport duty, some Native American sailors saw action on battleships. Wesley Youngbird, an Eastern Cherokee, served on the battleship *Wyoming*, and William Leon Wolfe, a Cree, manned "the massive twelve-inch gun on the forward deck of the *Utah*." Captain H. H. Hough, commander of the *Utah*, commented that "I know little of the individual cases in the 1,200 men on board the *Utah*, but the Indian, Wolfe, has forced his character upon my attention by his stalwart service and ability."[39] Of the twelve Indian navy recruits from the Chemawa Indian School in Oregon, three enlisted as firemen and the other nine as musicians. Recruits from the Phoenix Indian School enlisted for naval duty as carpenters, blacksmiths, and masons.[40]

American Indians proved a great deal during the war. Commissioner of Indian Affairs Cato Sells wrote, in 1919, that the deeds of Indian soldiers in World War I would "outlive all memorial bronze and marble" and "inspire the song and story of immortal tradition." However, as Jennings Wise has suggested, over-glorifying the exploits of Indian soldiers does them, and their descendants, a disservice by encouraging the perseverance of racial stereotypes.[41] Some Indian soldiers, on the other hand, probably did not object to the stereotypes and widespread acclaim they received for their contributions. In fact, as Robert Lowie has argued, throughout the nineteenth century an important inducement to get men from the various Plains tribes to make war was to gain the right to exhibit and recite their brave deeds in battle.[42] Thus, to be seen as a "warrior" and receive postwar accolades may have been the very ends that some Indian soldiers sought. Viewed in this light, to deprive them of the very attention that they craved would have been devastating.

Clearly, Native Americans made a significant contribution to the war effort. Some 12,000–12,500 Indians served during the war, about 25 percent of the adult male Indian population. Whether they served as infantrymen, truck drivers, or medics, or went aboard ships, most Indians performed their duties faithfully and with distinction. Brian W. Dippie estimates that at least 10 Native Americans received the Croix de Guerre and 150 others won decorations for valorous service.[43]

World War I provided thousands of Native American men with an opportunity to see the world and escape, temporarily at least, the isolation of reservation life. James McCarthy, a Papago veteran from Arizona, visited Kansas City, Chicago, and New York City while en route to his embarkation point on the East Coast. After a tour of downtown New York City, McCarthy marveled that "I had never seen such tall buildings like those—it made me dizzy just looking up at them."[44] Military service introduced soldiers from provincial backgrounds to new foods, equipment, and modern technology, and taught many the skills necessary to make a living in the postwar world. Service in the war also brought American Indians into close contact with other racial groups and broadened their understanding of, and appreciation for, a larger American society.

With the possible exception of those men who had attended government-administered Indian boarding schools that catered to a broad spectrum of Indian peoples (such as the Hampton Institute and Carlisle Indian Industrial School), military service brought Native Americans from different parts of the country together for the first time. Prior to the war, for example, a Cherokee farmer from Oklahoma was unlikely to know many Sioux people from the Dakotas, Chippewas from Michigan, or Yakimas from Washington. Serving together at training camp, traveling together aboard huge ships bound for Europe, fighting together in the trenches of France, or visiting with each other while on furlough, however, provided Native Americans from across the country with opportunities to become acquainted and, perhaps, to share their experiences as "doughboys" in Uncle Sam's army, as foreigners in war-torn Europe, or as minorities in an Anglo-dominated society. While in Europe, A'wa Tseighe, a Pueblo soldier from New Mexico, met and befriended McKinley Two Elk, an Oglala Sioux. Together, the two men performed Indian dances for other "doughboys." Shortly after the war, several hundred Native American veterans gathered for a reunion in Oklahoma, where they danced, sang, and reminisced about their wartime experiences. Among the tribes represented were Apaches, Comanches, Navajos, Papagoes, Sioux, Blackfeet, and, according to A'wa Tseighe, "lots kine [Indians] I didden never know before."[45] Consequently, service in World War I may have fostered, at least for a while, the development of a limited form of Pan-Indianism among veterans.

Once home, however, many Indian veterans, like other soldiers, eventually lost contact with their old comrades. In an era when interstate transportation and communication were still relatively undeveloped (especially in rural areas and on reservations), it would have been surprising if Indian veterans could have maintained their wartime relationships for any appreciable length of time. Nonetheless, at local meetings sponsored by veterans organizations such as the American Legion, Indian "doughboys" could gather together once more to remember fallen comrades, boast of heroic deeds, and commiserate over the hardships they suffered during the "war to end all wars."

Indian veterans returned home with pride, with self-confidence, and with a greater sense of national belonging and acceptance. Wartime experiences had broadened their outlook on life, and many were able to translate their training and newly acquired skills into better jobs and a more secure future at home. Others struggled to readjust to reservation life—haunted perhaps by the recent atrocities they had witnessed on distant battlefronts. Just a few decades earlier, many Americans had accepted the contention that Indians were a "vanishing race" and that their "inherent" backwardness and unwillingness to accept assimilation would doom them to inevitable extinction. Service during the war, however, offered convincing proof that Native Americans were vibrant and persevering peoples who had much to offer the majority culture. Viewed in this light, the war years may have helped hasten the evolution of popular misconceptions from the "Vanishing Race" scenario back to other stereotypes (that had never really died) which glorified the martial and virile attributes of Indian men—stereotypes that had important consequences for Indian soldiers and the types of duties they performed in World War I and future wars.

At Fort Wadsworth, NY in February 1913, Joseph K. Dixon (with top-hat at left) and Rodman Wanamaker launched their drive to erect a memorial to the American Indian. Tribal leaders from across the country were invited to participate in the ground-breaking ceremony. Courtesy the William Hammond Mathers Museum, Wanamaker Collection, Indiana University.

The Choctaw Telephone Squad set an important precedent for the now famous Navajo "code-talkers" of World War II. Pictured here left to right are Taylor Lewis, Mitchell Bobbs, James Edwards, Calvin Wilson, James Davenport, and Captain E.H. Horner. Courtesy the William Hammond Mathers Museum, Wanamaker Collection, Indiana University.

(*Opposite, top*) During the final Wanamaker Expedition in 1913, Joseph K. Dixon (center) had Indian leaders sign a Declaration of Allegiance to the United States government. Cut Finger, Southern Arapahoe, is pictured here at a ceremony in El Reno, Oklahoma. Courtesy the William Hammond Mathers Museum, Wanamaker Collection, Indiana University.

(*Opposite, below*) A sketch of the proposed Indian memorial. Once completed, the memorial would have housed an extensive Indian archives and photograph collection. War-time exigencies and lack of funding doomed the project. Courtesy the William Hammond Mathers Museum, Wanamaker Collection, Indiana University.

Survivors of the "Lost Battalion" at home at Camp Mills, New York. Robert Dodd, a Paiute, (back row, center) suffered wounds in the ankle and shoulder during the six-day episode. Courtesy the William Hammond Mathers Museum, Wanamaker Collection, Indiana University.

(Opposite, top) Group of Indian "doughboys" from Co. G, 13th Infantry. Service in the war provided Native Americans from across the country an opportunity to learn about other cultures and traditions. Pictured left to right are Hezekiah Chebatah (Comanche), Owen Yackeyonney (Comanche), Stacey Sitting Hawk (Southern Cheyenne), and Anton Meuteg (Aleut). Courtesy the William Hammond Mathers Museum, Wanamaker Collection, Indiana University.

(Opposite, below) Alphonse Bear Ghost, a Sioux serving in Co. M, 26th Infantry, suffered wounds in the Argonne Forest. His sergeant later commented that he "wished many times that all boys in the American Army were like Bear Ghost." Courtesy the William Hammond Mathers Museum, Wanamaker Collection, Indiana University.

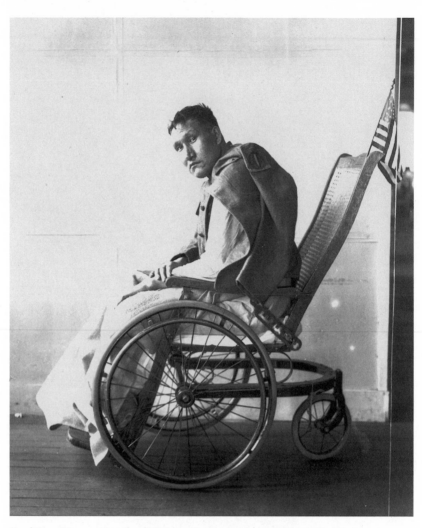

Fred Fast Horse, Rosebud Sioux, Co. F, Ammo. Train, 89th Division.
Injured and partially paralyzed during the Meuse-Argonne campaign, he
was sent home to recuperate at a military hospital in Greenhut, New
York. Courtesy the William Hammond Mathers Museum, Wanamaker
Collection, Indiana University.

William Leon Wolfe, Chippewa, served aboard the U.S.S. Utah during the war. He was one of approximately 1,000 Native Americans who saw duty in the U.S. Navy. Courtesy the William Hammond Mathers Museum, Wanamaker Collection, Indiana University.

Sam Thundercloud, a Winnebago serving in Co. D, 128th Infantry, was shot by a sniper while on scout duty at Chateau-Thierry. Of the thirteen Winnebagos who served in Co. D, two were killed and three others wounded. Courtesy the William Hammond Mathers Museum, Wanamaker Collection, Indiana University.

At a 4th of July memorial ceremony held at the Pine Ridge reservation in South Dakota, Joseph K. Dixon (left) extends his hand to a young Sioux veteran. Events such as these were common in the post-war era. Courtesy the William Hammond Mathers Museum, Wanamaker Collection, Indiana University.

John Miller (in uniform) and Charlie Wolf, veterans of World War I. Courtesy the Nebraska State Historical Society.

Banner from Sioux memorial flag presented at the 4th of July ceremony in 1920. Courtesy the William Hammond Mathers Museum, Wanamaker Collection, Indiana University.

Crow chief Plenty Coups gave a stirring eulogy at the Tomb of the Unknown Soldier on November 11, 1921. Courtesy the William Hammond Mathers Museum, Wanamaker Collection, Indiana University.

Joseph K. Dixon (center) introduced French military hero Ferdinand Foch to Crow chief Plenty Coups in November 1921 shortly before Foch's ceremonial adoption into the Crow tribe. Courtesy the William Hammond Mathers Museum, Wanamaker Collection, Indiana University.

AEF Cemetery no. 176 in Villers Tournaille, Somme. An estimated 300 Native American soldiers were buried here. Courtesy the William Hammond Mathers Museum, Wanamaker Collection, Indiana University.

5
American Indians as "Doughboys"
The Influence of Stereotypes

On the battlefields of France, Indian soldiers witnessed the devastating destruction and loss of life that characterize modern warfare. They fought, suffered, and died alongside their countrymen in the vast network of trenches that epitomized World War I. Indian troops had their share of heroes as well as those who could never reconcile themselves to the horrors and bloodshed of battle. Many, no doubt, struggled just to survive.

Unlike their Anglo, Mexican, and African American countrymen, however, Native Americans bore an added burden: the weight of their martial reputation. Other Americans expected Indian soldiers to live up to their historic prominence as fierce warriors and fighters. Such expectations were unrealistic, motivated by sensationalized press stories and dime novels rather than a realistic appreciation of Indian cultures. Jennings Wise, an AEF staff officer, accused the press of glorifying Native American service to satisfy "the national craving for a spark of romance in a war whose deep shadows seem unrelieved by color and the higher lights."[1] Common stereotypes of the period depicted Native Americans as "instinctive" soldiers possessing inherent martial qualities, as being endowed with strong masculine attributes that made them especially adept at warfare, and as "blood-thirsty warriors" particularly eager to fight.[2]

The romanticized portrayal of Native Americans as "instinctive" soldiers was the most common preconception. Caroline D. Appleton noted, in *Outlook* (a popular magazine of the day), that the Indians' "adroit tactics, sense of strategy, and feats of camouflage" were the "outgrowth of an ancient training in the science of war."[3] A similar article in *The Literary Digest* maintained that when it came to Indian fighting and scouting, "woodcraft was bred in their bones."[4] Another editorial suggested that "modern Indians in khaki ought to find many of their ancestral fighting instincts and methods immensely useful" as well as their utilization of the "tactics of frontier days." *The Native American* reported that "Indians are far keener soldiers than most white men. They can see danger quickly and take by instinct the best means out of it."[5]

A second popular stereotype purported that Native Americans possessed unique physical and emotional attributes that enhanced their abilities as soldiers. After accompanying a group of Iroquois soldiers on a patrol, William Beebe, a correspondent for *The Atlantic Monthly*, commented that the Indians were "athletic, wirey, virile, the menace of the German line throughout this whole sector."[6] Journalists Fullerton Waldo and Edwin Corle alluded to the legendary stoicism of Native Americans. Waldo remarked that "red Indians from Wyoming or Colorado were stoics of the high explosive shells and the poison gas as if the calumet went round at the council fire or the drums beat to a dance."[7] Corle, meanwhile, related the story of a Mojave veteran named Bluebird who, while near the French town of Catigny in May 1918, killed six German soldiers. Bluebird "picked off" the enemy soldiers, Corle maintained, "with the same emotions with which he lit cigarettes."[8]

In an editorial in *The Indian's Friend*, the author gave an account of the service of Native American troops near the Marne River and compared their physical capabilities to those of animals. Indian soldiers, he reported, after "scenting trouble . . . ran through the woods like deer" before diving into the river and swimming "like Hawaiians."[9] A write-up in *The American Indian Magazine* noted that flat feet, a common cause of rejection for military service among whites, was practically unknown among the Indians.[10]

A third popular preconception about Native Americans during the war depicted Indians as "bloodthirsty" and anxious to fight. One commentary suggested that Indian soldiers took "kindly to the trench warfare" and even "felt at home" in the trenches. An article entitled "Lo, the Rich Indian is Eager to Fight the Savage Hun" related the story of Jess Fixon, a Cherokee, who "wanted to go to France right away and bayonet the Kaiser all by himself." It claimed Fixon had said that Wilhelm II, the German leader, "killum papoose and killum squaw so Jess Fixon will find this Kaiser and stickum bayonet clear through. Ugh!" The piece also reported that Joseph Cloud, a Sioux, complained that he had not had enough time during the war "to lift any German's hair."[11] In a news item entitled "When the Chief Smiled," a Cherokee soldier was said to have smiled only twice in his life: once after army officials assigned him to the battalion scout platoon and again after he killed three Germans. A final example of exaggerated Native American bellicosity can be found in an article in *The Indian School Journal*. Allegedly, a

Sioux soldier "was so full of fight" that during the last two weeks of action he could not be kept in his dugout long enough to have his wound stripes sewn on his sleeves.[12]

Indians were also portrayed as ardent "whoopers" and, if one was to believe half of the media's assertions about Indian troops, there was not a single Native American in the AEF who did not, at one time or another, let out a "blood-curling" war whoop. A popular story was that story of Charlie Rogers, a Standing Rock Sioux assigned to the Eighteenth Infantry Regiment. In the heat of battle, Rogers, who was the "match for twenty Huns," reportedly "leaped over the parapet swinging his old rifle over his head. He let out a yell he had been saving for years, and it was a genuine war-whoop by one of the people who made war-whooping famous."[13]

For the most part, Native Americans accepted the stereotypes, perhaps because, as Alison Bernstein (who has studied Indian service in World War II) pointed out, they "tried to live up to their own, as well as the whites' perceptions of them as warriors."[14] Confronted with such high expectations of them, Indian soldiers must have felt considerable pressure to "measure up." Unlike African American soldiers, who were frequently held in contempt and struggled to earn the respect of their white peers, Indian soldiers entered the army with a degree of respect and acceptance already. Thus, it was theirs to lose. Native Americans probably realized that the only thing they had going for them, at least from the Anglo perspective, was their historic reputation as warriors. Combined with their own personal expectations and, for some, a desire to gain admittance into warrior societies, it would have been unconscionable to protest against dangerous assignments. A consequence of their acquiescence to the stereotypes was a casualty rate significantly higher than that of other soldiers in the AEF.[15]

While many Americans, on the one hand, were taken in by the romanticized notions of Indian fighting prowess, they were also convinced that in other respects Native Americans could not measure up to white soldiers. National "intelligence tests" suggested that full-blooded Indian men, who were generally less assimilated and more inclined to hold on to traditional Indian customs than mixed-bloods, possessed inferior intellects compared to *metis*. Implicit in the findings was the racist assumption that Anglo ancestry contributed to improved intelligence. Consequently, the wartime press frequently expressed amazement when full-bloods "made good" in the army, and editors found it newsworthy to inform their readers when a particular Indian war hero happened to be one.

Once in Europe, Native American soldiers performed a number of duties. While the majority served in combat arms such as the infantry (and, to a lesser extent, in the field artillery and cavalry), others fulfilled their military obligation as support staff, ambulance and truck drivers, mechanics, cooks, policemen, quartermasters, and medics. A postwar survey conducted of over 1,200 Indian soldiers reported that 744 (62 percent) had served in the infantry, 190 (16 percent) had served in the Field Artillery, and 100 (8 percent) in the Ammunition Train. The remaining 171 (14 percent) had served in other specialties. Of the 1,200 Indian respondents, 9 had been officers and 195 had served as noncommissioned officers (NCOs).[16] Because of the Indians' legendary reputation as guerrilla fighters plus popular stereotypes that encouraged the notion that Indians were "instinctive" soldiers, military officials assigned hundreds of Native Americans to special duties as scouts, snipers, and messengers. As the war progressed, unit commanders, in an effort to confuse German code breakers, used Indian soldiers to transmit telephone messages in their native languages.

Army scouts served primarily as observers and guides. During the day and through the night they reconnoitered No Man's Land for the location and strength of enemy positions. According to Major D. R. Mitchie, a British officer who gave lectures about identifying and training scouts during the war, a successful scout possessed "the cunning and agility of the fox," a good memory, and keen eyesight. Moreover, scouts needed "a placid even temperament" and the ability to "combine alertness and perseverance with bodily inactivity and patience."[17]

A scout platoon consisted of one sergeant, two corporals, and seven privates from each infantry company. Four scout platoons made up a complete battalion scout company. Members of scout platoons were often the best trained men and served half their time with the battalion intelligence section and half with their own units. Consequently, company commanders were often reluctant to release their best men for service with the intelligence section and promoted their scouts to the rank of noncommissioned officer (NCO) in order to prevent their deployment elsewhere. The result of such actions was a chronic shortage of well-trained scouts. To make up for the shortfall, military officials recommended that company commanders deploy increasing numbers of Indian soldiers as scouts.

In addition to the problem of a deficient number of trained white scouts, the army used Indians as scouts for other reasons. Support from the top military leaders was an important one. The commanding general of the AEF, John J. Pershing, had experience in working with Native Americans, as had U.S. Army Chief of Staff Hugh L. Scott. Both men had commanded units of Indian soldiers in the 1890s. During the Mexican border crisis in 1916, Pershing had employed a detachment of Apache scouts to aid the army in its efforts to capture Mexican revolutionary Pancho Villa. A number of Indian soldiers who fought for Pershing in Mexico later served in World War I.[18]

A third reason why military officials frequently employed Native Americans as scouts related to the popular preconception that Indians were "natural" soldiers, possessing "instinctive" traits that made them ideal scouts. Similar to acceptance of the media's racial assumptions pertaining to Native Americans, army officers tended to accept prevailing stereotypes that influenced their deployment of Indian soldiers. A memorandum entitled "American Indians as Battalion Scouts" provides convincing evidence that company commanders believed that Indians possessed inherent scouting abilities.[19]

Lieutenant F. G. Stevens, an instructor at the Army Infantry Specialists School, for example, maintained that American Indians were "superior to the average soldier for night work," and "were silent . . . knew direction, and were unafraid."[20] Captain Walter E. Guthrie, 114th Infantry Regiment, had used native scouts during the Filipino Revolution. He later put forward the idea that Indians possessed a development in the eye coming from long out-of-doors, trail-less environments. "They have a night vision and farsighted and discerning day vision," he asserted, "which is not possessed by many white men." Guthrie also submitted that the Native American color of countenance was a scouting advantage because "they show no reflecting facial surface in moonlight or flare glare. They are silent and self-oriented."[21]

In addition, the apparent willingness of Native Americans to serve as scouts gave impetus to such deployment. Some Indians accepted dangerous scouting missions to prove their worth as soldiers and to live up to their reputation as courageous warriors. Among Plains tribes in particular, being selected to lead a raiding party or patrol was seen as a high honor, and only those men with proven martial abilities were chosen. In the Crow tradition, for instance, one had to perform four feats in order to become a chief: lead a successful raid, capture tethered horses from an enemy camp, touch an enemy, and relieve a foe of his weapon. Scout and patrol duties during World War I provided Indian soldiers with opportunities to fulfill all these prerequisites for leadership (even taking an enemy's horse was not outside the realm of possibility), thereby contributing to the willingness of some Indian soldiers, particularly those with strong warrior traditions, to perform dangerous assignments.

Other Native Americans accepted scouting assignments simply because they enjoyed the duty. Alphonse Washington, a Native American from the Lumni Reservation in Washington, reportedly "took delight" in his duties as a scout for the 347th Machine-Gunners Battalion. Several Passamaquaddies of the 102d Infantry Regiment also volunteered for scout duty. Moreover, some military officials argued for the deployment of Indians as scouts because Native Americans "like to operate in movements that afford contact and association with each other and they enjoy the excitement incident to day and night patrols and raids."[22]

Army officials also were convinced that Native Americans would make good scouts because Indians possessed an inherent sense of direction. Non-Indian scouts apparently had to stop to consult their compasses in order to orient themselves, and, consequently, fell prey to German snipers. However, because Indians reportedly possessed a "true idea of North," army officials assumed that Native Americans would be less susceptible to enemy fire.[23] On one occasion, officers from the 142d Infantry Regiment selected five Indian soldiers to compete with an equal number of white soldiers in a crawling exhibition. The officers later reported that the Indians "proved their superiority by crawling blindfolded to the point indicated while the white men crawled in every direction but the right one." Lieutenant Owen H. Perry testified that during a patrol in woods "so thick that one could not see more than four yards ahead," he sent scout Henry George, a Nez Perce, in front to hold direction. Perry, who followed behind with a compass, found that "Private George invariably held right direction."[24] Further evidence of such "inherent" sense of direction came from an officer in the 309th Infantry Regiment. The officer reported that Private Rolland Little Elk, a Sioux, was "able to orient himself without difficulty, having a sense of direction both at day and at night."[25]

A few military officials even recommended that Native Americans be placed in aviation service to aid pilots. By watching out for important landmarks, they maintained, Indian navigators and observers could help pilots hold direction.[26]

Native Americans were also employed as scouts in order to provide an example for their comrades. Major R. Glyn, a British officer, noted that "the presence of Indians moving with characteristic quiet and stealth, taking forward positions by bounds and dropping for a moment for readjustment and cover" would educate new recruits more effectively than conventional models. In addition, Indian scouts could aid American intelligence officials by conducting raids on German positions and capturing prisoners for interrogation. If Native American scouts were captured, however, military officials believed that Indians, who by tradition could endure tortures without uttering a sound, would give little information of value to the enemy.[27]

Although popular stereotypes of legendary Indian military prowess influenced the army's decision to employ Native Americans as scouts, Indian performance was of equal importance in the assignment. Apparently, not all

Native American soldiers possessed the talents necessary to be successful scouts. Members of southwestern tribes, such as the Navajos, Hopis, and Zunis, military officials contended, made better messengers because of their endurance. Northern Plains tribes, such as the Cheyenne, Sioux, and Nez Perce, meanwhile, produced "fighting, aggressive, [and] resourceful scouts."[28] The army's continued use of large numbers of Indian scouts suggested that Native Americans performed their duties in a satisfactory manner.

Granted that misguided racial stereotypes influenced the way that military officials utilized Indian soldiers, there may have been an element of truth about some Native Americans having special abilities as soldiers. Rather than possessing soldierly attributes that were "inherent" or biological in origin, however, Indians from rural backgrounds may have learned certain skills that were lost to urban dwellers. Bruce Catton, the eminent Civil War historian, has written that the Confederate Cavalry enjoyed considerable success during the first two years of the Civil War due to the rural upbringing of Southern soldiers—many of whom had years of experience in working with horses—and because of Southern notions of chivalry. The majority of Union cavalrymen, on the other hand, came from big-city and nonagricultural backgrounds and "first had to be taught how to stay in the saddle."[29] If this indeed was the case, it would be reasonable to assume that men from rural areas (like Alvin York, for example) were sensitive about land forms and other natural conditions, were probably experienced hunters, and were more likely to be accustomed to engaging in outdoor activities than urban types. Those Indian soldiers coming from isolated reservations, therefore, might very well have possessed certain skills which officers, already conditioned by prevailing stereotypes, took as evidence that Indians were soldiers by "instinct."

Besides scouting, Native American troops served as snipers and messengers. Like scouts, snipers had to possess patience and keen eyesight. Major D. R. Mitchie, an officer in the British army, described the successful sniper as being "pain-staking, cool, and very patient." Accordingly, American military officials believed that Native Americans would make ideal snipers. "Chief" Wilson, for example, a Native American serving with the 144th Infantry Regiment, served as a sniper and allegedly killed at least ten Germans. Officers marveled at Wilson's "disposition to crawl into advance positions in No Man's Land on personal initiatives to shoot an enemy."[30]

Army commanders also used Indian soldiers as snipers because they observed that Native Americans used cover whenever possible and were very patient in waiting to get a good shot at the enemy. One officer maintained that the Indians were not very good "barracks soldiers" but, he added, if you gave them a rifle and the chance to go out and kill "Boche," Native Americans would "lie in a shell-crater all day" to get a shot at a German.[31]

To coordinate movements and maintain communication, the army used numerous "runners" to carry orders and instructions. Because of the enemy's ability to "listen in" on Allied telephone messages, runners became an essential mode of "safe" communication. Military officials often selected Native Americans, such as William Blindwoman, a Northern Cheyenne and graduate of Carlisle Indian Industrial School, as runners. His commander in Company H, Thirty-ninth Infantry Regiment, boasted that Blindwoman was "the most dependable runner and scout in the section," and he was assigned "the most difficult and important missions."[32]

Chester Armstrong Four Bear, a Sioux from the Cheyenne River agency in South Dakota, received training as a sniper and a message carrier. In the midst of heavy machine-gun fire in the fall of 1918, Four Bear carried a message from his company commander in the front-line trench back to regimental headquarters. As he maneuvered to the rear, the Germans unleashed a gas barrage that made it necessary for Four Bear to crawl much of the distance. Upon delivering the message, officials ordered him to report to the hospital for treatment. He refused, however, preferring to make his way back to his company near the front lines. On his way back to the front, Four Bear rescued a French messenger and rendered him first aid. In gratitude, the Frenchman took from his own breast a Croix De Guerre and gave it to Four Bear.[33]

Besides dispatching Native Americans as runners and messengers, army officials developed a novel method—one that proved immune to German eavesdroppers—of transmitting information via telephone.[34] In October 1918, officers of the 142d Infantry Regiment called on two Choctaw soldiers to transmit telephone messages in their native language. Because the 142d was occupying dugouts and houses recently deserted by the Germans, the Americans feared that every decipherable message going over the wires also went to the enemy. Consequently, the regimental commander, Colonel A. W. Bloor, turned to the Choctaws because, he believed, "it was hardly possible that Fritz would be able to translate these dialects and the plan to have these Indians translate telephone messages was adopted."[35]

After the 142d Regiment's initial experiment with the Choctaws, several Indian soldiers received instructions in how to transmit messages over the telephone. Lieutenant Black, a liaison officer, conducted their training, as did Lieutenant Ben Cloud, a Northern Cheyenne attached to the Forty-first Division.

A major problem confronting Black and Cloud grew out of the fact that

Indian vocabularies of modern military terms were insufficient. Many Indian languages are holophrastic (expressing a whole phrase or sentence in a single word) or polysynthetic (combining several words of a sentence into one word), which made it difficult for messengers to translate English directly into one of the Indian languages. Native American telephone operators overcame the problems by substituting Indian phrases for military terms. They translated "Third Battalion," for example, as "Three Grains of Corn"; they referred to a machine gun as "Little gun shoot fast," casualties as "scalps," and a poison-gas attack as "bad air."[36]

Although the use of Native Americans as telephone operators was not widespread, various units employed the tactic during the last two months of the war. In addition to the Choctaws, military officials used Comanches, Osages, Cheyennes, and Sioux to transmit messages. In their discussion of Osage telephone messengers, Wendell Martin and Alphonzo Bulz, veterans of the Thirty-sixth Division, remarked that the Osages "used to love to talk on our telephones and they'd talk in Osage. We used to wonder if the Germans could ever interpret those calls." If the Germans could, they mused, "it would have confused the hell out of them."[37] Paul Picotte, a Yankton Sioux, expressed great pride about Indian contributions during the war. In fact, he went so far as to make the dubious assertion that Indian telephone operators won the war single-handedly! "That World War was ended by the Indian boys who were in the service," he boasted. "They were eventually put up to the front . . . in the communication system, and they talked in Indian . . . and the war came to an end."[38]

While Native American telephone operators perplexed German code breakers, the presence of American Indian troops on the Western Front had an important psychological impact on the enemy as well. The German people held a long-standing affinity for Native Americans, one that stretched back to the nineteenth century. From the 1880s to the 1910s, Native Americans had performed throughout Europe in various "Wild West" shows. Such performances included war dances, mock battles and hunts, and, in a few instances, the erection of Indian villages complete with tepees and campfires.[39]

The German interest in Native American cultures was also influenced by popular literature. The western novels of late nineteenth-century German author Karl May (who visited the United States in 1908 and met with some Tuscaroras, but never made it west of Niagara Falls), "established a deeply effective romantic-emotional tie to the American Indian." In *Winnetou*, a novel about a Mescalero Apache chief, May described the Apaches as a noble and honorable people. Nevertheless, he provided a lengthy discussion of Apache torture techniques, scalping, and massacres. He also characterized

Native Americans as extremely adept and efficient fighters. Indians, according to May, could throw a tomahawk and cut off the tip of an outstretched finger at a hundred paces.[40]

In Germany on the eve of World War I, books that discussed Native American history and culture were very popular. Europeans translated into German, and published in 1912, Dr. Charles Eastman's book *Indian Boyhood*. One year later, the Germans published a fourth printing of the work.[41]

A decade after World War I, Hans Rudolf Reider summed up the reasons for German interest in Native Americans. He wrote that "the Indian is closer to the German than to any other European. This may be due to our stronger leaning for that which is close to nature." In addition, Reider asserted that the Native American "is model and brother for us during our boyhood; among the dreams and longings of those years he remains one of our most cherished recollections." Therefore, when German troops encountered Native American soldiers on the Western Front, they may have experienced conflicting emotions about fighting their childhood heroes. Rudolf Conrad has noted, however, that German enthusiasm for Indians never seems to have abated because of such "isolated indications of lacking reciprocity."[42]

While the German affinity for Native Americans may have continued through the war, German propaganda painted a much more negative picture of Indians than had Karl May. A piece in the *Rhenish Westphalian Gazette*, for example, indicated that there were no Native Americans fighting on the Western Front. Indians were dying out, the newspaper reported, and they were "thoroughly degenerated from drink" and, thus, unfit for combat.[43] Perhaps the propaganda was aimed at reassuring Germans that their soldiers did not have to face in battle the kind of fierce enemy that Karl May and earlier German authors had depicted in their novels about the American West.

Atrocity stories generated another popular propaganda technique. According to Harold D. Lasswell, the stories yielded a crop of indignation against the "fiendish perpetrators" of alleged dark deeds, and satisfied certain "powerful, hidden impulses" of combatant nations.[44] Articles in the *Norddeutsche Allgemeine Zeitung* resurrected images of past Allied brutalities by recalling England's use of American Indian auxiliaries in the late eighteenth century. The British reportedly paid the Indians thirty-four shillings for every scalp taken from the American colonists.[45]

German military officials held great respect for Indian soldiers. An officer captured by units in the Thirty-second Division during the Battle of Soissons asked his captors if the division consisted of Indians. He commented on the bravery of Indian soldiers and noted that they were superb fighters. Another

German POW told members of the Canadian Expeditionary Force's Twenty-fourth Battalion of the Victoria Rifles that his superiors had warned him not to be taken prisoner by Canadians because they were all "red Indians" who would scalp him. Captured documents also illustrated German appreciation for the value of Indian soldiers as night workers and scouts. During the St. Mihiel Offensive, for example, a colonel in the Ninety-seventh Landwehrs issued an order to his battalion commanders that additional snipers be detailed specifically to kill Indian soldiers. The colonel characterized Native Americans as "greatly superior" to the North African troops serving in various French regiments. A letter captured from a German soldier assigned to the Sixth Jaeger Regiment stated only half-facetiously that the "Indians of the Sioux tribe were identified in one of the last attacks. After the war Karl May can write another book about his experiences with the Redskins."[46]

The report of a captured American officer whom the Germans had interrogated provides further evidence of German concern with fighting Indian soldiers. The officer stated that the Germans showed considerable anxiety when learning of the high numbers and disposition of American Indians among AEF units. In response, some American military officials, to demoralize the Germans, suggested that a limited number of night raids be conducted using men camouflaged as Indians in full regalia.[47] Thus, Native Americans, through their service as scouts, messengers, and telephone operators, aided the Allied victory and perhaps helped indirectly by demoralizing the enemy.

When the war ended in November 1918, army officials, impressed by the service of Native Americans, expressed interest in more efficient utilization of Indian troops in the future. The primary advocate for a greater military role for Native Americans was Lieutenant John R. Eddy, Thirty-ninth Infantry Regiment. A former Indian bureau employee, Eddy began his BIA career in the spring of 1905, working as a clerk for Frank Mead, the general supervisor of Indian reservations. Later that year he transferred to the San Xavier agency in Arizona where he helped supervise agricultural activities among the Papagos. Roughly a year later, Eddy received another transfer, this time to the Tongue River agency (later renamed the Northern Cheyenne reservation) in Montana. For the next eight years he served in a dual capacity as agency superintendent, and as the superintendent of the Tongue River Indian School before resigning in November 1914.[48]

Soon after the United States entered the war, Eddy joined the army and received a commission and an assignment with the Thirty-ninth Infantry Regiment. His decade-long experience in working among Native Americans apparently remained on his mind. In the summer of 1917, he submitted a proposal to Colonel Robert McClure, First Division, to constitute a tactical unit of Indians in each division for advance contact work at the front. Having lived among the Northern Cheyennes for many years, Eddy had probably heard about the exploits of Lieutenant Edward "Ned" Casey and the famed "Cheyenne Scouts" who had served in the army during the 1890s. This knowledge may have given him the initial inspiration to organize a special Indian tactical force. Although army officials did not adopt his plan, after the war Eddy requested that a detailed report of Native American achievements be made, both for future military use and as a recognition of Indian service in the AEF.[49]

On January 10, 1919, Eddy received orders to proceed to general headquarters for temporary duty with the historical section. Within a month, Eddy convinced his superiors to distribute a questionnaire he prepared to over fifteen hundred combat units in the AEF. After his superiors gave their consent, Eddy distributed the queries. William Bruce White has written that Eddy was convinced that innate Indian traits made them superior scouts and designed the questionnaire to elicit the results he wanted.[50]

The Eddy document posed several general questions: Did Indians stand the nervous strain in battle? Did they prove to be natural leaders? Did they associate readily with white men? Had they demonstrated fitness for any special arm? In addition, the questionnaire posed a number of questions concerning Indians as scouts: What capacity had Indians shown for courage and endurance? What about their keenness of senses and dexterity? Had Native Americans demonstrated good judgment and initiative? What about their ability to utilize mechanical devices and read maps?

Responses to the questionnaire lent support to Eddy's contention that Indians made ideal scouts. They also reflected prevailing Indian stereotypes. In general, the respondents concluded that Native Americans stood the nervous strain of battle, associated readily with whites, and possessed superior keenness of senses and dexterity. But the completed questionnaires also revealed that Native Americans lacked leadership qualities and exercised only "fair" judgment and initiative. Many officers rated Native American ability to use mechanical devices as "poor."[51] More important, however, the completed questionnaires indicated that several officers in the army accepted popular preconceptions regarding Native Americans as fact and evaluated their Indian troops accordingly.

As mentioned earlier, one common preconception was that Native Americans possessed inherent physical attributes that especially suited them as soldiers. Captain Otho W. Humphries, 167th Infantry Regiment, remarked that American Indians under his command had shown "remarkable dexterity and keenness of senses, often-times being the only ones in a party to discover the presence of the enemy."[52] Indian soldiers in the Eighteenth Infantry Regiment reportedly possessed "hearing and eyesight better than that of white men."[53] Lieutenant Ray H. Duncan, 142d Infantry Regiment, noted that "the Indian has demonstrated his keenness of sight to us on many occasions; he can see at night like a cat."[54] In addition, Captain M. D. Steen, 141st Infantry Regiment, maintained that Indians possessed a "sense of hearing . . . exceptionally keen, and they could readily hear the breaking of a twig and detect the location." Other officers complimented Native Americans for the "accuracy and speed with which they could crawl."[55]

Some military officials countered, however, that Native Americans possessed physical attributes that undermined their efficiency as soldiers. First Lieutenant Lusien B. Coppinger reported that Indians seemed to lack muscular control and that "an Indian company in line will extend about three feet further than a company of white men of equal number." This result, he noted, was due to their large waist measure. Captain E. A. Simpson, 142d Infantry Regiment, complained that Native Americans were not the equal of white men in hiking ability—a deficiency which a medical officer attributed to the "fact" that "their feet were not as large as those of white men."[56]

The responses to the Eddy questionnaire echoed other popular stereotypes. Captain John L. Morely, 142d Infantry Regiment, spoke of the Indians' "inherent bravery" and "bloodthirsty desire" to go forward and to undertake dangerous missions without regard for their personal safety.[57] Lieutenant Colonel William J. Morrissey seconded Morely's depiction with his observation that in bayonet training, Indians not only displayed a keen interest but exhibited "great energy, spirit, and dash."[58] The personnel adjutant of the 358th Infantry Regiment, Captain John N. Simpson, remarked that Indian soldiers were "not afraid of hell itself," adding that "if we had had more Indians, we would have killed more Germans. They did not believe in taking prisoners."[59]

Respondents also characterized their Indian soldiers as stoic. Officers described Private John Elk, a Sioux with Company D, 139th Infantry Regiment, as "very cool and calm but very quiet . . . [he] very seldom smiles."[60] Herman Yon, a Sioux in Company C, 307th Supply Train, reportedly possessed "many of the traits found in Indians, *viz*: quiet, independent, doesn't take naturally to military restrictions."[61] Another officer characterized Native American soldiers as possessing as keen a sense of humor as any average white man," although mixed-bloods seemed to possess an "extraordinarily keen sense of humor" and did not seem so "reticent about it."[62]

Popular conventional images regarding Native Americans also gave impetus to negative evaluations of Indian soldiers. Among the most common complaints was alcohol abuse. Lieutenant Whitfield A. Shepard, Thirty-ninth Infantry Regiment, reported that Private Moran Lester, a Chickasaw, was "a good industrious soldier when sober, but he cannot be trusted with money, when it is possible to use some for the purchase of alcohol."[63] Private Samuel A. Roy, a Chippewa with Company E, 310th Infantry Regiment, apparently indulged "in alcoholic stimulants to such an extent as to make him very unreliable." His commanding officer charged that Roy "seems to have no sense of responsibility, having on two occasions gone absent without leave (AWOL)."[64] Lieutenant A. E. Smith, Seventh Engineers, in his evaluation of Private Joseph Esau, a Pawnee, noted that "he has a failure common among all men of his race. This same medium got him into serious difficulty after his arrival in France but . . . he is trying to do his best to overcome this failure."[65] Not all officers, however, shared the criticism. In his remarks on Indian troops, Lieutenant C. B. Cates, Sixth Marine Regiment, commended his Native American soldiers for their sobriety.[66]

Officers also complained that Indian soldiers were illiterate, unintelligent, or both. Lieutenant F. B. Taylor, Sixty-fourth Infantry Regiment, commented that John Doublehead, a Cherokee, "does not speak very good English and perhaps this is one reason why he is poor in carrying verbal messages."[67] Some officers apparently mistook an Indian's inability to speak English as proof of ignorance. Tecumseh Anna, a Choctaw with Battery B, Sixteenth Field Artillery, was described as "not very intelligent. On the front he was used in the echelon where he performed good manual labor. His knowledge of the English language is very poor."[68] Captain A. G. Price, Seventh Infantry, reported that Edward Pine, a Chippewa, was "very illiterate, unintelligent and of low mentality. Believe he is below the average type of American Indian."[69]

Other criticisms of Indian troops included their apparent lack of initiative and leadership abilities, their inability to handle mechanical devices, and their disinclination to accept military discipline. Captain Carl C. Brown, 144th Infantry Regiment, suggested that if Indian soldiers had any judgment or initiative, it "was not noticeable," while Captain Henry K. Cassidy, 165th Infantry Regiment, commented that Native American soldiers displayed no leadership and were content to follow orders at all times, "never showing any initiative."[70]

The fact that few soldiers received adequate training in mechanical devices, such as electric signaling devices or telephones, did not prevent officers from concluding that Native Americans were inept at such pursuits. Lieutenant Ray H. Duncan, 142d Infantry Regiment, commented that "the average Indian is not very proficient in the use of buzzers and mechanical devices, but the educated Indian who has been instructed in the use of such instruments has proven himself to be very accurate and reliable."[71]

Such was the case with Private Ray C. Sanook, a Cherokee assigned to the Sniping, Observation and Scouting Section of the First Battalion, 319th Infantry Regiment, Eightieth Division. Officers commented that Sanook, a former Carlisle Indian Industrial School student, "had proven to be a good leader in the ranks" and was quite familiar with maps and map reading. While at the front he made a map showing differences in elevation by color. The map was said to be "one of the best pieces of work done in the Section and was considered very useful and practical."[72]

Finally, some officers criticized Indian soldiers for their lack of military discipline and distaste for routine drill. Lieutenant Lusien B. Coppinger, who had trained Indian troops at Camp Bowie, Texas, noted that Native Americans were "self-conscious, easily amused, and take a great interest in field work as opposed to close order drill."[73] Military authorities brought Private John Ratt, a Cherokee, before the adjutant for failing to salute an officer. In defense of the violation of military etiquette, Ratt responded that in his hometown of Wellington, Oklahoma, "when me meet man there we speak to him one time. No speak any more to same man all day. Down here me salute everytime me pass man?"[74] Officers in Company B, First Machine-Gunners Battalion, meanwhile, were critical of Private George Kaquatosh, a Menominee, because of his "extremely unsoldierly appearance."[75]

Not all Indian soldiers, however, received criticism for the way they looked. Captain M. R. Harrison, commanding Battery C, Seventeenth Field Artillery, described Private Frank Osborne as "exceptionally clean and very well liked by men in the battery."[76]

With the completed questionnaires to bolster his arguments, Eddy urged army officials, in May 1919, to endorse his plan to deploy Native Americans in special units as scouts and rangers. He argued that the typical Indian soldier possessed a remarkable sense of direction, went about his duties uncomplainingly, and had "unlimited patience and reserve." Furthermore, Eddy asserted, the typical Indian soldier was a good shot, crawled "habitually" on night patrols, had non–light reflective countenance at night, was silent at work, and proved to be "stoical under fire." Thus, Eddy concluded, Indians were exceptionally qualified by natural characteristics and disposition as scouts for service in modern warfare.[77]

Eddy envisioned the creation of divisional ranger companies comprised of 6 white officers and 250 enlisted Indians per division. Native American graduates from prominent Indian schools, such as Carlisle Indian Industrial

School in Pennsylvania and Haskell Indian School in Kansas, would be encouraged to enlist. Leading Americans who knew the Indians intimately, such as historian George Bird Grinnell, would assist by encouraging Native Americans to volunteer for ranger duty. Members of specific tribes would be strongly recruited: the Hopis, Zunis, and Navajos, for their talents as long distance runners; Cheyennes, Sioux, and Blackfeet, for their fighting ability.[78]

The Indian rangers would be equipped with a rifle, bayonet, pistol, and trench knife. They would wear field service uniforms and heavy moccasins. In addition to conducting scouts, the rangers would be required to draw maps of the terrain they had recently patrolled. The fact that Indians were "always oriented," together with their "native ability to draw," Eddy argued, made such tasks simple. In open warfare, rangers would search out and destroy enemy machine-gun nests, effect advance observation and contact, and kill enemy snipers and scouts.[79]

After penetrating enemy lines, rangers would send back messages via pigeons or rocket signals. Because they were required to maintain isolated advance positions, caches of canned rations would be buried at regular intervals to provide rangers with a readily accessible food supply. In the daytime, rangers would communicate with each other by using Indian sign language. Stimulus for rangers to serve would result from "frequent recognition of especially worthwhile accomplishments."[80]

The army never implemented Eddy's program, but as Jennings Wise pointed out three years after the war, Eddy's report was worthy of the most serious study and consideration. According to Wise, the report "tersely epitomized the history of the suffering, the experience, and the splendid service of the American Indian in the ranks of Democracy."[81]

Although Wise may be correct, the Eddy report holds even greater significance in what it reveals about non-Indian perceptions of Native Americans during World War I. The questionnaires and Eddy's plan to organize Indian ranger companies indicate that many whites continued to view Indians more as romanticized nineteenth-century warriors than as fellow countrymen worthy of equal rights and citizenship. Moreover, the questionnaires shed light on Native American contributions during the war and help explain their high casualty rate.[82]

Thus, several things become clear about American Indians as doughboys. The army's use of Indian telephone messengers set an important precedent for the future. During World War II, military officials utilized Navajo marines to communicate messages in the Pacific theater. The famous Navajo "code-talkers" baffled Japanese intelligence crews in a manner reminiscent of the Choctaws during World War I. In a study of the potential utilization of American Indians as communication linguists in 1950, the National Security Agency pointed to the 142d Infantry's experiment of October 1918 as the precedent for such use.[83]

From Chateau-Thierry (where the AEF helped stop a major German offensive) to the final campaign between the Meuse River and Argonne Forest, Indian soldiers fought in every major engagement. The presence of Indian scouts and snipers may have been a cause of consternation among German troops, who feared having to meet the fierce warriors described in the novels of Karl May. Indeed, Germans were so fearful over the prospect of fighting American Indians that German newspapers tried to hide the fact that Native Americans were on the Western Front.

The Eddy questionnaires bear ample proof that most American officers held Indian soldiers in high esteem, praising them for their courage, fortitude, and loyalty. Nonetheless, some also harbored strong negative feelings about Indian soldiers, criticizing them for their lack of military discipline, their illiteracy, and their alcoholism. Popular stereotypes—both positive and negative—certainly played a key role in shaping the officers' assessments.

Although they possessed few of the rights and privileges of their countrymen, Native Americans proved their loyalty and willingness to defend their homeland by fighting and, in some cases dying for their country. The wartime sacrifices of the "first Americans" went a long way toward convincing non-Indians that Native Americans were worthy of respect, equal rights and citizenship, and that they were capable of playing an important role in American society. Like other racial and ethnic minorities serving in World War I, many American Indians hoped that fighting for freedom, democracy, and self-determination abroad would translate into a more vigorous application of these principles at home—as is seen in the next chapter.

6
American Indians and Other Minorities in World War I

THE RESPECT AND ADMIRATION ACCORDED TO AMERICAN INDIAN SOLDIERS during World War I was unique. Compared to other American minority groups serving in the war, Native Americans enjoyed a degree of popular esteem and national gratitude that came reluctantly (if at all) for African Americans and Mexican Americans. Nevertheless, useful comparisons can be drawn regarding the experiences and treatment of minority soldiers in the American Expeditionary Force (AEF). The comparisons include an examination of draft policy, efforts at segregation, popular stereotypes, and the performance of ethnic minorities in combat. The results should help illuminate and explain race relationships in the United States and provide a better understanding of Anglo perceptions of Native Americans in the second decade of the twentieth century.

Similarities can be drawn as well between the army's use of Native American soldiers and the way in which other Allied powers utilized racial minorities. Canada, for example, employed roughly three thousand to four thousand Native American troops as well as Asian American and African American soldiers. France deployed colonial units from West Africa, and the British did likewise with troops from India. Similar to racial minorities in the AEF, Europe's colonial troops endured unfair stereotypes and racial discrimination. An examination of their role in World War I, therefore, can help place the American army's treatment of Native American troops within a more cosmopolitan perspective and shed light on how racism and popular preconceptions influenced their service.

Like Native Americans, African Americans had a long history of military service.[1] Nonetheless, many Americans, southern whites in particular, distrusted the army's use of black troops. Some questioned the loyalty and trustworthiness of African Americans while others doubted their abilities as soldiers. A good many southerners also worried about how military service might impact the blacks' willingness after the war to tolerate second-class treatment. An editorial in *The New Republic* cautioned that black soldiers would acquire "a new sense of independence" that would make them fomenters of unrest among their people. The August 1906 raid in Brownsville, Texas, where black soldiers faced accusations of rioting in response to local discrimination, only exacerbated the paranoia of southern whites regarding black troops. After Woodrow Wilson's election as president in 1912, some southern congressmen and military officials suggested, without success, that black units be disbanded altogether.[2]

African Americans served in World War I for diverse reasons. Like Native American soldiers, many blacks fought to defend their country, prove their loyalty, gain social status, and improve economic mobility. Contrary to the Native American population, however, all African Americans possessed citizenship, albeit of a second-class variety. Black leaders hoped that serving in the war would prove their people's worthiness to exercise the rights and privileges accorded other citizens and perhaps would diminish white resentment toward the black population. Emmett J. Scott, an African American and a special assistant to the secretary of war, noted that black soldiers realized that they could not be in a position to demand their rights unless they fully performed their duties as American citizens. Through military service, therefore, blacks fought indirectly for justice in the courts, better schools, the abolition of Jim Crow laws, fair wages, and improved housing.[3]

Some African American leaders discouraged black participation in the war effort because of the army's policy of segregating black troops and its reluctance to employ black officers to lead them. The majority of African Americans, however, supported the war effort with enthusiasm. In his annual report to the secretary of war, Provost Marshal General Enoch H. Crowder commended black troops as being filled with the same "feeling of patriotism," and the same "martial spirit," that fired their white fellow citizens in the cause of world freedom. Emmett Scott likewise suggested that one of the brightest chapters in the whole history of the war was the black man's "eager acceptance of the draft" and his "splendid eagerness to fight."[4]

Notwithstanding their fitness and eagerness to serve, the army's application of the Selective Service Act was unfair to both African Americans and Native Americans. As noted earlier, noncitizen Indians were exempt from compulsory service, but registration boards occasionally misclassified them as Class I to lessen the draft burden on whites. Not until the last few months of the war were noncitizen Indians granted official approval to enlist—although many had managed to do so "unofficially" earlier in the war due to lax enforcement by draft boards needing to fill quotas. In contrast, the federal government restricted black enlistments, allowing only enough African American enlistees to bring the existing four black regiments (Ninth and Tenth Cavalry Regiments and Twenty-fourth and Twenty-fifth Infantry Regiments) to full strength. Therefore, an overwhelming majority of the 367,710 blacks inducted for duty were draftees. Similar to those who employed discriminatory draft procedures on Indian reservations, registration boards in the South frequently denied claims for exemption from black registrants and placed them in Class I. This may help to explain why over half of the black registrants during the war received Class I designations compared to one-third of whites. Moreover, during the first two draft calls, military officials inducted 367,710 African Americans, a one-in-three acceptance rate compared to only one-in-four for white registrants.[5] Thus, like Native Americans, blacks served in disproportionately large numbers during World War I.[6]

A notable distinction between the black and Indian experiences in the war was that African Americans served in segregated units. While they opposed segregating Indian soldiers, government and military officials apparently considered African Americans a "special case," and the segregation of black soldiers continued through World War I.

An important reason for the inconsistent policy was that many whites refused to serve with blacks.[7] In July 1917, Representative John C. McKenzie of Illinois, a member of the House committee on military affairs, stated bluntly that "white men as a rule do not want to serve with Negroes, but the same prejudice does not exist toward the Indians."[8] A couple years later, fellow committee member Frank L. Greene of Vermont suggested that "the white man does not want to go in there with those organizations of Negroes; he does not want to serve there." "On the other hand," he continued, "the white man is glad to have his Indian neighbor right in the ranks with him."[9] Consequently, black troops received military training apart from other American soldiers, and the army also transported them in segregated trains and ships.[10]

Popular stereotypes exerted a strong influence over the types of duties assigned to Native American and African American soldiers. Popular preconceptions of African Americans, however, differed dramatically from those of American Indians. They included the notion that blacks were intellectually inferior, docile, and submissive. Eugenicists and other "experts" regarded blacks as "sub-species of mankind" with admirable physical strength, but with mental constitutions "very similar to that of a child."[11] Other stereotypes depicted African Americans as sexually promiscuous and likely to commit crimes of passion. Ironically, blacks were also seen by many whites as deeply religious and inherently cheerful.

The notion that the intelligence of blacks was inferior to that of whites received reinforcement from army intelligence tests administered to all inductees after their arrival at training camps. Because the tests were prepared with an educated, white, middle-class test group in mind, however, their validity is dubious. In his examination of test scores among black soldiers at Camp Lee, Virginia, for example, George O. Ferguson concluded that of the 5,425 blacks tested, 3,285 (over 60 percent) were illiterate as compared to only 18 percent of white soldiers. In addition, Ferguson maintained that the median mental age of white soldiers was approximately thirteen years old, while the median mental age of blacks was just over ten.[12] Such "scientific" evidence seemed to confirm notions of white superiority.

In a letter to J. W. Dady, the superintendent of the Red Cliff agency for the Chippewas in Bayfield, Wisconsin, Miss Lou B. Robison, a journalist who was investigating the role of Native Americans in the war, commented on the intelligence of blacks and Native Americans. She stated that African Americans, as a race, were "irresponsible." According to psychologists, she continued, blacks were "incapable of high mentality, except in exceptional cases, or when due to a mixture of white blood." To compare the Indian to the black man, Robison concluded, "is an insult to the Indian."[13]

A second stereotype depicted African Americans as docile and submissive, a personality trait that perhaps carried over from their experience as slaves. In an article in the *Journal of the Military Service Institution*, Major Robert L. Bullard described black soldiers as submissive, faithful, and subordinate. Moreover, black officers reportedly lacked initiative and self-control, and were incapable of exercising effective discipline over their troops. Such popular preconceptions justified the army's policy of using white officers to command black regiments.[14]

A third conventional image of African American troops suggested that blacks could not control their sexual passions and, therefore, posed a threat to white women. Consequently, AEF officials expressed considerable concern over deploying black troops in France. To prevent possible miscegenation, some African American troops received orders not to talk with French women, and white officers placed strict curfews and travel restrictions on black troops on furlough.[15]

A final stereotype characterized African Americans as deeply religious and cheerful. An article appearing in the January 1919 edition of *The Literary Digest* maintained that "next to a camp-meeting, the [black man] feels more at home amid a deadly clash of armed forces than he does at work in the corn-fields," and the "inferno of hot work in the line evoked the religious fervor" of African American troops. A black soldier reportedly exclaimed that "when Fritz spotted us hell bus' wide open an tu'n all dem onregen'ret niggers into a ragen' prayeh-meetin."[16] Another editorial made the dubious assertion that black soldiers sang plantation songs in the trenches and that "the terrors of shrapnel, gas, and high explosives, the grim life in the trenches, were made bearable by the unfailing good nature" of African Americans. Colonel James A. Moss, commander of the 367th Infantry Regiment, characterized the black soldiers under his command as "by nature of a happy disposition" and "very amendable to discipline."[17]

Largely in response to such conventional images, military officials assigned the majority of black troops to duties as "stevedores" (those seen as mentally or physically unfit to fight) in labor units. John W. Chambers has estimated that nearly 75 percent of all African American troops served as stevedores. Although blacks in 1917–1918 made up approximately 10 percent of the American population, they made up one-third of the laborers and only one-thirtieth of the combat forces in the AEF. Stevedores performed backbreaking and mundane but important work. They loaded and unloaded ships; built piers, roads, and warehouses; cut wood; drained swamps; and buried the dead. Charles H. Williams has explained that "the Negro was regarded by many army officials as specially adapted to this work because of his previous experience and his cheerful disposition." Most African American soldiers in World War I, consequently, were more often than not laborers in uniform.[18]

There were two black combat divisions in the AEF: the Ninety-second (which included the 365th, 366th, 367th, and 368th Infantry Regiments) and Ninety-third Division (which included the 369th, 370th, 371st, and 372d Infantry Regiments). Once in France, however, units in both black divisions fought in the French sector rather than with their American comrades. Like other American troops, blacks in the AEF served extended periods of time at the front and suffered heavy casualties. The Ninety-third Division, for example, lost 3,166 killed or wounded, one-third of its soldiers. Units and individuals from both divisions received citations for valorous service. The 365th Infantry Regiment earned the French Croix de Guerre, and 167 men in the Ninety-third Division received decorations, including the Distinguished Service Cross and the Legion of Honor. Privates Henry Johnson and Needham Roberts, both members of the 369th Infantry Regiment, repelled a German patrol of twenty-four men, although each of the Americans had been wounded several times. Johnson reportedly killed four Germans with his bolo knife, while Roberts hurled grenades "even while the hands of a muscular German were about his throat."[19]

German troops apparently feared fighting black troops about as much as fighting Native American soldiers. Consequently, German propagandists aimed their tracts at fomenting disloyalty among African American units. An article in *The Literary Digest* reported that it was seldom that German troops would hold out when the "yelling, sweating [African Americans], jumped into their trenches." Emmett Scott noted that Germans regarded black troops "with unusual fear," and they allegedly offered a four-hundred-mark reward for the capture of African American soldiers.[20]

While it focused on diminishing the mythic fighting ability of Native Americans and denying that Indians were even fighting on the Western Front, German propaganda worked to undermine African American loyalty by stressing the racial inequities that blacks endured in the United States. German propaganda placed particular emphasis on lynchings in the South and promised African American troops that they would receive much better treatment if they crossed over to the German lines. As Harold Lasswell has written, "the propaganda was directed to stir up trouble continuously between whites and blacks of any nature and description."[21]

Despite their exemplary service and commendations, an incident during the Argonne Offensive cast a cloud of doubt over the fighting abilities of black American soldiers. In the midst of heavy combat, in September 1918, some units in the Second Battalion, 368th Infantry, reportedly broke formation and retreated without orders. Officers in the Ninety-second Division later claimed that their superiors had ordered the retreat, but many military officials charged the 368th with cowardice. General John J. Pershing and Secretary of War Newton D. Baker ignored the incident, however, and commended the service of black troops in no uncertain terms. Pershing wrote that "I cannot commend too highly the spirit shown among the colored combat troops, who exhibit fine capacity for quick training and eagerness for the most dangerous work."[22]

Through their assistance in World War I, African Americans demonstrated their loyalty to the United States. By doing so they hoped to secure all the rights and privileges promised them as citizens. As Emmett Scott noted, through service in the war the black soldier received "a keener and more sharply defined consciousness, not only of his duties as a citizen but of his rights and privileges as a citizen." James P. McKinney, a soldier in Headquarters Company, 371st Infantry, summed up African American experiences in World War I in this way: Black troops "assumed the burden of democracy along with white and red troops. We did our share to keep America unchained, and we are all proud that we did it."[23] Finally, in his discussion of African American veterans, Kelly Miller, dean of the College of Arts and Sciences at Howard University, declared that the black soldier "is no longer Negro, nor Afro-American, nor colored American, nor American of African descent, but he is American—simply this, and nothing more."[24]

The army's treatment of Mexican American soldiers during the war was similar to that accorded Native Americans as well. Like many of their countrymen, Mexican Americans served to demonstrate their loyalty and they volunteered in disproportionately large numbers. Such a demonstration was especially important to Americans of Mexican ancestry because of the widespread anti-Mexican sentiment that existed in the United States. Border violence along the Rio Grande had erupted during the Mexican Revolution in 1910. In 1916, President Wilson sent American troops into Mexico to capture Pancho Villa and put an end to Mexican raids north of the border. Such incidents provoked a strong anti-Mexican backlash in the United States— particularly in the Southwest.

In 1917 many Americans suspected the Mexican government of possessing pro-German sympathies, a suspicion compounded by the publication of the Zimmerman telegram. Unfortunately, few Americans differentiated between Mexican nationals and Mexican American citizens. That being the case, people of Mexican ancestry were often considered untrustworthy and viewed with suspicion. Mexicans in Los Angeles, California, for example, faced accusations that they were intriguing with German spies. In Texas, "vigilante groups ran wild in an orgy of violence—harassing, intimidating, shooting, and killing dozens of defenseless Mexicans and Americans of Mexican descent." Throughout the Southwest, the wartime media warned of the ominous presence of the "Bronze menace."[25]

Similar to the Indian population on the eve of World War I, the legal status of people of Mexican ancestry in the United States was diverse. Some Hispanics were native-born American citizens or naturalized citizens; others were Mexican citizens in the process of naturalization; and some were Mexican citizens who did not wish to become citizens of the United States at all. In the wake of political turmoil in their homeland, however, thousands of Mexicans emigrated (either legally or illegally) to the United States after 1910. The outbreak of the war in Europe served to increase American demands for labor and provided further impetus for Mexican immigration northward. Pedro Castillo estimates that between 1917 and 1921 as many as 72,000 Mexicans crossed into the United States legally. Matt Meier and Feliciano Rivera have estimated that during the same period roughly 100,000 crossed illegally.[26]

After the American declaration of war in April 1917, all Mexican American males and Mexican aliens between the ages of twenty-one and thirty-one registered for the draft (as required by the Selective Service Act). Reminiscent of the difficulties facing local boards with Native American registration, draft officials had to determine the citizenship status of Mexican registrants. During the first registration period in June 1917, only those Mexican aliens who had declared their intention to become naturalized American citizens (declarant aliens) were liable for the draft. Non-declarant aliens, therefore, received exemptions. To discourage non-declarant aliens from claiming exemption after the June 1918 registration period, Congress amended the Selective Service Act. Thereafter, non-declarant aliens could still claim exemption from compulsory military service, but by doing so they forfeited any future chances for American citizenship.[27]

In the Southwest, where the Hispanic population was large, the draft law created a host of new problems. During the first registration period in June 1917, non-declarant aliens were counted for state quota purposes, which raised the total number of men drafted from a particular state, but then those aliens received draft exemptions. In response, local boards, in an attempt to ease the draft burden on white registrants, began to intentionally misclassify non-declarant Mexican aliens as Class I. Because the burden of proving one's citizenship lay with the registrant (and few Mexican nationals possessed passports, birth certificates, or other legal documents), local boards interpreted this to mean that Mexicans without documentation (or those who did not speak English and did not understand the requirements for exemption) were liable for the draft. John W. Chambers estimates that as many as 200,000 non-declarant aliens were illegally drafted and certified as Class I during the war, and perhaps 9 percent of the AEF were noncitizens. According to the provost marshal general's office, between June 1917 and June 1918, 59,145 Mexican aliens registered for the draft, 26,114 were called, and 5,794 accepted for service.[28]

Although Mexican American enlistment was proportionately greater than their representation in the population as a whole, Anglo Americans still remained critical of Hispanic service due to the large number of Mexican draft resistors. Many Mexican nationals and even naturalized Mexican American citizens, fearing with good reason that they might be drafted into the United States Army, fled south and back to Mexico. This wartime exodus-in-reverse was examined in the 1930 report of a California state-appointed Mexican Fact Finding Commission. The commissioners concluded that "the number of naturalized Mexican women in 1920 was almost double that of naturalized Mexican males," which they believed offered proof of Mexican draft evasion. The stigma of Mexican "slackers" persisted up to World War II.[29]

With problems similar to those facing Native American soldiers, many Mexican American troops did not speak English and were often subject to prejudice from Anglo officers. Like American Indians, Hispanics were integrated into white units, although some companies, especially in the 125th, 141st, 325th, 359th, and 360th Infantry Regiments, contained large numbers of Mexican American men. Also like their Native American counterparts, Mexican American soldiers participated in the major AEF campaigns from the St. Mihiel Offensive to the Meuse-Argonne campaign. Three Mexican Americans received the Distinguished Service Cross, and Marcelino Serna, a Mexican immigrant from El Paso, Texas, received seven decorations for valor.[30]

Hispanic soldiers, like their African American and Native American countrymen, fought for freedom and democracy as well as for improvement in their status at home. In her study of Mexican American soldiers from Texas, Carole E. Christian has written that they "fought for greater acceptance of Hispanics by other Texans and for more opportunities after the war ended." She argues further that Mexican American participation in the war hastened their acculturation and entrance into the American mainstream. Hispanic veterans "strove to awaken the political consciousness" of the Mexican American population and contributed to the organization, in 1928, of the League of United Latin American Citizens (LULAC).[31] Meier and Rivera have contended that the war "broadened Mexican Americans' cultural horizons and raised their levels of expectations." The most important development resulting from World War I for Mexican Americans, they concluded, was that "for the first time thousands left their familiar Southwest environment."[32] The same argument can be made for Native Americans and rural African Americans.

Useful parallels also can be drawn between the United States' use of Native American soldiers and the Canadian government's policy of enlisting racial minorities. During the first year of the war, Canadian officials prohibited the enlistment of Native Americans, blacks, and Asians. Skepticism about their fighting abilities and the belief that "killing Germans was the privilege of white troops" kept Canadian minorities out of the war until the end of 1915. Because of high casualty rates and a severe manpower shortage in the Canadian Expeditionary Force (CEF) in the fall of 1915, restrictions against Indians ended, and thousands of Native Americans entered the military. Similar to their brethren in the United States, noncitizen Indians in Canada were exempt from compulsory military service, although many enlisted to prove their loyalty to Great Britain or to escape the confines of reservation life.[33]

In spite of the fact that some Canadian recruiting officers "winked at the regulations and enlisted individual Indians into white units," several all-

Indian units were established during the war. The 135th Middlesex Regiment contained soldiers from the Ojibway, Oneida, and Munsey tribes, while Saugeen Indians from Georgian Bay were assigned to the 160th Bruce Battalion. Approximately three hundred Iroquois men, disregarding the Iroquois Council's decision to refrain from sending its men to fight "unless asked to do so by the king himself," enlisted and were assigned to the 114th Battalion of the Haldiman Rifles. An additional five hundred Native Americans fought in the 107th Battalion.[34]

Similar to African Americans in the AEF, Indians in the CEF often received assignments in labor units where they worked shoulder to shoulder with black Canadians building roads, digging ditches, and loading ships. Others fought in infantry units, where they served as scouts and snipers. Approximately thirty-five percent of them were voluntary enlistees. Despite language difficulties with Indian soldiers, Canadian officers gave them favorable ratings and several Native American soldiers in the CEF won decorations for valorous service. Cameron Brant, the great-great grandson of famed Iroquois leader Joseph Brant, commanded a platoon of the Fourth Canadian Infantry Battalion until he was killed near Ypres, Belgium. Francis Pegahmagabow, an Ojibway from the Parry Island reserve in Ontario, served as a sniper in the First Canadian Infantry Battalion and received three decorations for marksmanship and scouting skills. Henry Norwest, a Cree from Alberta, also served as a sniper and was credited with 115 observed hits before being killed in action shortly before the war ended.[35]

The major European powers' utilization of racial minorities from their colonies during World War I was, in many respects, similar to America's use of its internal minorities. The French deployed Senegalese soldiers from West Africa, for example, and the British called upon their colonials in India for reinforcements on the Western Front. In many ways, Native Americans themselves constituted a colonial force. They lived on isolated reservations segregated from the dominant Anglo culture, but remained subject to, and dependent on, white political rule. Like the European colonials in Africa and Asia, many American Indians did not possess citizenship or the franchise.

The French use of Senegalese troops dates back to the 1820s, after the end of the Napoleonic Wars. In 1857 French officials formed the first Senegalese Battalion, under the direction of French West Africa governor Leon Faidherbe. French authorities believed that the Senegalese Battalion would complement their efforts to transform the colony into a commercial asset for France. For the next forty years the Senegalese Battalion (or the Senegalese *tiralleurs*, as they were sometimes called) aided in the maintenance of order in West

Africa. In 1909 Lieutenant Colonel Charles Mangin, chief of staff in French West Africa, recommended that Senegalese troops be recruited for duty in Morocco and Algeria, to bolster French military presence in northwest Africa. Although they had no plans to assimilate West Africans into French society, policymakers in Paris argued that military service would "be an important aid in bringing civilization to the [Senegalese] natives."[36]

Consequently, in February 1912 the French government adopted compulsory military service in West Africa and dispatched officials to administer the draft. All men between the ages of twenty and twenty-eight were required to serve for two years. Similar to methods employed by the United States government to encourage Native Americans to enlist for military service, the French called on local leaders and clerics to rally support for the draft. Despite their efforts, opposition to conscription came from two quarters: from the French landowners in West Africa and from the Senegalese people themselves. French landowners opposed the draft because it threatened to deplete their labor supply. Senegalese men, fearing that they would be deployed far from home, evaded the draft by escaping into the forest and, in some instances, maiming themselves.[37]

With the outbreak of World War I in August 1914, French authorities called on their Senegalese colonials to fight against the Germans in Africa (for example, in Togoland, a German protectorate) and in the trenches of Western Europe. Thus, on August 10, Senegalese troops stationed in Morocco departed for France, and like the experiences of some Native Americans their voyage to Europe was a terrifying ordeal and seasickness was common. Morale plummeted as they watched their homeland disappear to the south. Many feared they would never live to touch African soil again.[38]

Once in France, military officials segregated the Senegalese into isolated camps and forbade them from mingling with the local population. Nonetheless, French propaganda depicted the Senegalese as *"les bon sauvages"* who possessed all the "primitive, natural qualities" of bravery, loyalty, and trustworthiness. Popular preconceptions suggested that the Africans were warriors by tradition and would make good shock troops. One French soldier commented that "the blacks were faithful, loyal and tireless in their periods of active military operations," but "they could not undertake missions requiring intelligence." Still, he continued, "their lack of nervous system made them cool under the most trying situations, and their bravery, even to the point of rashness, was conspicuous." Partly because of their reputation for bravery, the French deployed the *"Force Noire,"* as the Senegalese were also called, in hazardous combat zones. Their casualty rate, consequently, was significantly higher than that of their French counterparts.[39]

The service of Corporal Hamilde Annonetti is a vivid illustration of the mixed reputation of the Senegalese. After suffering the effects of a poison-gas attack while serving on the Western Front, Annonetti was taken to a relief station from where he reportedly begged to go back to the firing line to finish his attack. He escaped from the hospital and dragged himself back to the front, where he renewed his offensive. He reportedly killed five Germans who were manning a machine gun, but lost both his legs in the ordeal.[40]

German propagandists played upon the worst stereotypes associated with African soldiers. They alleged that Africans collected ears and heads and that they "committed atrocities which set at defiance not only the recognized usages of warfare, but of civilization and of humanity." The Germans also charged that French soldiers allowed Senegalese troops to stand guard over innocent women and "expose them to their animal passions."[41]

Like Native American troops, the French Senegalese fought to uphold their martial traditions, for economic advancement, and for social mobility. In addition, the Senegalese served "to assert their worth as human beings before men who had [formerly] viewed them as brutes." The French government drafted or enlisted between 130,000 and 200,000 West African troops for service in the war, and Senegalese efforts had an important impact on the their relationship with France. Conscription, high taxes, and economic instability in Senegal bred a spirit of rebellion. French promises of pensions, land grants, and citizenship for veterans did little to alleviate the Senegalese discontent. Their service, Alice Conkin has suggested, "engendered attitudes and expectations which, but for the war-time encounter, would have been unthinkable."[42] Having fought and died alongside their white counterparts, Senegalese soldiers no doubt questioned the alleged superiority and invincibility of their French landlords. Service in World War I, therefore, may have encouraged racial pride and confidence among the Senegalese people, as it did for American Indians fighting in the AEF and serving at home in the United States.

The experiences of Native Americans in the war also can be compared to those of British colonial troops from India. The British began using Indian soldiers in the late seventeenth century to help protect the interests of the East India Company. Such use expanded through the eighteenth century and, from the 1850s until the start of World War I, the British maintained approximately 75,000 men in India as well as a 160,000-man Indian army. In August 1914 the Indian Army consisted of 155,423 combat troops, including 15,000 British officers and over 45,000 soldiers in noncombat units. The duties of British and Indian troops in South Asia were to maintain internal security, defend India's frontiers, and protect the colony in case of an attack by another European power.[43]

The composition of Indian units was unique. Unlike Native American soldiers, Indians served in segregated units. In response to the hierarchial caste system that divided the Indian population into hundreds of distinct social and religious groupings, however, Indian companies initially incorporated soldiers from the same caste. As late as 1912 30 percent of Indian infantry units were still organized according to caste. Moreover, certain castes were perceived to be more martial than others. The British "martial race theory" contended that people from hot, flat regions in India made poor soldiers, while those from cold, hilly regions were good soldiers. They also considered particular ethnic groups in India to be more warlike than others. The Rajputs, Jats, Dogras, Pathans, Gurkhas, and Sikhs, for example, were considered martial races. Consequently, the British labored to ensure that members of the so-called martial castes dominated the ranks of infantry and cavalry and placed them in special "class regiments."[44]

Following the start of World War I, British officials expressed hesitation about deploying Indian soldiers in Europe. Some policymakers argued that military service would aid in the acculturation of Indian soldiers and would encourage their loyalty to the crown. Opponents of such deployment, on the other hand, feared that removing large numbers of British and Indian soldiers from the colony would undermine English control over India. Moreover, the British believed that such utilization might encourage the Indians after the war to demand concessions—maybe even independence—for "bailing out" Great Britain.[45]

On August 25, 1914, the British government decided against using Indian troops in Europe, but it soon reversed the decision. At the Battle of La Cateau on August 26, the British lost eight thousand men and thirty-eight artillery pieces. Fears of greater British casualties in the future prompted policymakers to overlook their initial misgivings about using Indian soldiers. Consequently, on August 27 the British government issued new orders for the deployment of two Indian divisions on the Western Front.[46]

The First Army Corps set out for France from Bombay and Karachi, India, in September 1914. Ill-equipped and poorly prepared for modern warfare, the First Army was deficient in strength by over five thousand men, a brigade short of a typical British Army Corps. Nonetheless, by the end of October 1914 units of the Third (Lahore) Division and the Seventh (Meerut) Division occupied a sector on the front.[47]

Similar to stereotypes regarding the martial prowess of Native Americans, troops from India were depicted as instinctive warriors and "bloodthirsty barbarians" who were especially eager to fight. Sir James Willcocks, a general in the British army, described Indians as a "race of born fighters," while W. Kerr Connell, another British officer, maintained that although "the 'noble Red Man' is a myth, the noble Sikh is a great reality." An article in *The Literary Digest* claimed that the Indians' "arms always throbbed for swords with which they might slaughter the enemies of the British government." In addition, young men from India were reportedly wandering around like "madmen" wanting to enlist. German propaganda, meanwhile, depicted soldiers from India as barbarians who fought with poison knives and drank the blood of their enemies. The Germans alleged that Indian troops who came across wounded enemy soldiers would "mutilate their faces with knives, and cut their throats."[48]

Indian colonials in the First Army Corps enjoyed limited success. Many earned the respect and admiration of their British officers (hundreds of Indian soldiers won honors or rewards and twelve won the Victoria Cross), but numerous problems undermined the Indians' achievements. Jeffrey Greenhut, in his examination of Indian infantry on the Western Front, argues that the South Asian soldiers were only partially loyal to the British, and service in the trenches tended to erode what loyalty existed. Indian soldiers also had a hard time acclimatizing to weather conditions in Europe; the cold, damp climate apparently undermined their morale.[49]

Reports of desertion and treason among Indian troops were common. In February 1915 Indian soldiers, quartered in barracks at Singapore, mutinied in hopes of sparking a popular uprising in India against British colonial rule. A month later, twenty-four Indian soldiers went over to the German lines. Many Indian soldiers reportedly maimed themselves in order to escape further service in the war. During their first two months at the front over one thousand Indian soldiers sought treatment for self-inflicted wounds to their left hands. In response, British military officials issued warnings that if discovered attempting to maim themselves, the soldiers would be court-martialed and shot.[50]

Leadership in Indian units was another problem. If their white officers were killed, the efficiency of Indian soldiers deteriorated rapidly. According to Jeffrey Greenhut, Indian troops viewed their officers as much more than military leaders; officers were teachers, advisers, and, at times, "father substitutes." Thus, when an officer suffered wounds or died in combat, his Indian troops were devastated. Replacements often lacked any knowledge or respect for Indian languages, cultures, or traditions.[51]

Poor training and a lack of experience in trench warfare led to high casualty rates among Indian soldiers. Many inexperienced troops needlessly exposed themselves to enemy fire, while cold weather and exhaustion under-mined their health and morale. An estimated five hundred Indian officers and twenty thousand Indian soldiers suffered wounds or died in Western Europe during the war. Consequently, just a year after the First Army Corps was deployed on the Western Front, British military officials issued orders to withdraw all Indian troops from Europe. Overall, of the 850,000 men that India committed during World War One, 49,000 were killed in action—a 5.7 percent casualty rate.[52]

Despite the obvious prejudice and danger, the opportunity to serve the crown made many Indians feel appreciated and important. Although they "failed to adjust to the novelties of industrialized and bureaucratized war-fare being fought on the Western Front," Indian soldiers fought with cour-age and recorded many deeds of heroism.[53] Like minorities serving with the French, Canadian, and American armies, Indian troops suffered from the effects of popular preconceptions and unrealistic expectations of their fight-ing abilities.

Indian soldiers also learned a great deal from their tenure in the military. Wartime service introduced many young Indian soldiers to new technology, military discipline, new varieties of food, and the English language. Of even greater importance, the war years brought Indians of all castes and ethnicities into intimate contact with each other, which, in some ways, undermined the hierarchial class system of India. On the other hand, military service tended to reinforce traditional cultures and customs among Indian troops. British officers, for example, respected Sikh prohibitions against cutting their hair and allowed Gurkha troops to engage in their ceremonial beheading of goats. Thus, wartime service tended to reinforce traditional Indian cultures while, at the same time it introduced Indians to European lifestyles and technolo-gies.[54] Despite their relatively short period of service on the Western Front, India's contributions to the British war effort were at least as great as that of any other European colony.[55]

As one can see, Native American experiences in World War I paralleled those of other minority groups. Generally speaking, racial minorities fought for many of the same reasons: (1) for short-term employment and to escape poverty; (2) to demonstrate their loyalty and patriotism for the mother coun-try; (3) to gain and/or retain respect and appreciation from the dominant population; and (4) to improve the social and political status of their breth-ren after the war.

The prevalence of popular stereotypes concerning minority soldiers dem-onstrates a further similarity. Although the conventional images were not always the same, they exerted a strong influence on the duties assigned to minority soldiers. Certain ethnic or tribal groups, consequently, received the most dangerous assignments while others served in labor units.

A final similarity was that white policymakers in the United States and Europe hoped that military service would hasten the acculturation of their minority soldiers and expedite their adoption of "civilized" behavior. Close contact with white soldiers, government officials believed, would go a long way to help educate minority peoples about "proper" conduct and discipline.

In many ways, the wartime experiences accomplished these goals, and many veterans returned home with a heightened awareness of the world around them and a keener appreciation for the rules and regulations that governed European-based societies. Lessons learned during World War I encouraged some minority groups in the postwar era to fight for racial equality and to demand the rights of citizenship. The idea of self-determination as applied to Europe could not be kept from filtering into imperial relationships elsewhere, as evidenced by the growing movements to end colonialism in India and Ireland. In the United States, the summer of 1919 (alias the "Red Summer") signaled the beginning of a series of violent race riots as African Americans reacted to continued discrimination and "colonialism" at home. For Native Americans the decade of the 1920s witnessed the growth of important reform organizations that sought to ensure a greater degree of Indian self-determination and cultural pluralism. Ironically, the contributions of Indian soldiers abroad and of their families at home (which is the subject of the next chapter) prompted the BIA to accelerate—rather than to reconsider—its efforts to assimilate Native Americans.

7

The Indian Homefront
and the BIA

INDIAN SOLDIERS WERE NOT THE ONLY NATIVE AMERICANS WHO SERVED
their country during World War I. Indian civilians, women in particular, supported the war effort in several important ways. Many purchased war bonds
or contributed money to the Red Cross. Some worked in shipyards, aircraft
plants, and other war-related industries. In response to new initiatives from
Cato Sells, the commissioner of Indian affairs, Native Americans participated in the "Great Plow Up" and brought a larger percentage of their lands
under cultivation, providing vital food and raw materials for the war effort.
In an effort to hasten the assimilation process and terminate federal guardianship of American Indians, Sell stepped up his prewar policy of establishing "competency commissions" to determine if individual Indians were
"competent" to manage their own affairs.[1] Consequently, between 1917 and
1919 thousands of Native Americans received fee patents to their lands.

The war also affected Native American cultures. In spite of persistent efforts by the Bureau of Indian Affairs (BIA) to hasten assimilation, Indian
cultures and traditions exhibited great resilience during the late nineteenth
century. But as the twentieth century began, many ceremonies and rituals,
particularly those connected with hunting and warfare, lost their former
prominence and vitality. During the war, however, tribal dances, giveaways,
and feasts became prevalent again among some Indian peoples as a way of
recognizing their veterans' accomplishments, just as their warrior ancestors
had done in the past.

Native Americans on the homefront also faced tough problems. Indian
health and education services, for example, already in deplorable condition,
declined even more between 1917 and 1919 as federal officials sought to
curtail public expenditures in order to finance the costs of the American
Expeditionary Force (AEF).

Thousands of Native Americans demonstrated their loyalty and support by participating in the government-initiated bond and stamp drives that were common during the war. To help finance the American war effort in the spring of 1917, Secretary of the Treasury William McAdoo initiated a campaign to sell savings bonds and war stamps. Coming in various denominations and accruing an interest rate of approximately 4 percent, "Liberty bonds" became an important symbol of status and evidence of patriotism. Government-sponsored propaganda reminded citizens that purchasing bonds and stamps was a national duty and an important way of supporting American boys overseas.

Native Americans participated with enthusiasm, and during the first bond issue in the spring of 1917 they purchased over 4.6 million dollars worth of bonds. During the second and third bond issues, they bought an average of 4.3 million dollars worth, a per capita subscription of approximately 50 dollars for every Indian man, woman, and child. By the war's end, Native Americans had purchased over 25 million dollars worth of Liberty bonds, a per capita investment of about 75 dollars. Members of the Five Civilized Tribes of Oklahoma accounted for nearly half of the investment, purchasing 10,250,000 dollars worth of bonds and 986,300 dollars in stamps.[2]

American Indians bought Liberty bonds for several reasons. An important motivation was patriotism and a sincere desire to aid the American war effort, but there were other factors. The BIA, for example, encouraged Native Americans to purchase bonds and employed important Indian spokesmen to appeal to their brethren's generosity and willingness to sacrifice. In addition, Indian school publications boosted bond sales by running articles that commended those tribes or individuals who purchased more than their fair share.

Commissioner Sells encouraged Native Americans to purchase Liberty bonds because, he believed, it would teach Indians the money-saving habit, help develop "good character," and hasten assimilation. Furthermore, Sells saw the sale of Liberty bonds and war savings stamps as an opportunity for spreading the "gospel of thrift" among the Indians in the hope of forming in them "the beginnings of provident and progressive habits." Accordingly, in April 1918 the commissioner wrote that he wanted to see "a Liberty Bond in every American home . . . in the home of every Indian and every employee of our service." He instructed reservation superintendents to urge upon each reservation employee and each Indian the advisability of purchasing bonds as an investment and "the necessity of doing so as an aid to our country."[3]

Reminiscent of the way that it encouraged Native Americans to register and enlist for military service, the BIA employed influential Indian leaders to boost Liberty bond and stamp sales. In his 1917 report, Sells noted that several Apache scouts were liberal purchasers, as were the widow and son of Geronimo. The *New York Times* reported that Chief Strongheart, a Yakima and the son of Running Elk, an aide to Theodore Roosevelt during the Spanish-American War, visited several military posts in the fall of 1918 to organize support for war savings stamps and Liberty bonds. Meanwhile, Chief White Elk, a Cherokee, along with his wife "Princess Ah-tra-ah-saun," a Klamath, spoke in behalf of bond sales in Oregon, California, and New York. The couple reportedly succeeded in selling in one week more than 1.8 million dollars worth of Liberty bonds.[4]

Indian school publications also encouraged Native Americans to invest their money in bonds and stamps. An article in *The Native American* reminded its readers that "many of our Indian boys are on foreign soil and must be brought home. . . . A new loan will be floated soon. . . . Will the Indians carry on to the end?" *The Indian School Journal* reported that "Oklahoma Indians are taking an active part in the 'win the war' campaign" through their purchase of over four million dollars worth of Liberty bonds. *The American Indian Magazine* commended the Osages for subscribing 226,000 dollars during the third bond drive.[5]

In an effort to boost bond sales even more, Secretary of the Interior Franklin K. Lane in June 1917 suggested that tribal funds be invested in Liberty bonds. The Treasury Department, he reported, held "Indian tribal funds amounting to probably more than five million dollars" that was drawing little or no interest. Lane believed that Native Americans (not to mention the federal government) might be served better if the Interior Department invested the money in Liberty bonds that bore 3.5 percent interest.

To ascertain the legality of the proposal, Lane asked Walter W. Warwick, the comptroller of the treasury, for his opinion. On June 9, Warwick responded in the negative. He stated that "it is clear that the [Indian] moneys now on deposit in the Treasury . . . can be used only for the purposes which the law or treaty prescribe." Therefore, Warwick continued, further legislation by Congress would be necessary before tribal funds could be withdrawn and invested in Liberty bonds.[6]

Meanwhile, Secretary Lane had asked Senator Henry F. Ashurst of Arizona to submit a resolution that would allow him to invest individual Indian funds in Liberty bonds. On June 1, Ashurst, together with Senator Henry L. Myers of Montana, introduced Senate Joint Resolution 73, a bill "authorizing the Secretary of the Interior to invest Indian funds in government bonds." On June 11, the Senate approved the bill. The measure empowered the secretary of the interior to invest (with or without Native American consent) any Indian funds or moneys in the fifteen- to thirty-year 3.5 percent gold bonds where, in the secretary's judgment, "the interests of the Indians and of the United States justified such investment." A month later, the Senate referred the bill to the House where the committee on Indian affairs began deliberations on the measure. Despite the committee's positive report, the House of Representatives, already busy with other war-related legislation, did not ratify the bill until May 25, 1918.[7]

When Native Americans attempted to redeem the Liberty bonds that Secretary Lane had purchased for them, problems arose. Because the bonds were in his name, Lane had discretion over the time when they could be liquidated. Illustrating what some have called "classic" Indian bureau paternalism, Lane frequently denied Indian requests to cash in their bonds and have the proceeds relinquished to their control because he assumed that the Indians would make poor use of the money. In December 1918, for example, George Whiteturkey, a Cherokee, requested that the Interior Department redeem all Liberty bonds and war savings stamps purchased in his name. Lane responded that he had deposited the bonds and stamps in the Treasury "for safe-keeping." Furthermore, because Whiteturkey was already earning about five thousand dollars a year from oil royalties, Lane reasoned that the Native American did not really need the money.[8]

Department of the Interior officials gave similar rationale for their refusal to redeem bonds for Mrs. Sallie Morrison, a Native American from Oklahoma. When Morrison requested that the Liberty bonds purchased for her son Jerry be turned over to her, Assistant Secretary of the Interior S. G. Hopkins responded that "you are not now in need of [the money] for maintenance and support" so "it is deemed inadvisable to disturb it."[9]

Even those Native Americans whom the BIA had declared "competent" experienced difficulties in gaining control over their Liberty bonds. In June 1918, Secretary Lane had purchased three thousand dollars worth of Liberty bonds for Clifford Johnson, a Cherokee. Seven months later, however, the BIA declared Johnson to be "competent to transact his own business affairs" and he petitioned the Department of Interior for control of his bonds. Regardless of Johnson's new status, Lane ruled that the grant of competency removed only those restrictions on land and did not apply to Liberty loans. He denied Johnson's request.[10]

Thus, while they were "competent" enough to fight and die for their country, to possess clear title to their lands, and to transact their own business affairs, Native Americans apparently were not competent enough to make effective use of bond proceeds. Although it claimed to have the best interests of Native Americans at heart, the Interior Department's policy on Indian-owned Liberty bonds demonstrated that some of the concerns of American Indians still remained subservient to those of the federal government.[11]

In addition to supporting the Liberty bond and war savings stamp drives, Native Americans aided the Red Cross. Commissioner Sells estimated that ten thousand Indians joined the Red Cross during World War I and that they were "mingling their efforts with the whites and are glad to do their work for the good it accomplishes rather than from a spirit of racial emulation." In addition to gifts of money, American Indians staged auction sales, knitted sweaters and hospital garments, and sent thousands of Christmas boxes to loved ones in the AEF. Native Americans living on the Pine Ridge reservation in South Dakota conducted an auction sale and raised fourteen hundred dollars for the Red Cross in one hour. A group of Indian boys from the File Hills reservation in Saskatchewan, Canada, were reported to have formed a marching band and played concerts to raise money for Red Cross relief efforts in Belgium. Several Indian ranchers donated cattle or sheep to the Red Cross, and in Montana Native American farmers contributed sacks of wheat to the organization. The *New York Times* reported that several boys attending an Indian school in the Pacific Northwest (the Chemawa Indian School in Salem, Oregon, perhaps) collected two thousand pounds of sphagnum moss for use in surgical pads. *The Indian's Friend* noted that Cheyennes living near Clinton, Oklahoma, donated an antique peace pipe to the Red Cross, and that every family in Santa Ana Pueblo, New Mexico, had purchased a Red Cross membership.[12]

Some Native Americans, especially the Plains tribes, apparently associated Red Cross activity with the Sun Dance. Both the Red Cross and the Sun Dance, for example, were often associated with the care and recovery of sick and wounded people; both shared the cross emblem; and both employed the color red, which is considered by some Indian people to be sacred. Several Native Americans apparently fulfilled their Sun Dance vows by contributing to the Red Cross or donating livestock and property, and a few Sun Dance participants reportedly wore a Red Cross on their chests in lieu of the traditional chest and back skewers.[13]

Among the most important contributors to Red Cross fund raisers and activities were Indian women. In historic times, Indian women helped outfit and equip their loved ones with food, clothing, and other supplies. What they did after preparing their men for battle, wishing them luck, and hoping for their safe return varied from tribe to tribe. Mandan women fasted when their brothers were away on war expeditions, while Apache women were supposed to pray for their husbands every morning for four days. Among some tribes, women accompanied their loved ones into battle, where they prepared food, dressed wounds, and occasionally fought beside the men.[14]

A popular story during World War I was that of an impoverished seventy-five-year-old Ute woman named Pe-retta. During a tribal gathering where reservation superintendent Albert H. Kneale addressed the Utes concerning Red Cross needs, Pe-retta contributed five hundred dollars, leaving only thirteen dollars in her savings account. Her sacrifice to the war effort gained considerable notoriety after Commissioner Sells published the story, which appeared in several Indian journals and magazines.[15]

Indian women also knitted socks, mufflers, sweaters, and hospital garments for American soldiers. Commissioner Sells reported that Mrs. Sarah Valandre, a Sioux from South Dakota and a "champion knitter," began a soldier's sweater at 2:00 P.M. and completed the garment eight and a half hours later. *The Indian School Journal* related the story of an elderly Cherokee woman who was knitting a sweater for the Red Cross. "Umh, me help; me don't like Churmans," she stated, and began to speed up work on the garment. Native American girls at the Hampton school in Virginia aided the war effort by packing "comfort kits" that contained bath towels, combs, toothbrushes, shaving equipment, and handkerchiefs. They forwarded the kits to Indian soldiers serving in Europe.[16]

Native American women performed other important work. In response to Food Administration director Herbert Hoover's call to conserve food, Indian women planted "Victory Gardens" and canned food. Many Indian women worked for the BIA as cooks, teachers, laundresses, clerks, seamstresses, and assistant matrons at Indian boarding schools. Others served as nurses both at home and in Europe. Miss Effie Barnett, a Choctaw and graduate of Presbyterian College in Durant, Oklahoma, and Agnes Anderson, a member of the Callam tribe and a graduate of the Cushman Indian Trades School, served as an army nurses in France. Lula Owl, an Eastern Cherokee, also entered the army's medical corps as a nurse and enjoyed the distinction of being the only Eastern Cherokee officer in the war. A few Indian women provided entertainment for American troops overseas. Tsianina Redfeather, a Cherokee from Muskogee, Oklahoma, had two brothers serving in the army. She sang in France both to entertain American doughboys and to "bring about a better understanding between her race and the white people." Iva J. Rider (alias "Princess Atalia"), a Cherokee, served on the entertainment committee of the Young Woman's Christian Association (YWCA), as did Anne Ross, the great-great granddaughter of Cherokee chief John Ross. After the war, Native American women in California established the "Wigwam Club" to raise money for disabled Indian veterans. Members sold handmade Indian crafts, such as paintings and moccasins, and organized an annual picnic to attract attention to their cause. Thus, World War I provided opportunities for Indian women to continue a long tradition of service in time of war.[17]

The war years may have influenced Anglo perceptions of American Indian women. According to Pamela M. White in her examination of Native American women in western Canada and their impact on Canadian Indian policy, the war years modified the way that the Canadian government viewed Indian women. Prior to the war, it viewed Native American women as "a nuisance" and their lifestyle as "inappropriate" and "untidy." In response to their wartime contributions, however, Indian women "were seen to have measured up to the non-Indian population" for the first time.[18]

In the United States, Anglo perceptions of Indian women underwent a similar change. Prior to the war, many Americans erroneously compared the position of women in Indian society to slaves or draft animals. Indian women, many Americans believed, possessed no rights or liberties and exercised little influence in tribal affairs. In 1890, for example, Commissioner of Indian Affairs Thomas Jefferson Morgan characterized the position of women in Indian society as one of "servility and degradation."[19] In 1902 William R. Draper, in a poorly informed and racist article published in *Cosmopolitan*, described courtship practices among Native Americans and the role of Indian mothers. If an Indian woman has "a gentle, sweet voice," Draper maintained, "she may have many duskey wooers," but otherwise she is "doomed to be sold as a slave to some buck." When an Indian baby reaches the age of three, he continued, "its mother loses interest in it completely, and it is not yet old enough to be deserving of any attention on the part of the father."[20]

A decade later, Cato Sells illustrated his own lack of understanding about Indian cultures by describing the role of Native American women as "barbaric" and calling on government-administered Indian schools to instill in their pupils a "truly chivalrous spirit that recognizes and respects the sacredness of womanhood." In some of the nation's Indian boarding schools, administrators restricted their students' freedoms for fear that the Native Americans' "natural sexual promiscuity" would take over if they were not closely supervised.[21]

During the war years few Americans complained about the status of Indian women or their activities on the homefront. In fact, they praised Native American women for their thrift, hard work, and patriotism. Instead of expressing concern about the "servility" or "natural promiscuity" of Indian women, BIA officials marveled at the Native American spirit of service, generosity, and fidelity to country.

The media also focused on the positive contributions that Indian women were making to the war effort. *The Indian School Journal,* for instance, commended Indian service on the homefront as evidence that Indian women too were "one hundred percent Americans." In its May 1918 issue, *The Indian School Journal* published a speech given by Clara Root, an Arapaho student at Chilocco Indian Agricultural School, who enumerated the devastating costs of the war and argued in favor of President Wilson's plea for disarmament and the establishment of a League of Nations. After the war, Edgar B. Meritt, the assistant commissioner of Indian affairs, wrote about the improving economic status of Indian women and their abilities as mothers. He stated that many Indian women were earning a good living through native arts, such as lace making and beadwork in addition to looking after the welfare of their families. No mother, he continued, "is more devoted to her children than the Indian mother."[22] Thus, through their contributions during World War I, Indian women took a large step in discrediting popular misconceptions regarding their role in Native American society.

While stereotypical images of Indian women underwent a transformation of sorts during the war, BIA policy exhibited remarkable consistency in pursuing its late nineteenth-century goals. The individualization and assimilation of Native Americans, together with the termination of federal guardianship, had been the primary objectives of the BIA following the passage of the Dawes Act in 1887. During the war years they remained the most important goals in Indian policy.

This is not to say that BIA policies were effective, however, or influential to the public at large. Historian Frederick Hoxie has contended that the "campaign to assimilate the Indians" was "fundamentally altered" after 1900. While reformers continued to work for "the incorporation of Native Americans into the majority society," Hoxie maintained, "they no longer sought to transform the Indians or guarantee their equality." An integral part of the Hoxie thesis is that Indian policymakers after 1900 took a much more pessimistic view about the Native Americans' ability to change. He alleges, for example, that by 1915 "the public was growing accustomed to viewing the Indians as members of one of the world's many 'backwards races.' "[23]

There is much truth to Hoxie's thesis. A portion of the American public and some reformers may very well have questioned the long-held policy of assimilation after 1900 and, consequently, altered their expectations regarding the ability of Native Americans to enter the social and political mainstream as equals. As the twentieth century progressed, for instance, educators increasingly emphasized a vocational rather than liberal curriculum for their

Indian pupils, while government policymakers continued to express doubts about whether Native Americans were capable of exercising the rights and responsibilities of citizenship.

Despite such indications of declining public expectations, a reexamination of the Cato Sells administration (particularly the second half of his administration), the outbreak of World War I, and their combined impact on federal Indian policy poses a challenge to Hoxie's thesis. As John R. Finger has pointed out, Hoxie failed to "give proper attention to the effects of World War I in promoting a more optimistic vision of assimilation among officials in the Indian Office."[24] If this, in fact, was the case, then federal Indian policy during the war years might more accurately be interpreted as a continuation of nineteenth-century policies—and a departure of sorts from Hoxie's theory of a fundamentally altered Indian policy after 1900.

To many BIA officials, World War I provided new opportunities to "transform" Indians into "real" Americans, and imbued administrators with renewed energy and optimism. In a letter to the editor of *The American Review of Reviews* in May 1918, for example, Sells wrote that "a few words can scarcely describe the progressive awakening of the Native American in recent years." Indian soldiers serving alongside whites, he continued, were gaining "an education that will lead them away from tribal relations, and give them a definite comprehension of the genius of American institutions."[25]

The renewed hope in the traditional policy of assimilation received a voice in popular literature as well, standing in sharp contrast to the "pessimism" suggested in the Hoxie thesis. Emma Matt Rush wrote, in *Overland Monthly*, that service in World War I served to "amalgamate and unite the American races into one grand composite, in unison and in harmony, working together, side-by-side, fighting side-by-side."[26] An editorial appearing in the January 1926 edition of *Current History* predicted that the BIA planned to use Indian veterans as the foundation to build a "new Indian race," one that would "continue to bear the name but not the characteristics of the dying, primitive, race of old." Moreover, the editorial continued, the "changed status" provided by the ex-serviceman would lead to improvements in sanitation, education, and industry, an interest in government, and "intelligent citizenship."[27] Even J. Walker Fewkes, the chief ethnologist of the Bureau of American Ethnology, lamented in 1918 that "the American Indian is rapidly losing many of his instructive characteristics in his amalgamation into American citizenship."[28]

Thus, while Hoxie's contention that federal Indian policy changed after 1900 may hold some validity during the administrations of Commissioners

Francis E. Leupp (1905–1909) and Robert G. Valentine (1909–1913), it does not adequately take into account the war's influence on Indian policy and Cato Sells's renewed optimism for a complete "transformation" of Indian peoples and their assimilation into the majority society. During World War I and the immediate postwar era at least, Indian policy was marked by continuity with the goals of the post–Dawes Act reformers rather than by change.

Further evidence that points to the continuing dominance of assimilation was Commissioner Sells's three-pronged strategy during World War I. First, he encouraged Native American participation in the war effort, both in the military and on the homefront. Second, he urged Native Americans to boost agricultural production. Finally, he accelerated the movement to discontinue federal guardianship over competent Indians that had been inaugurated during the administration of Robert G. Valentine. Such a strategy, Sells believed, would increase Native American desire for "individuality, self-reliance, initiative, and ability to stand alone." Sells boasted that his Indian policy could "not fail to dissolve tribal bonds, remove inter-racial barriers, rescue the Indian from his retarding isolation," and "absorb him into the general population with the full rights and immunities of our American life."[29]

Bureau of Indian Affairs policymakers were convinced that military service would hasten Indian assimilation. In 1917, Sells wrote that the war was teaching Native Americans "its profound lesson that the highest authority and best social welfare must spring from a free and self-governing people." Moreover, he maintained, military service provided Indian soldiers with a "clearer vision of what constitutes well-organized society."[30] Fighting beside white men, Sells argued further, would provide the "associational contact" needed for Indian soldiers to move away from tribal relations and toward "civilization."[31]

The second BIA goal was to boost agricultural production on Indian-owned lands. On April 9, 1917, soon after Congress declared war on Germany, Sells sent an urgent telegram to Indian-service superintendents throughout the country. Perhaps caught up in the excitement of America's entry into the war, Sells informed his employees that the "war situation makes it imperative that every tillable acre of land on Indian reservations be intensively cultivated this season to supply food demands." He directed superintendents to call farmers and leading Indians together "immediately" and to get organized. "There can be no delay," Sells warned; this is of the "highest importance and requires aggressive action."[32]

Hence, the BIA began a two-year crusade to convert Native Americans, particularly in the West, into successful and productive farmers and ranchers. Although government officials and reformers for decades had tried to encourage Native Americans to adopt farming or stockraising, the renewed effort between 1917 and 1919 was more forceful and, because of the country's entry into World War I, even urgent.

The program had several important objectives. Its immediate goal was to aid the U.S. war effort through the production of foodstuffs and commodities (such as wool for uniforms). Its long-range goals were similar to those of earlier reform efforts: to encourage Indian self-support, to instill in Native Americans the value of hard work and industry, and most importantly, to hasten assimilation. The campaign to boost Indian agricultural production, Sells noted in 1917, would hasten the final solution of the "Indian problem" for the "obvious reason" that the Indians would gradually achieve self-support and become independent by means of their increased industrial activity.[33]

There may have been additional motivations for the BIA's campaign. White farmers and ranchers in the West resented Native Americans for not making efficient use of tribal lands. America's entry into World War I exacerbated such sentiments, because many western farmers coveted Indian lands and felt the "urge to cultivate every tillable acre" to aid the war effort. As a result, the BIA came under increased pressure from western land interests to force Indians either to become better farmers or to give up their lands. Secretary of the Interior Franklin K. Lane, a Californian, warned that "idle Indians on idle land must lead to the sale of the lands, for the pressing populations of the West will not long look upon resources unused without strenuous and effective protest." Some western politicians even suggested without success that the government draft Native Americans into federal service as farmers or farm laborers.[34]

David L. Wood, who examined Indian agriculture during the war, argued that the BIA had an additional motivation for encouraging Indian agricultural production. Indian-bureau officials, Wood maintained, hoped to demonstrate their own loyalty and thereby avoid public criticism by getting Native Americans to use more acres.[35]

The BIA encouraged Native Americans in several ways. First, on April 12, 1917, Sells instructed Indian-service employees to "get into the field early and stay late, encouraging and assisting Indian farmers in every possible way." They were to "appeal to the patriotism of the Indians" by showing them how they could serve their country effectively in the present emergency by "exerting themselves to the uttermost in the production of foodstuffs." In addition, some government spokesmen warned of widespread famine and starvation if the Native Americans did not "do their part" by cultivating more land.[36]

Second, the BIA persuaded Native Americans to support agricultural fairs, where the men could display their agricultural products and livestock and Indian women could show off their processed foods and native handcrafts. Awards and prizes would be awarded for the best exhibits. The most famous of the fairs, which first took place in 1904 at the Crow reservation in southern Montana, had become a popular annual event, and by the time the United States entered World War I there were over fifty agriculture fairs in operation in the West. According to Sells, "the spirit of rivalry and competition is a strong incentive to success among Indians as well as whites," and he praised the agricultural fair as one of the most effective means of "stimulating the enthusiasm of Indians along industrial lines."[37]

The media also exhorted American Indians to boost agricultural production and conserve food. An editorial in *The American Indian Magazine* encouraged Native American farmers to double their efforts to produce food supplies and "faithfully cultivate" their farms, while a piece in the *Oglala Light* called on its readers to participate in "Potato Week" so as to save wheat for the war effort. By doing this, magazine editors maintained, Indians would "bring an increased hope of a world wide victory to all mankind" and "save the world from misery." An article in *The Native American* also discussed the need for Indian farmers to mobilize. "The European war which we have entered is to be won by the mobilization of not only men," it suggested, "but of our money, our shops, [and] our farms." A commentary in *The Indian School Journal*, entitled "The Farmers' War Responsibility," predicted that "the American farmer . . . will determine the trend of human history for all time to come" and be a decisive factor in influencing "whether autocracy or democracy shall rule the world."[38]

Other editorials viewed the war as an appropriate time to alter significantly the relationship between Indian peoples and the federal government. A commentary published in the fall edition of the *Word Carrier of the Santee Normal Training School* declared that "the time is ripe for a more progressive treatment of the Indians. The war has changed the situation with them as it has changed most of the other relations in life." A rather mean-spirited editorial in the *Oglala Light*, meanwhile, claimed that Native Americans had been a "burden on the American people" and had "subsisted from the American ration table" without worry or trouble on their part. The American people, the author went on to warn, "are going to need their rations for other purposes from now on and no able-bodied person has the right to expect any help except such as he gives himself."[39]

Native American responses to the BIA's agriculture campaign were encouraging. Many Indian men, some of whom had never tried farming or made enough money from land or oil leases, began farming for the first time. Shoshones from the Wind River reservation in Wyoming brought one thousand new acres into cultivation, and Native Americans on seven different Montana reservations added over twelve thousand new acres. On the Fort Berthold reservation in North Dakota, members of the Mandan, Hidatsa, and Arikara tribes in one district alone farmed eight thousand new acres. In Arizona, farmers devoted a large percentage of Indian lands to long staple cotton, and the BIA had plans of converting fifty thousand acres of Indian-owned lands in the Southwest into cotton farms. Commissioner Sells estimated that during 1917 the amount of land under cultivation on seventy-three reservations increased by over 31 percent. Between 1916 and 1919 the total number of Indian-owned acres under cultivation increased approximately 12 percent, from 678,527 acres in 1916 to 759,933 acres in 1918.[40]

The value of Indian crops also rose sharply as European demands for American agricultural goods expanded. In 1916 the BIA estimated the value of Native American agricultural products at 5.2 million dollars. A year later the number had climbed over 50 percent to 7.9 million dollars. By the war's end the value of Indian agricultural products had risen another 22 percent to 9.7 million dollars. Altogether, their value increased by nearly 75 percent during the war years.[41]

The number of Native Americans engaged in raising livestock expanded as well. In 1916 there were an estimated 43,309 Indian stockraisers. The number climbed 9 percent in 1917–1918 to 47,174. The size of Indian-owned cattle herds experienced similar growth. In response to wartime inflation and heavy American beef exports to Europe, cattle prices soared and Indian cattlemen took advantage of the opportunity to maximize profits. In 1916, for example, Native American ranchers owned 276,769 head of cattle. By the end of 1918 Indian-owned cattle herds had increased by nearly 20 percent to 329,613 head.[42]

Despite the substantial increases in Indian agriculture, the BIA came under increased pressure from western land interests unimpressed with Native American efforts and impatient to get their hands on Indian lands. The BIA responded by encouraging hundreds of Native Americans to lease their lands to white farmers and ranchers who had more experience and possessed better equipment. As Janet McDonnell has noted, "World War I increased pressures on Indian land, for wartime demand for food, fuel, and raw materials intensified the drive to . . . encourage Indians to lease or sell their idle land." Commissioner Sells justified the measure with the concession that even with "our utmost efforts it is beyond the physical capacity of the Indians to bring under cultivation all the surplus land on different reservations." Thus, the

BIA took "aggressive steps" to lease as much of the "surplus land" as possible.[43]

According to leasing regulations published in July 1916, leases of Indian lands were to be small scale and temporary in nature. Unallotted dry land could be leased for five years and irrigated land for ten years. Allotted lands could be rented only if the Indian allottee was unable to farm. Lands of minors could be leased only until the child reached adulthood, and allotments of deceased Indians with undetermined heirs could be let for one year.[44]

In 1918, however, BIA officials were allowing large-scale lease agreements involving thousands of acres. In April, Secretary of the Interior Franklin Lane approved a deal whereby Thomas D. Campbell, an agricultural engineer from Grand Forks, North Dakota, and head of the fledgling Montana Farming Corporation (MFC), received permission to develop 200,000 acres of farmland on the Crow, Fort Peck, Blackfeet, and Shoshoni reservations in Montana and Wyoming. The Native American owners were to receive 10 percent of the crop for the first five years and 20 percent the subsequent five years. Unfortunately, meager harvests and a declining market after the war resulted in the MFC's collapse, although Campbell continued farming wheat lands on the Crow reservation for another decade. Indian leasers never received much more than a dollar an acre, although they had expected at least twice that amount.[45]

Despite such disappointments, several Indian tribes leased substantial portions of land to white farmers and cattlemen. In South Dakota, for instance, wealthy cattlemen leased nearly all of the Pine Ridge reservation as cheap grazing land. By the end of Sells's administration, white lessees were farming six times as much Indian land as the Native Americans. All told, the number of leases on allotted Indian land increased by 22 percent, from 16,500 in 1915 to 20,226 in 1918. The number of leases on unallotted Indian land increased dramatically from 51 in 1915 to 1,088 in 1918. Renting their lands, even during wartime, seemed easier for Native Americans and perhaps was more profitable than farming it themselves.[46]

Indian farmers faced several problems that curtailed their transition from subsistence to commercial agriculture. Insufficient capital and inadequate training prevented many of them from making use of new mechanized farm implements. Most Native American farmers, accordingly, continued to work their land with hand tools and horse-drawn machinery.[47]

Poor weather conditions also undermined Indian agricultural pursuits during the war years. Severe droughts followed by equally devastating winters combined to wreak havoc upon Indian livestock raisers and farmers living in the West. In the desert Southwest, Navajos suffered considerable loss of sheep in consequence of drought and hard winters. On the northern plains, meanwhile, Chippewa farmers from the Rocky Boy reservation in Montana also suffered from the effects of dry weather conditions. In 1917 their farmlands yielded less than three bushels of wheat per acre. The year before they had harvested more than ten times that amount. The Board of Indian Commissioners commented, in 1918, that the Rocky Boy Chippewas had cultivated over a hundred acres of new land, even though the previous summer had been so dry that a number of white homesteaders had threatened to leave the northern plains.[48]

Native American stockraisers also experienced problems during the war years. As beef prices rose steadily during World War I, the BIA encouraged Indian cattlemen, many of whom had been raising cattle for decades, to sell their animals to maximize profits. White ranchers also encouraged Indians to sell their herds. Once Indians got rid of their cattle, they reasoned, there would be little reason for Native Americans to refuse to lease their lands. Some people, such as the Oglala Sioux and Blackfeet, sold their entire herds (including their breeding stock) and after the war had to completely restock their pastures. In the desert Southwest, meanwhile, unethical traders urged Navajos to sell their sheep, arguing that they would never again receive such high prices. According to Russel Barsh, BIA employees, often in collusion with large cattle companies, were able to buy or lease most of the good Indian grazing land on some reservations by the late 1920s.[49]

Drought and harsh winters further reduced the size of Indian cattle herds. Of course, white cattlemen who leased Indian rangelands were not immune from the severe weather conditions and declining beef prices after the war, and as a result many reneged on their lease payments, leaving their Indian landlords economically destitute. E. A. Hutchinson, the superintendent on the Arapaho reservation, commented that Indians who leased their allotments to whites "for a bagatelle" were "aimlessly drifting . . . waiting for something to turn up." Not surprisingly, it was the Indians who entered the Great Depression a decade before the rest of society.[50]

For Native Americans who owned no land or cattle, the short-lived agricultural boom during the war years provided them with employment opportunities, and several hundred Native American men and women worked for farmers and ranchers. Commissioner Sells encouraged such employment. He stated that farming enterprises in various sections of the country needed Indian labor, and the Indians, if not profitably occupied with their own allotments, needed jobs. Students from the Phoenix Indian School in Arizona, for instance, gave up their summer vacations to work for local farmers. An additional four hundred Indian school students from the Southwest worked for the American Beet Sugar Company in labor camps that stretched across the central plains from Garden City, Kansas, to Rocky Ford, Colorado. Some government officials recommended that members of the Apache, Mohave, Navajo, Pima, Papago, Maricopa, and Yuma tribes be transported to Arizona to work on cotton farms. Indian policymakers, however, feared that such a "mixed community," composed of members of several tribes who are temporarily without the "safeguards of reservation jurisdiction," would be hard to control and apt to develop "deplorable" living conditions.[51]

Hundreds of Native Americans, particularly graduates of Indian vocational institutions, worked in the nation's factories during the war. The Carlisle Indian Industrial School in Pennsylvania sent dozens of its students to the Ford factory in Detroit, Michigan, to learn the various aspects of the automobile industry. The young men worked under the supervision of a Native American overseer and agreed to refrain from drinking alcohol, to pay their debts, and to save a portion of their earnings. In addition, they labored eight hours a day and spent four nights each week taking courses in mechanical drafting and technical automobile engineering. Commissioner Sells estimated that over three hundred Indians received such factory training. An additional fifty Native Americans worked at the Hog Island shipyard in Philadelphia. Others gained employment as mechanics in tractor factories and in the aircraft industry. Indian school students in Washington gained employment in shipyards and lumber mills, where they earned as much as ten dollars a day.[52]

In a final strategy to hasten Indian assimilation, Commissioner Sells's April 1917 "Declaration of Policy" accelerated the discontinuation of federal guardianship and the bestowal of fee patents to competent Indians. Such a policy, he argued, would allow the BIA to give even closer attention to the "incompetent" Indians so that they could more speedily achieve "competency."[53]

To implement the policy, the BIA turned to the Burke Act of 1906. Sponsored by Republican Congressman Charles H. Burke of South Dakota and enjoying the support of Commissioner Francis Ellington Leupp, the law amended the Dawes Act of 1887 by declaring that no Indian would be automatically granted citizenship until the twenty-five year trust period on his allotment expired. To reward those Native Americans deemed "competent" enough to manage their own affairs, however, the Burke Act authorized the secretary of the interior, at his discretion, to issue fee patents and grant citizenship prior to the expiration of the trust period. Although designed, in part, to prevent the conferring of citizenship upon those Indians who were not ready for it and to enable the BIA to better protect allottees against unscrupulous whites, the act's competency clause invited abuse and contributed to a dramatic decline in Indian landholdings.[54]

Both Secretary of the Interior Franklin Lane and Commissioner Cato Sells supported the continued allotment of Indian lands and the immediate and vigorous application of the Burke Act's competency clause.[55] Francis Paul Prucha has asserted that Sells "combined a deep concern for Indians who needed the help of the government" with a "ruthless determination to rid the government of responsibility for those Indians whom he judged able to manage fully their own affairs." Accordingly, in 1914 Secretary Lane encouraged Sells to establish a commission to determine the competency of Native American allottees, and the two men agreed that the Flathead Indian reservation in Montana would be a good place to test their plan. To head the newly established competency commission, Lane and Sells selected Major James McLaughlin, the former agent at the Devil's Lake agency and Standing Rock agency in Dakota Territory and, after 1895, an inspector for the Interior Department, and Frank A. Thackery, the superintendent of the Pima and Maricopa agency in Arizona. The BIA established additional commissions in 1916.[56]

The general criteria in determining Indian competency were literacy and self-sufficiency, but several problems undermined the commissioners' abilities to judge Indian candidates. Bad roads, poor weather, and isolated reservations hampered the effectiveness of the competency commissions and perhaps enticed some commissioners to issue fee patents without ever actually visiting the Native Americans in question.[57]

Many Indian allottees resisted the issuance of fee patents, thereby causing further problems. Receiving full title to their allotments made Indian-owned lands subject to taxation and exacerbated the Native Americans' chronic lack of capital. Additional problems occurred when whites coaxed Indians with fee patents to take out loans by using their allotments as collateral. When they failed to repay their debts, the Indians lost their lands. Members of the Cheyenne and Arapaho tribes reportedly received fee patents against their will. The best Cheyenne and Arapaho farmers were damaged severely in 1917, Robert Nespor has written, "not by the weather or the market," but by an Indian Department policy that forced fee patents upon the best farmers. Ben Buffalo, a prominent Cheyenne farmer prior to the war, lost his allotment in 1921 in part because he could not make his property-tax payments. In order to force reluctant Indians to accept full title to their allotments, competency commissions sent the documents by registered mail so that Native Americans would have to accept them.[58]

In hopes of expediting the disbursal of fee patents during World War I,

Commissioner Sells's April 1917 "Declaration of Policy" stated that patents in fee would be issued to all adult Indians of one-half or more Indian blood who were found to be competent. Moreover, graduates of government-administered Indian schools, upon reaching the age of twenty-one and who had demonstrated competency, also would receive full title to their lands. Consequently, the number of fee patents issued rose dramatically during World War I. During the decade that preceded the war the BIA issued 9,894 fee patents, roughly 1,000 per year. Between 1917 and 1919, however, it issued 10,956 patents, an average of 3,652 per year.[59]

Not surprisingly, Indian land sales increased as well. Between 1915 and 1916, Native Americans received 6,993,390 dollars from land sales. Between 1917 and 1918, proceeds from land sales nearly doubled to 11,751,769 dollars. Ironically, Sells's policies undermined, rather than encouraged, Indian self-support and resulted in a massive disintegration of Indian lands. By the 1930s, therefore, about one-third of the Indians' allotted acreage nationwide had been lost, and there were an estimated 150,000 landless Indians.[60]

Another integral part of the BIA's attempt to hasten Indian assimilation was the eradication of Indian tribal relations and the acculturation of the Native American population. During the war, the BIA along with its advisory body, the Board of Indian Commissioners (BIC), tried to limit the performance of Indian dances and ceremonies by implying that they were acts of disloyalty and an attempt to subvert the will of the government. By the war's end, however, Commissioner Sells had apparently resigned himself to the fact that traditional Indian cultures continued to persevere. "The 'Welcome Home' which Indians give their young men returning from military service," he wrote, "is usually of the most cordial and commending character. Occasionally they feel," he continued, "that by reviving the native costume and some form of old war-time dances they can best express complete approval of those who enlisted under the banner of American freedom."[61] Consequently, many aspects of traditional Indian cultures gained renewed importance and vigor during World War I, allowing young people to witness, perhaps for the first time, aspects of their cultures about which they had only heard from elders.

Many Native American peoples honored newly inducted soldiers with elaborate going-away rituals. Such a ceremony occurred among the Standing Rock Sioux in South Dakota. In December 1917, the Sioux honored seven young inductees with a parade, with songs, and with patriotic speeches. Members of the White Horse Brigade (a traditional warrior society), mounted on horses and with other older warriors, escorted the young men into town amidst the "chanting of the 'ancient Indian warriors' parade song." Apache recruits from the White Mountain reservation in eastern Arizona were honored with a war dance before entraining for Camp Cody, New Mexico.[62]

Traditional Indian war songs also gained renewed popularity. The Native Americans sang chiefly about the American flag and their responsibility to it, about their experiences in World War I, and about their valorous deeds in combat. Instead of creating entirely new songs, however, Native Americans simply put new words to old melodies. Andrew Blackhawk and Jim Carimon, both Winnebago veterans who had fought in France, composed a song that included the lyrics:

> I love my flag,
> so I went to the old world to fight the Germans.
> If I had not loved the American flag,
> it would not have come back,
> but now we are still using it.[63]

The Sioux replaced warrior-society songs about traditional Indian enemies with songs about non-Indian enemies. Lakota war songs contained such verses as:

> The Germans retreat crying.
> The Lakota boys are charging from afar.
> The Germans retreat crying.
>
> Lakota boy, the Germans,
> whose many lands you have taken,
> are crying like women there.
>
> German, I have been watching your tracks
> Worthless one! I would have followed you
> wherever you would have gone.[64]

Traditional Native American dances, feasts, and giveaways also gained popularity among some Indian peoples. In November 1918, Aaron McGaffey Beede, an Episcopal priest and missionary, witnessed a Sioux victory dance held at Fort Yates, North Dakota. According to Beede, it was the "first time this dance has been held since the evening after the Little Big Horn battle of June 25, 1876." Participants in the victory dance combined traditional Indian symbols, such as the sacred tree and the wolf, with patriotic symbols, like the American flag. Interspersed with the victory dances were a series of speeches and calls for donations to the Red Cross and the United War

Work Campaign, an organization established during the war to raise money for the welfare of American veterans, particularly those who had suffered wounds fighting for their country.[65]

Occurring simultaneously was a victory dance held at Cannon Ball, North Dakota. This dance differed from the one at Fort Yates in that a crude representation of German Kaiser Wilhelm II was erected. At the appointed time, warriors crept forward and shot at the effigy until it fell down. Afterward, four children previously selected for the purpose counted coup on the Kaiser. Next, four men counted coup, the first of whom rode the horse of a Sioux soldier killed in World War I.[66]

In June 1919, forty Pawnee veterans, some dressed in their army khaki uniforms and others in full native regalia, participated in a victory dance. At another Pawnee dance, the mother of a soldier carried a German helmet on a pole topped by a captured knife, reminiscent perhaps of the scalp poles used commonly in the nineteenth century. Elderly members of the Comanche tribe used a traditional dance to recognize their veterans as warriors, although some tribal elders dismissed the fighting in France as just a "shooting war" that provided no real opportunity for Indian soldiers to demonstrate their manhood. An article in *The Literary Digest* described two dances sponsored by Bacon Rind, an Omaha, whose son George was in the A.E.F. At the first celebration, the host served fresh beef and disbursed presents of pipes, horses, and blankets. At the subsequent gathering, there was much dancing and singing and a "livelier exchange of peace presents" than at the first gathering.[67]

Myrtle Lincoln, an Arapaho, and Birdie Burns, a Cheyenne, both witnessed traditional dances during and after the war. Lincoln attended a "Scalp Dance" (or Victory Dance) held in 1919 in honor of Indian veterans from Canton, Oklahoma. Reportedly, a young Cheyenne veteran brought an actual German scalp for the occasion. The veterans sang and danced all night around a huge bonfire. A few Native Americans mounted horses and rode through the streets.[68]

Birdie Burns was on hand at a "Give Away Dance." In addition to enjoying a night of singing and dancing, she remembered, Indian veterans received a new name. According to Burns, the recipients, after receiving the name, stood on a new blanket and covered themselves up. At this time, friends and relatives placed gifts of food and shawls next to their loved one.[69]

Not all Native Americans experienced the same resurgence of traditional dances and social activities enjoyed by the aforementioned groups. Naomi W. LaDue, a Chippewa, remembered the war years as being rather dull! Indian dances and powwows, she recollected, "kind of died down." After all, "they took a lot of boys around here, alot [sic] of the young men." Better educated and acculturated Indians, meanwhile, may have scorned the return of traditional native cultures. One Indian pastor admonished his congregation for participating in traditional dances. "Now that our young men are going to war," he exclaimed, and at the "very time when we ought to be more Christlike, some are falling back to the heathen dance for their comfort."[70]

In 1918 the BIC expressed concern about the resurgence of the "Squehealous Dance" among the Lumnis in Washington. The Lumnis claimed that performing the dance could cure disease and cited examples of how "regular" doctors had been unable to heal their Indian patients. After careful consideration, the BIC ruled that the performance of the Squehealous Dance was a "reversion to pagan rites" and that it could not see "anything but evil" in permitting its continuation. Accordingly, it demanded that the dance be prohibited.[71]

Native American participation in traditional Indian death rituals also regained importance during World War I. Such was the case at the funeral of Lee Rainbow, a Yuma who died in France. In keeping with their tradition, the Yumas cremated the body and casket high upon a huge pyre. The October 27, 1918, edition of the *New York Times* reported that at the funeral of Allen Otterman, a Sioux soldier, a young Indian man on horseback led the funeral procession to the cemetery. A crowd of Native American men and women followed close behind chanting lamentations for the dead.[72]

World War I also affected Winnebago burial rituals. According to Winnebago tradition, warriors commanded the spirits of the men they killed in battle. Following the death of a Winnebago woman named Hino'nika, therefore, her people sent for four young Winnebago veterans. Each night for four consecutive nights, the young men related songs and stories of their exploits during the war. On the fourth night, just before morning, Hino'nika's spirit was "to begin its journey to the spirit land." Consequently, each of the four Indian veterans addressed the spirit of a German soldier whom he had killed, telling him to accompany the spirit of the woman, to bring wood for her evening fire, carry her tobacco, and provide her with food. The Winnebagos considered that they were honoring the spirits of the Germans by this commission, showing they trusted them because of their bravery.[73]

Native American participation in World War I strengthened traditional Indian cultures and values. Through dances, songs, feasts, giveaways, and death rituals, American Indians demonstrated that their rich cultural heritages and traditional ceremonialism were still intact, even after decades of federal policies aimed at eradicating them. As William K. Powers has suggested, the effect that World War I and Indian entry into the military had on native cultures was to guarantee that many social institutions would "maintain a sense of relevancy despite their anticipated degeneration and obsolescence."[74]

While Native Americans enjoyed a cultural renaissance of sorts during World War I, the status of Indian health care, notoriously inadequate to begin with, deteriorated rapidly. The cost of medical supplies, in the face of mounting price inflation, soared. The inflationary trend coincided with the government's attempt to cut appropriations for non–war related projects. As a result, the BIA received no additional government funding to procure essential medical supplies and provisions.[75]

A shortage of qualified medical personnel also undermined the effectiveness of Indian health care. In response to the wartime demand for qualified medical personnel, many doctors and nurses abandoned the Indian service for lucrative medical careers elsewhere. At the war's end the Indian medical service was one-third its earlier strength. The number of regular physicians was down by 39 percent, the number of contract physicians was down by 13 percent, and the number of nurses declined by 45 percent.[76]

Trachoma and tuberculosis, among the most devastating diseases that afflicted Indian peoples prior to World War I, continued to devastate Indian communities during the war years. The BIA estimated in 1918 that over 30,000 of 64,272 Native Americans examined suffered from trachoma and 23,000 from tuberculosis. A government-appointed health team, after investigating conditions on the Blackfeet reservation in Montana, reported that "so many unreported cases of tuberculosis were found that the reservation sanitarium was soon filled to its capacity." Bureau officials placed most of the blame for the high tuberculosis rate on the unsanitary living conditions and the tendency of many Native Americans "to neglect seeking the physician's aid until the appearance of warning symptoms" and their disinclination to accept the "white man's" medical methods.[77]

American Indians also suffered a high infant mortality rate. Out of 5,571 Indian births in 1918, for example, 1,541 children died (nearly 27 percent) before the age of three. Commissioner Sells expressed particular concern about the matter. "We can not solve the Indian problem without the Indians," he wrote in 1916, "we can not educate [Indian] children unless they are kept alive." He introduced a new campaign to "save the babies" that called for improved sanitary conditions in Indian homes, better nutrition for expectant Indian mothers, and the establishment of a system of cooperative information to educate Native American families about proper child care.[78]

In addition to trachoma, tuberculosis, and a high infant mortality rate, Native Americans also suffered from numerous epidemics such as smallpox, measles, diphtheria, rabies, whooping cough, and an equally unwelcome new-comer during World War I, influenza. A smallpox epidemic hit the Navajos in Arizona in 1916 and within a year had spread to the Hopis and Navajos in New Mexico.[79]

The influenza pandemic of 1918–1919, however, was by far the worst catastrophe to hit Indian country in decades. It originated in February 1918 in San Sebastian, Spain. By May the "Spanish flu," as it was called, had spread through France, Scotland, Greece, Italy, and Egypt. Not long after-ward the deadly virus reached the United States. From October 1918 through March 1919, 73,651 American Indians (about a quarter of the Indian popula-tion) contracted the flu. Symptoms included high fever, swollen glands, head-aches, dizziness, nausea, a rapid pulse, and sore throat. In many cases, the Spanish flu developed into pneumonia, which resulted in the deaths of hun-dreds of thousands of Americans. Jo Ann Blythe has estimated that over 548,000 Americans died of complications derived from the "Great Flu Epi-demic of 1918."[80]

American Indians living on reservations were especially hard-hit. *The Native American* reported that four hundred Sioux from the Pine Ridge reservation succumbed from the flu, and two hundred more died at the Rose-bud reservation. *The American Indian Magazine* carried the story of Jesse Cornplanter, a Seneca, who, upon returning home from Europe, learned that his parents, sister, brother-in-law, and two children had all died during the influenza epidemic. Clara Winona Goodbear, a Cheyenne, caught the flu in 1918 and "got sick with it and pretty near died." Sadie Weller, a Caddo vet-eran, contracted the flu in 1918, and, like thousands of other victims, devel-oped pneumonia. He remained bedridden for a year and, before he finally recovered, his weight dropped to under one hundred pounds. An estimated 9 percent (6,270) of the 73,651 Native Americans who contracted the flu died. All told, 2 percent of the entire Indian population succumbed during the epidemic. The mortality rate was four times greater than that of white Ameri-cans living in large cities.[81]

Tuberculosis, smallpox, and influenza aside, some government policy-makers perceived alcoholism and peyote use as the greatest threats to Indian health and welfare. In 1918, Commissioner Sells applauded legislation de-signed to strengthen the prohibition of illegal liquor sales on Indian reserva-tions. To demonstrate the Indian bureau's resolve to curb alcohol consumption, Sells withheld annuity payments to Osage people in response to alleged alcohol abuse on their reservation. He insisted that he would disburse the annuities only after "the chiefs and headmen of the [Osage] tribe shall have pledged themselves to use all their influence" and to "make all proper exertions to prevent the introduction and sale of such liquor in their country." When the Osages took the matter to court, the judges upheld Sells's action.[82]

The Board of Indian Commissioners expressed even greater concern about alcohol consumption among Native Americans. In its annual report in 1917, the board, in a classic attempt to micromanage Indian affairs, recommended that Indians be forbidden to purchase lemon and vanilla extracts. Board members reasoned that "when Indians buy vanilla extract to the amount of a dozen bottles at a time it must be evident to anyone that the intention is to use it for other purposes than for flavoring."[83]

The rising popularity of peyote use among Native Americans and the establishment in 1918 of the Native American Church were also a source of government consternation. Native Americans who used peyote claimed that the dried tubercles ("peyote buttons") of the cactus plant enabled users to have visions, brought them into a direct relationship with the supernatural, and promoted internal peace. For some Indian users, peyote offered a temporary escape from the devastation to native cultures wrought by Anglo civilization and laws. Ray Blackbear, a Kiowa-Apache, suggested that some Indian soldiers carried pouches of peyote for protection when they went to France during World War I.[84]

Despite such claims, missionaries, with local, state, and federal authorities, denounced peyote use as a "harmful, debasing, sinful, and habit-forming drug," and attempted repeatedly, with limited success, to pass legislation prohibiting its use. The Indian Rights Association and the National Indian Association supported such efforts and wrote articles that condemned peyote use as physically harmful and morally evil. The National Indian Association wrote, in December 1918, that "the menace of peyote is still great" and called for a "strict prohibitory law" to curb its consumption. An article in *The Indian School Journal* cautioned that "this deadly drug appears to be getting a firmer hold on our red brethren as their meetings are more numerous and they are eating more of the stuff."[85]

Similar to the retrenchment evident in Indian health-care services, Native American education facilities "decreased in number and declined in quality" during World War I. At the Cushman Indian Trades School, in the Pacific Northwest, administrators suffered from inadequate supplies, the loss of one-third of its faculty, and the death of ten of its students from complications associated with the flu epidemic. At the Oglala Indian Training School, located on the Pine Ridge reservation in South Dakota, the cost of coal, flour, lard, bacon, sugar, and beef shot up nearly 60 percent and school officials feared that they might have to close the institution. In keeping with the assimilationist leanings of the BIA, however, Sells sought to disband reservation and off-reservation Indian schools and encouraged Native Americans to enroll in regular public schools, where close contact with white children would, he presumed, hasten their absorption into Anglo society.[86]

Consequently, in his April 1917 "Declaration of Policy," Sells called for the elimination of "ineligible" students from the government Indian schools. "In many of our boarding schools," he declared, "Indian children are being educated at Government expense whose parents are amply able to pay for their education and have public school facilities at or near their homes." Therefore, Sells resolved, "such children shall not hereafter be enrolled in Government Indian schools supported by gratuity appropriations" unless the parents paid the necessary costs themselves.[87]

Continuing the policies of Estelle Reel, the prior superintendent of Indian education, Sells insisted that a vocational education would best suit Indian students and equip them for self-support. The central idea of the course of study for Indian schools, Sells maintained, was the elimination of "needless studies" and the employment of a "natural system of instruction." Such a system, he continued, would allow "Indian boys and girls to design and make beautiful and useful things with their hands" and encourage their transition into "all-round efficient citizens."[88]

In February 1916 Sells introduced a new scheme for Indian education. It included a curriculum that combined both academic and vocational instruction (with a heavy emphasis on the latter) and a new system of student classification. He divided the new course of study into three categories: (1) the primary division, which included the first three grades; (2) the pre-vocational division, which included grades four through six; and (3) the vocational division, which contained grades seven through ten. Primary and pre-vocational students were to receive an education that paralleled public school courses, in addition to introductory vocational classes. Coursework for the vocational division, however, was planned with the vocational aim "very clearly and positively dominant, with especial emphasis on agriculture and home-making." Students in the vocational division would spend half a day receiving academic instruction in mathematics, geography, history, and language, and half a day taking vocational courses in agriculture, harness making, blacksmithing, carpentry, cooking, and sewing.[89]

Indian schools taught thousands of Native American children the rudiments of the English language and provided some with the skills necessary to earn a living as farmers, carpenters, or industrial workers. Nevertheless, critics denounced Sells's education program as "stagnant" and "unrealistic," containing a "curriculum of low expectations" that sentenced "Indians to lives of manual labor and poverty." Reformers also denounced the often brutal methods of discipline utilized in Indian schools and likened such measures to "Prussian brutality." Moreover, BIA officials and educators demonstrated contempt for Indian heritages and cultures and designed their curricula with a clear racial bias.[90] With the assimilation of Native Americans into the dominant Anglo culture as the BIA's paramount objective, few Americans would have expected anything different from Cato Sells and his staff.

The war years can be seen as a "cultural watershed" in modern Native American history. Despite BIA efforts to undermine Indian cultures and tribalism, hasten assimilation, and handle related issues, many aspects of differing Indian cultures and traditions gained renewed importance and vitality in 1917 and 1918—but again the degree of cultural regeneration differed significantly based on a particular tribe's history, geographic location, level of acculturation, and involvement in the war effort. For many Indian peoples, the cultural manifestations arising out of their service in World War I enabled the younger generations to witness and participate in ceremonies and rituals associated with Indian warfare. The war years, consequently, strengthened Native American customs and traditions until legislation could be passed to ensure their survival.

Thus, life for Native Americans on the "homefront" was full of inconsistencies. While the BIA advocated Indian economic self-sufficiency and independence, it insisted simultaneously upon maintaining its paternalistic control over Indian life and refused to allow many Native American families control over their own finances and property. While reservation officials encouraged and exhorted Indian men to increase the amount of acreage under cultivation and become more efficient farmers and ranchers, the insistence during World War I that Indians sell their stock devastated tribal economies and led to the wide-scale leasing of reservation lands to non-Indians. The policy of assimilation gained some headway as Indian families bought Liberty bonds and war savings stamps, as young men enlisted in the military or found employment in factories, and as Indian women joined the Red Cross and served as nurses and entertainers overseas. In many parts of the country, on the other hand, traditional Indian ceremonies and dances gained renewed popularity and relevance, which guaranteed their survival for at least another generation.

Finally, while the majority of American Indians demonstrated that they were ready and willing to support the war effort and defend their country, thousands did not even possess American citizenship, and fewer still had the right to vote. It is not surprising, therefore, that during the postwar era a growing number of Indian reform movements demanded that the federal government grant citizenship to all Native Americans living in the United States—which is one of the subjects in the next chapter.

8

Indian Veterans
in the Postwar Era

ON NOVEMBER 11, 1918, DAN RAINCLOUD, A RED LAKE CHIPPEWA, was plowing a sixty-acre plot at the Wahpeton Indian School in Minnesota. It was hard work and Raincloud was anxious to finish the task before the weather turned too cold. Suddenly, he heard bells ringing and whistles blowing back at the school compound. Dropping his work, the young man raced back to the school to find out what had happened, and upon arriving he witnessed great excitement and rejoicing. An armistice had been signed. World War I was over![1]

Following the war's conclusion, American soldiers eagerly waited to be sent home. Samuel LaPointe, an Indian soldier serving at Headquarters, American Second Army, wrote in January 1919 that "time seems to drag and pass along so slow these days. It seems that way since the 11th of November. Everybody is waiting to be sent home and that's what makes times travel too slow."[2] Upon receiving their discharge papers, a uniform, coat, pair of shoes, and a bonus of sixty dollars, the "doughboys" bid their units farewell and returned home to embark on new careers or to pursue old ones.[3]

Some soldiers received a hero's welcome, while others returned home quietly and without fanfare. For a brief time after the November 1918 armistice, Americans continued to believe that they had helped "make the world safe for democracy" and that the fighting in Europe had marked the "war to end all wars." However, following the United States' rejection of the 1919 Treaty of Versailles, widespread disillusionment replaced the postwar euphoria, and American veterans confronted the realization that their sacrifices had failed to usher in the era of world peace that President Woodrow Wilson had envisioned.

Like their non-Indian countrymen, Native American veterans came back home with a sense of pride in their accomplishments and with expectations for a brighter future. The nation lavished praise on American Indians, both for their exploits abroad and for their contributions at home. Ironically, thousands of Indian soldiers and over a third of the Native American population did not possess citizenship; fewer still enjoyed the right to vote.

Indian veterans received the praise and admiration of a grateful nation.[4] Provost Marshal General Enoch H. Crowder commended Native Americans for demonstrating their "traditional aptitude" for a military career and for "nobly showing their zeal for the great cause." Former Army Chief of Staff Hugh L. Scott added that Indian soldiers "played a higher part in the war on the side of patriotism than the ordinary white man" and that "we may indeed all be proud of our red race and its record in the World War." If he compiled the complete record of Native Americans in the war, Commissioner of Indian Affairs Cato Sells concluded grandiosely, it would be "a voluminous narration of scenes, episodes, eloquent appeal, stirring action, and glorious sacrifice" that should be written into "a deathless epic by some master poet born out of the heroic travail of a world-embattled era."[5]

As a token of its gratitude, the federal government, on the second anniversary of the armistice, selected the Crow chief Plenty Coups to place a wreath upon the Tomb of the Unknown Soldier at Arlington National Cemetery. The elderly Indian leader also presented a magnificent eagle-feather bonnet and a decorated coup stick to honor those killed in World War I. Afterward, Plenty Coups, in his native language, addressed those assembled. "I am glad to represent all the Indians of the United States in placing on the grave of this noble warrior this coup stick and war bonnet, every eagle feather of which represents a deed of valor by my race." He concluded his speech with a prayer: "I hope that the Great Spirit will grant that these noble warriors have not given up their lives in vain and that there will be peace to all men hereafter."[6]

In the years following World War I, the federal government awarded several Indian tribes with American flags and certificates of appreciation. The certificates, which the president personally signed, expressed the nation's thanks for the Native Americans' "unswerving loyalty and patriotism," their "willing sacrifices," and the "bravery of their sons in the military and naval service of the United States." In the fall of 1924, President Calvin Coolidge sent certificates to the Five Civilized Tribes of Oklahoma, to the Yumas at the Fort Yuma Indian reservation in southern California, to the Sioux living on the Cheyenne River reservation in South Dakota, to the Tulalip and Yakima Indians of Washington, and to the Warm Springs Indians of Oregon. Native Americans received the certificates with great enthusiasm and staged large feasts and ceremonies to commemorate the event. The Yakimas, for instance, held a huge barbecue while the Yumas incorporated the certificates into their

"Ceremony of the Dead" and flew the American flag above their "Temple of the Dead."[7]

The Eastern Cherokees of North Carolina were proud of their military service as well. At tribal meetings they adopted unanimously a resolution that pledged their continued loyalty to the United States and requested that the army's enlistment records "contain some evidence of their being Indians." In addition, they vowed to keep a "full and true record" of the military history of those tribal members who had volunteered for service during the war and to "perpetuate the record of their service in the proper archives of the tribe."[8] Among the Sioux, meanwhile, it became a custom for many traditional parents to select only those who had served their country honorably during World War I to participate in a naming ceremony, and bestow upon their children an Indian name.

Although it displayed its appreciation and gratitude for Indian military service through its presentation of certificates and American flags, the federal government proved much more reluctant to enact legislation to curb Indian unemployment, to aid Indian farmers and ranchers, or to halt the erosion of the Native American land base. President-elect Warren G. Harding seemed a hopeful leader for Native American causes. Although he had indicated little interest in Indian affairs as a United States senator, he was expansive in his promises to a delegation of Indian leaders at an August 1920 meeting. As president, he vowed to ensure that "Indians receive their freedom and that they become equal with all other races that have had the freedom of this great liberty-loving country." Also taking the opportunity to criticize America's role in the Treaty of Versailles and the League of Nations—which many Republicans opposed—Harding announced that he favored a bestowal of "democracy, humanity, and idealism" on Native Americans "whose lands the white man took, rather than waste American lives trying to make sure of that bestowal thousands of miles across the sea."[9] Such empty talk earned Harding the nickname "The Great Bloviator," especially when during his inaugural he promised an ambiguous "return to normalcy." When applied to Indians, "normalcy" meant a return to government indifference, second-class treatment, and neglect.

Unfortunately for Indians, Harding's selection of Senator Albert B. Fall of New Mexico to head the Department of the Interior did little to advance "democracy, humanity, and idealism" in Indian country. An arch foe of conservation and Indian property rights, Fall, whose involvement in the notorious Teapot Dome scandal led to his dismissal from office in 1923, opposed reforming the administration of Indian affairs. Along with Charles H. Burke, Harding's commissioner of Indian affairs, Fall adopted an obscurantist position regarding Indian policy and worked to undermine the budding reform movement of the 1920s.[10]

Thus, at a time when strict budgetary constraints and laissez-faire economic policies were the norm, increased appropriations for the Indian bureau were, at best, a low government priority. Consequently, many Indian veterans returned home to reservations plagued with persistent problems such as high unemployment and illiteracy, and with few prospects for upward mobility. Some Native Americans understandably became disillusioned. The more assimilated and educated Indian veterans had expected that having risked life and limb in the war, they would be entitled to a greater voice in the democratic process at home. The Indians' return to government indifference, disenfranchisement, and reservation squalor, in many respects, paralleled that of black veterans who returned to discrimination, poverty, and Jim Crow.

The task of finding jobs confronted many veterans upon their arrival home. Considering the seemingly insurmountable problems that characterized life on many remote reservations, the task must have appeared herculean. Some veterans had learned new skills from their tenure in the military, but they were not always successful in translating the skills into civilian occupations, because reservations rarely afforded Indian men the opportunity to practice them. That being the case, Indian veterans responded in diverse ways to secure employment in the postwar era.

Despite the scarcity of economic opportunities, most Indian veterans returned home to their reservations. The overwhelming majority had been born on reservations, had family members and close friends living there—often in a communal setting—and may have never considered seriously living off the reservation. Furthermore, reservations provided a sense of security and familiarity that must have been comforting to many returning veterans—the reservation, after all, was home. For others, tribal lands were sacred and an important part of their Native American heritage. Indian soldiers had fought in the war, at least in part, to protect their lands and families. Naomi W. LaDue, a Chippewa from Minnesota, recalled that many Indian veterans—full bloods in particular—returned to reservations after the war. During World War I, she remembered, "there were more Indians, you know, real Indians that went [off to war] and they were more apt to come back to the reservation than mixed bloods."[11]

Moses Trudell, a Santee Sioux from Nebraska who had served in the AEF's Sixth Division while in France, and George Jewett, a Cheyenne River Sioux who, in addition to fighting on the Western Front had played on the American Expeditionary Force's championship football team, returned to their farms after the war ended. Henry Tallman, a Navajo and former student at the Albuquerque Indian School in New Mexico, returned to his reservation to tend horses and sheep.[12] Veterans who attempted to take up agricultural pursuits had their work cut out for them. A nationwide agricultural recession and poor weather conditions between 1918 and 1920 doomed many Indian farmers and ranchers to economic uncertainty. Gordon MacGregror, who has studied living conditions on the Pine Ridge reservation in South Dakota, wrote that the loss of the cattle economy during the war, together with the demise of Indian dryland wheat farming due to the drought of the early 1920s, "appears as the most significant single catastrophe in the history of Pine Ridge people" and was as devastating to them as the disappearance of the buffalo.[13]

Other veterans who had leased their lands to non-Indians or, perhaps, had never owned any farm land to begin with found temporary employment performing manual labor. Residents of the Blackfeet reservation in Montana, for example, earned several thousand dollars in 1921 and 1922 by cutting wood and hauling it to the agency. When they applied to Superintendent F. C. Campbell for rations, saying that they had no money and could not get work, Campbell hired able-bodied Indian men to cut the wood into stove-length pieces and paid them in cash so they could buy food and supplies. The role of the Native American in the postwar economy, therefore, has been described as that of a "super-exploited victim." Federal agents leased Indian lands at low fees to non-Indians; Native American labor was used on a temporary basis for unskilled farm tasks; and Indians "consumed rather than produced."[14]

Some Indian veterans, unable to make an adequate living, left reservations to seek their fortunes elsewhere. Guy Lambert, a Yankton Sioux, enlisted in 1916 and during World War I was stationed along the Mexican border. After the war, he served as an Indian policeman on various reservations in South Dakota and was later ordained as a deacon in the Episcopal church. Chester A. Four Bears, a Cheyenne River Sioux, enjoyed a career in show business as a bronc rider, tap dancer, and singer. In 1923, he performed before the Queen of England. Andrew DeRockbrain, a Standing Rock Sioux, worked as a cowboy after the war. In the late 1920s, however, he was "discovered" and spent several weeks in California shooting a movie about the Little Bighorn battle. DeRockbrain made nearly one thousand dollars for his efforts and later mingled with the likes of Anthony Quinn, Clark Gable, and Gary Cooper.[15]

While these fortunate men were exceptional cases of off-reservation Indians "making good" in the postwar era, there is additional evidence to sup-

port the contention that significant numbers of Indian veterans left reservations after World War I. In response to a BIA questionnaire circulated in
1920 requesting information about Native American wartime contributions,
several reservation officials responded that they could not complete the questionnaires because many of the veterans formerly under their jurisdiction
were no longer living on the reservations. R. R. Wadsworth, a BIA official
working with Chippewas on the White Earth reservation in northwestern
Minnesota, for example, wrote that "owing to the fact that a great many of
our Indian ex-soldiers are scattered over the reservation, and outside the
reservation, it is doubtful if our report can be made complete." H. M. Tidwell,
superintendent of the Pine Ridge reservation in South Dakota, responded
that "a great many of these Indians are living off the Reservation, and what
are here are scattered from one end to the other." Granted that some of these
veterans may have lived off-reservation before the war, it appears likely, as
Donald Parman has written, that "World War I set a minor precedent for the
more sizeable off-reservation exodus Indians made after World War II."[16]

Reenlisting for military service also provided an important source of off-
reservation employment for Indian veterans. Several Eastern Cherokee veterans from North Carolina returned home, but soon recognized the limited
opportunities on the reservation. Consequently, some of them reenlisted.
Thomas L. Slow, a Sioux from North Dakota, reenlisted in April 1919 with
the "prospect of learning something" from the vocational training classes
offered by the army. James McCarthy, a Papago veteran, received his discharge on May 8, 1919, but he signed on for three more years the same day.[17]

Authorities also encouraged Ojibway veterans living in Minnesota to re-
enlist and, according to Josephine Gwin Wadena, a Chippewa resident of the
White Earth reservation, many Indian soldiers from that reservation did so.
In December 1919, Major Leroy H. Watson, a recruiting officer stationed at
Camp Grant, Illinois, reported that the Chippewas were "thoroughly satisfied with the treatment that they received in the army" and were therefore
"in the right mood at the present time to listen to us and many are already
interested" in reenlisting. Drawing on the experiences of earlier recruiters,
Watson proposed working through the local leaders to encourage Chippewa
cooperation and suggested that the educational and trade schools in operation at Camp Grant "would be of immense value to the Indians and would
prove of great advantage to them on their return to civil life." After review-
ing Watson's plan for reenlisting Indian veterans, Assistant Commissioner
of Indian Affairs Edgar B. Meritt announced that the Indian office had no
objection to any adult able-bodied Indian enlisting in the army.[18]

As is the case after every war, many veterans who had witnessed horrific suffering and death found it difficult to adjust to civilian life. Alfrieda Garnenez, a woman of mixed Sioux-Navajo ancestry from Shiprock, New Mexico, remembered that her Sioux grandfather, the "son of Chief Bonnet Tail," was one of the first men from his reservation to enlist. After he returned home he refused to talk about the war and expressed scorn for those who did. "The Man that really went through it, that went through torture like that," he said, "they'll never come out and talk about it."[19] Frank Fools Crow, the Oglala Sioux spiritual leader, recalled that many of the Sioux soldiers who went off to war came home wounded and crippled. "Others were physically well," he remembered, "yet never mentally the same again." Mental illness was uncommon among the Sioux, Fools Crow maintained, until the veterans came home after World War I.

Indian soldiers who had traveled overseas and even many of those who remained stateside experienced different cultures and lifestyles. Those who fought in Europe witnessed the poverty and suffering of war-torn France and may have returned home with a better appreciation of the United States. Moreover, having trained, fought, and lived beside whites for several months, Indian veterans developed a better understanding of American society as seen through the eyes of their white comrades. The same can be said of the lessons gained by white troops serving with Indians. More than likely, some Indian "doughboys" developed a more positive attitude about Anglo society and Euro-American political and economic values.[20]

It was inevitable, therefore, that some Indian veterans—particularly those from unassimilated and isolated groups—brought home new ideas and habits that were considered inappropriate by tribal elders who were struggling to maintain traditional Indian values. Frank Fools Crow, for instance, lamented that Sioux veterans brought back "worldly and selfish attitudes" which weakened the Sioux nation as did the loss due to the young men killed or wounded. Some veterans, consequently, may have felt like newly graduated Indian school students—too "Indian" to be fully accepted as equals in white society, but too "assimilated" to easily reenter Indian society.[21]

In an attempt to cope with postwar feelings of maladjustment and alienation, some veterans sought escape through alcohol and drug use. Others, hoping that a return to traditional ways might provide some direction to their lives, found solace through the ministry of the Native American Church. Others simply became dependent upon the government for their subsistence or dropped out of sight altogether.

Such was the case with Joseph Oklahombi, a Choctaw and one of the most decorated Native American veterans of World War I. After the war, Oklahombi returned home to his wife and family in southeastern Oklahoma. Illiterate and unable to find work, the war hero took to drinking and was soon destitute. He finally found a job paying two dollars a day loading lumber for a local lumber and coal company, but, in 1932, he was again unemployed and seeking a veteran's pension (about twelve dollars a month) to stay alive.[22]

Felix Renvielle, a Sisseton Sioux veteran with the 341st Machine-Gunners Battalion, fought in the Argonne Forest and received dozens of wounds after being hit by shrapnel. The fighting in his sector had been so fierce, in fact, that the medic who had come to his aid had been shot and killed. Left on the field as dead for over a day, Renvielle was later discovered by a burial detail. His wounds were so severe that army officials, believing that the young Indian would not live, sent his parents a death certificate. Although he survived and returned home safely, Renvielle's wounds prevented him from working and he remained permanently disabled for the rest of his life.[23]

The *New York Times* reported, in July 1921, that another Sioux veteran, Na-Hiv-A-Ta, a highly decorated sniper during World War I, was stranded and penniless in Columbus, Ohio. He had been making his way across the country, trying to get home to the Pine Ridge reservation in South Dakota. Some local veterans groups came to his aid, however, and "Indian Joe," as the article referred to him, "accepted, for the time, a vaudeville position in a local amusement park."[24]

An important source of comfort and support for Indian veterans came from other veterans. In the fall of 1920, George Peake, a Potawatomi, Henry J. Flood, a Sioux, Anderson W. Cash, a Sioux, and Dr. James W. Levy, a Cherokee, founded "American Indians of the World War" (AIWW), an organization headquartered in Minneapolis that was designed to foster a closer relationship between Indian veterans and "to weld the thoughts of [its] members along lines of mutual interest."[25] Corresponding with their efforts was the creation in Canada of the "League of Indians of Canada," an organization of Indian veterans that sought to safeguard their rights as Canadians and their identity as Indians.[26]

More important and long-lasting, however, was the organization of several American Legion posts on Indian reservations. Henry Tallman, a Navajo who had served in the First Division, organized the first Legion post on the Navajo reservation in Arizona. Eastern Cherokee veterans established the Steve Youngdeer Post on their reservation in western North Carolina, and Sioux veterans, meanwhile, built the Chauncey Eaglehorn Post on the Rosebud reservation in South Dakota.[27]

While veterans groups struggled to publicize Indian wartime contributions and provide Native American veterans with comfort, understanding, and an organizational framework within which they could reflect upon their military experiences, the federal government in the postwar era provided only sporadic relief for destitute veterans and their families. Instead, discrimination, fraud, bureaucratic mismanagement, and an insatiable demand for Indian lands remained the hallmark of Anglo–Indian relations after World War I. In January 1919, Ben Stonecool, a Pitt River Indian from California, wrote to officials in the Bureau of Indian Affairs (BIA) to complain about the poor living conditions on the Pitt River reservation. Stonecool complained that "all the land we got is up on [a] hill-side among the rock where we can not get no water." Moreover, he continued, the local white population was treating his people poorly. "They wont let us Indians eat in hotel or sleep in rooming house," he charged, and when his people were served, the whites "bring food out in [a] dish-pan like they [were] going to feed [a] dog or hog."[28]

Conditions on the Blackfoot reservation in northern Montana were even worse. In a letter to General Pershing, dated December 10, 1921, Joseph Dixon, the leader of the Wanamaker Photographic Expeditions and a leading advocate of segregated Indian units in the military, wrote that many Blackfoot veterans were "dying by the roadside" from sheer hunger and that "their hunting grounds have been pre-empted and their land filched." So desperate were reservation residents, Dixon continued, that "to keep from starving they had killed and eaten all the prairie dogs which had formerly had their habitat thereabout, and also had resorted to eating skunks." The BIA, in response to the crisis, was doing little, if anything, to help the Blackfeet, Dixon alleged, and the young Indian men who had fought for Pershing in France "are now likewise wounded, helpless and suffering with their fathers whom they cannot help."[29]

Living conditions on the various Chippewa reservations in Minnesota were poor as well. In a scathing critique of the BIA, Theodore D. Beaulieu, a Chippewa and the vice president of the Society of American Indians, stated that his people lived under an "undemocratic bureaucracy, are compelled to pay double taxation, and are denied the privilege of word or suggestion as to the manner of the disposition of their tribal funds." He charged that BIA officials controlled tribal moneys and used them mainly for the purpose of paying themselves "fat salaries" and perquisites that included modern homes, automobiles, and chauffeurs, while the Chippewas were "struggling against want, hunger, and disease."[30]

In New York, meanwhile, state officials ruled that Native American veterans residing on reservations were not entitled to receive state bonuses accorded to other New York veterans. In June 1921, the New York State Bonus Commission, along with New York Attorney General Charles D. Newton, ruled that because American Indians were not citizens of the state of New York, they were ineligible to receive bonuses. The decision produced a firestorm of criticism from members of the League of Six Nations (Senecas, Mohawks, Oneidas, Tuscaroras, Cayugas, and Onondagas) as well as from the press. Arthur C. Parker, a prominent state archeologist, museum curator, and a Seneca, stated that if the Indians living in New York did not receive their bonuses, "it will be the cruelest cut the race has ever received during all its melancholy history." Furthermore, he maintained, it would lead the Indian "to believe that he was an outcast, fit to share in his country's perils, but one to be excluded from the feast in the day of rejoicing."[31]

New York Indians received support from the state's press. Editorials in the *New York Telegram*, the *New York Tribune*, the *Albany Journal*, and the *Schenectady Gazette* pointed out the injustice of the Bonus Commission's ruling. The *New York Telegram*, for instance, noted, in an article entitled "Even Bravest of N. Y. Indians Can't Share Soldier Bonus," that "even though they may wear decorations won for valor on the field," Indian veterans would not receive their share of the soldiers' bonus.[32]

In response to pressure from the League of Six Nations and the press, Attorney General Newton in August 1921 reversed his decision and called on the Bonus Commission to award the Indians their bonuses. In a letter dated August 12, 1921, Newton reasoned that although the Indians of New York were not citizens, they were still residents of the United States and of New York State "within the meaning of both the federal selective service acts and the New York Soldiers' Bonus Act." His opinion was that noncitizen Indians, when otherwise qualified, were entitled to share in the New York soldiers' bonus.[33]

In hopes of focusing national attention on the issue of Indian rights, various Indian groups in the postwar era sought unsuccessfully to recruit the support of international organizations like the League of Nations. In 1919, the Society of American Indians even tried to gain inclusion in the Paris Peace Conference. Gertrude Bonnin (Zitkala-Sa), the secretary of the Society of American Indians, presented the Indians' case. Such inclusion, she argued, would be proof that the federal government recognized and appreciated Indian contributions during World War I. Though unsuccessful, her actions may have prompted those taken a few years later by Iroquois leaders in Canada, who hoped that an appeal to the League of Nations and to the International Court of Justice at The Hague might lead to improvements for the native peoples residing north of the United States. In December 1923, the *New York Times* reported that a delegation of sixteen Arapahos from Wyoming had arrived in Paris to ask the League of Nations to intervene in their behalf with the United States government so that Native Americans "might have the same rights and privileges as other Americans."[34]

The movement to deprive Native Americans of their land continued during the postwar era. In 1918, Senator Henry F. Ashurst and Representative Carl Hayden of Arizona, Senator Albert B. Fall of New Mexico, and Representative A. J. Gronna of North Dakota worked to pass legislation to open Indian reservations in the West to mining. The lands reportedly contained minerals needed for the war effort. Because, as Lawrence C. Kelly has noted, the bill would, in some cases, "make possible profits of such magnitude as to make gratuity appropriations for the tribes concerned unnecessary" and because of congressional concern about the staggering cost of the war, the bill passed soon after World War I.[35]

The quest for Indian lands in the West continued in 1922, when Senator Holm O. Bursum introduced the infamous Bursum Pueblo land bill. Designed to "quiet title to lands within the Pueblo Indian land grants" that had been in dispute for decades, the Bursum bill placed the burden of proving title to Pueblo lands on Indians. For the next two years, proponents of the measure (including Secretary of the Interior Albert Fall and Commissioner of Indian Affairs Charles H. Burke) and opponents (which included the Indian Rights Association and John Collier's newly established American Indian Defense Association) debated over the Bursum bill until the compromise Pueblo Land Act became law in June 1924.[35]

In the fall of 1923, Gertrude Bonnin, with Matthew K. Sniffen of the Indian Rights Association and Charles H. Fabens of the American Indian Defense Association, conducted an inspection of Indian affairs in Oklahoma. They charged that the Five Civilized Tribes were "being, and have been, shamelessly and openly robbed in a scientific and ruthless manner" by the judges, lawyers, legal guardians, and other state officials of Oklahoma. Bonnin and her associates also expressed disgust that "flappers" were marrying Indian men and then divorcing them in order to receive handsome alimony settlements. The authors were equally critical of legislation passed in June 1918 that made the lands of full-blood members of any of the Five Civilized Tribes subject to the laws of Oklahoma, and thus easy prey for land grafters. "There is no hope for any reformation of the present system," the authors lamented, "and if action is delayed for a few years there will be no Indians with property to be protected."[37]

Secretary of the Interior Franklin K. Lane's proposal to provide farms for American veterans of World War I represents a final example of government apathy for Indian welfare in the immediate postwar era. Shortly after the war, Secretary Lane distributed a pamphlet entitled "Hey There! Do You

Want a Home on a Farm?," in which he outlined his plan to provide former "doughboys" with farms. American veterans who had served during the war and had received an honorable discharge were eligible. If they were willing to work on draining, clearing, irrigating, and improving unused land that the Interior Department had reclaimed, veterans would receive, at bargain prices, a farm, stock, and implements. Payment for the farms would be spread over several years, at 4 percent interest.[38]

The plan, at least from a Native American viewpoint, had two serious drawbacks. The first problem related to where the government would secure the "unused" land. If the United States government followed the Canadian government's example, unused Indian lands would be turned over to non-Indian veterans. In her study of Indian farmers in western Canada, Sarah Carter demonstrated that Native Americans living in Saskatchewan eventually gave up sixty thousand acres to the Canadian soldier settlement Board. Some American policymakers had similar ideas. In December 1918, J. W. Dady, the superintendent of the Chippewas' Red Cliff school and agency in Bayfield, Wisconsin, wrote a letter to Commissioner Sells regarding Lane's plan. Dady recommended that consideration be given to some of the tracts of land belonging to Indians who "have more land than they need."[39]

The second problem was that Secretary Lane did not design his scheme to include many Native American veterans. In March 1919, Albert Isham, an Indian veteran from Wisconsin, wrote to Lane on behalf of several Indian veterans requesting that funds be made available for the improvement and cultivation of their allotments. The secretary responded on March 27, stating that his plan involved aid only to returned soldiers who had no land, and therefore Native Americans with allotments did not qualify.[40]

Thus, Native American veterans returned home to familiar problems that had undermined Indian social and economic viability for decades. While it was willing to acknowledge the Native American contribution to the war effort, the federal government limited its gratitude to symbolic gestures such as disbursing certificates of appreciation and American flags. Rather than providing real aid to curb chronic unemployment on reservations and to bolster faltering farms, government policymakers opted for symbolism over substance. Native Americans, consequently, found themselves abandoned. In May 1923 newly appointed Secretary of the Interior Hubert Work (who had replaced the scandal-tarnished Albert Fall) called for the establishment of a "Committee of One Hundred" to advise the federal government on how it might improve Indian administration and the BIA's relationship with Native Americans. Although the committee advocated that appropriations be made for reforms in Indian health and education, congressional indifference prevented the enactment of most of its recommendations.[41] Five years later, the publication of Lewis Merriam's *The Problem of Indian Administration* provided startling evidence of Indian poverty, disease, and suffering and became a blueprint for the subsequent reform efforts of the 1930s.

Ignoring the stubborn endurance of problems throughout Indian country, government officials and the popular media in the postwar era went to great lengths to demonstrate how military service (though brief in duration) had expedited Indian assimilation. With allotment and Indian education coming under increasing scrutiny and criticism, Commissioner Sells publicized (and often exaggerated) how military service had "transformed" Indian veterans. By doing so, he aimed to prove that the government's long-held goal of assimilation—though battered and bruised—was still a viable policy.

The commissioner had expected that the war would bring "civilization" to Native Americans. In his 1919 annual report, therefore, Sells included a section entitled "War as a Civilizer," where he provided several examples of how the military service had "improved" Indian character and thus fulfilled his earlier predictions. "The great lesson mastered by American soldiers, as their achievements clearly show," Sells maintained, "was to get things done. No Hindenburg line across the field of civil progress can stand against such fellows. They are destined for tomorrow's leadership." Moreover, he continued, the war "wondrously multiplied" Native American interest in trade, industry, education, and the professions. The same sort of "splendid initiative and self-reliance" that Native Americans learned during the war, Sells concluded, "should find final expression in action wherever the Indian soldier returns to his people."[42]

Reports from reservation superintendents, Indian school officials, and Indian veterans themselves seemed to confirm such pronouncements. The Board of Indian Commissioners reported that the "12,000 Indian boys who served this Nation in the World War" provided an indication of "the great progress of a people who are not so very far away from the blanket, the skin tent, and the war trail." Bureau of Indian Affairs officials, perhaps telling their boss what he wanted to hear, reported that Indian veterans returned home well disciplined and speaking better English, with improved manners and greater motivation. Others commented on the Native Americans' "broadened outlook" on life, industriousness, and civility.[43]

In an evaluation of Indian veterans living in northern California, one Indian school superintendent wrote that "in every case that I have encountered where an Indian has returned to this jurisdiction I have found that the Indian young man was greatly bettered through his work in the Army, both physically and mentally." A reservation official from Oklahoma commented that "one Cheyenne, typical, no-account, reservation Indian with long hair went to France, was wounded, gassed, and shell-shocked." After the war, the official continued, the Cheyenne reported to the agency office "square shouldered, level-eyed, courteous, self-reliant, and talked intelligently. A wonderful transformation, and caused by contact with the outside world. He is at work."[44]

The superintendent of the Five Civilized Tribes marveled at the "transformation" of the "full-blood" veterans under his jurisdiction. "I am convinced," he wrote, "that the Indians in the military service, especially the full-bloods, have received inestimable benefit from their association with white comrades and the training to which they have been subjected." In addition, he reported, "a number of full-blood Cherokees lately returned from the army, none of whom could speak a word of English on their entering the service, now talk English fluently."[45]

Bureau of Indian Affairs officials in Minnesota commented on the improved discipline and industriousness of Ojibway veterans. "The steady grind of daily work," one superintendent wrote, "has always been distasteful to the Indians . . . [but] I believe that the service in the Army in common with so many others will show them that it is only by 'sticking to it' that they can succeed." Another Minnesota official noted that "there seems to be a more general willingness among the young men who have returned to engage in a useful occupation which affords them an opportunity to earn support." He attributed the change to their "contact with life foreign to reservation conditions" that resulted in fostering "generally advanced ideas."[46]

The head of the Sherman Institute, a large Indian school located in Riverside, California, epitomized the results of Indian experience in the war as follows:

> He has lost much of his timidity.
> He has greater self-confidence.
> He is more courteous and more polite.
> He has been made to feel that he is as capable of fulfilling his obligations to his country as any other race of people.
> He understands more fully his patriotic duty to his country.
> He realizes more than ever that there is a place for him in the community: that he is a unit in the great Commonwealth.
> He has seen and learned many things of educational value, and delights in telling of his experiences whether in Army camps, or the Navy, or abroad.
> He has improved perceptibly in the use of English.

His contact with the outside world and his associations with disciplined men has meant for him much mental discipline. As a result of such discipline he returns to school a better and more desirable student, and he becomes a better citizen.[47]

Several Indian veterans testified to the notion that military service had somehow "transformed" them and broadened their outlook on life. Louis Atkins, a Potawatomi from Oklahoma and a former member of the 103d Field Artillery, Twenty-sixth Division, had been gassed while in action near Verdun. Upon his return home, he reportedly stated that "I feel that I can look the whole world in the face now that I went and have come back. The realization of duty well done is satisfying."[48] John Gunn, a Laguna veteran, testified that "I can say that I got a great deal of benefit from [military service], being with white soldiers all the time. I was treated fine by the white boys."[49] Philip Frazier, a former student at the Santee Normal Training School in Nebraska before serving in the 355th Infantry Regiment, wrote that "the war game has shown us how to make a stand for truth in the face of death. The American Indian has proven himself a worthy citizen" and "thus, with a broader mind and a larger heart, we are coming home."[50] An editorial published in *The American Indian Magazine* quoted an Indian veteran as saying that "in my travels with the army I have seen a great world. I did not know till then that I had been living in a reservation wilderness." The author went on to describe the Indian veteran as an "Indian Soldier Disciple" who "brings home to his race stories of human enterprise and world activities such as they have never dreamed."[51]

Other Indians attested to the notion that wartime service exerted strong influences on them. The "war was a great lesson to us," wrote Thomas G. Bishop, a Snohomish from Tacoma, Washington, and secretary-treasurer of the Society of American Indians. "While it cost greatly in lives, many of our people were tremendously advanced and they learned a great deal, and now they are seeking for more privileges and chances in the same channel."[52] Henry M. Owl, an Eastern Cherokee, commented on the potential of military service to promote important changes in traditional Indian cultures. Because of Indian participation in World War I, he reasoned, "my people are fast discovering the futility of tribalism and are gradually stepping into the body politic as citizens worthy of recognition."[53]

The popular media, not surprisingly, followed the government's lead and further encouraged the notion that wartime service had miraculously transformed Indian men. By doing so, the media continued its long tradition of telling readers what they wanted to hear and believe about American Indians—irrespective of the facts. Twenty years before, magazines and newspapers were filled with editorials forecasting the end of the "Vanishing Race." During World War I, however, the press changed its tune and published hundreds of stories commenting on the Indians' "inherent" and "instinctive" martial attributes and how the Germans had better watch out! With the war's end, the press changed gears one more time and emphasized how Indian veterans had been transformed and were now ready and willing to take up a more responsible role in society.

Thus, the media, mirroring society, continued naively to depict Indians as it hoped and expected to see them, rather than as what Native Americans actually were—complex and diverse peoples who defied simplistic definitions and characterizations. An article in *The Literary Digest*, for example, reported that many Indian veterans had been "completely regenerated" in the service, and the army experience had proved, for most of them, the "most important educational factor of their careers." A piece appearing in *Overland Monthly* just months after the war remarked that Native Americans had achieved equality in Anglo society. "The upright and honest Indian stands today shoulder-to-shoulder with the white brother, in an even race against the rise and fall of modern activities."[54] Native American veterans would return home "full of courage and ambition, with a more perfect stature, with a broader view of the world"—an editorial published in *The Indian School Journal* predicted—and they "will prove to the people that their vision is focused on a prosperous future."[55]

Military service may have helped propel some veterans into tribal leadership positions. Among many Indian peoples, but particularly the Plains tribes, being a successful warrior was an important prerequisite for political power; tradition dictated that "any power exercised within the tribe was exercised by the total body of responsible men who had qualified for social eminence by their war record and their generosity."[56] During the 1890s, for example, Sioux soldiers who had served in the regular army gained the respect and admiration of their people and many became important tribal leaders. It is likely, in fact, that a few politically ambitious Indian men actively sought military service during World War I as a means of gaining power. While wartime service certainly would not have been the only reason why veterans rose to positions of tribal leadership (one's level of education, economic status, personal reputation, family, ability, and level of commitment would have also factored in), military experience gave men from tribes with strong martial traditions a distinct advantage over those who had never served.

There are numerous examples of Indian veterans of World War I who later became important tribal leaders. Victor M. Locke, a Choctaw veteran of both the Spanish-American War and World War I, became a tribal council-man in 1903, was a delegate to the Republican national convention held in Chicago in 1904, and later became the tribe's principal chief. Jesse Cornplanter, a Seneca who served in the 147th Infantry Regiment, Thirty-seventh Division, lived through a poison-gas barrage during the Meuse-Argonne Offensive and suffered from neurasthenia for the rest of his life. Despite the ailment, Cornplanter became a well-known artist, author, and storyteller and was an active participant in the Iroquois' deliberations concerning the Indian Reorganization Act. John J. Mathews, an Osage veteran, enlisted in the cavalry in 1917, but later switched to the aviation branch of the Signal Corps and served as an aviator in France. After the war he graduated from the University of Oklahoma, studied at Oxford, and became a noted scholar, author, geologist, rancher, and tribal council member. His history of the Osages is still considered the standard work on the tribe.[57]

There are other examples. John Mackey, Sr., a Santee from Nebraska, and George Jewett, a Cheyenne River Sioux from South Dakota, both became important tribal spokesmen. Mackey served with the mounted cavalry in France during the war. He gained employment with the Works Progress Administration during the Great Depression and was "instrumental in the negotiations and writing of the first Santee tribal constitution." Jewett, who had returned to his South Dakota farm after the war, was later selected in 1934 to be part of a Sioux delegation to Washington, D.C. Upon his return to the Cheyenne River reservation, Jewett spoke in behalf of the Wheeler-Howard bill.[58]

Steve Spotted Tail, a Brule Sioux from the Rosebud reservation in South Dakota, enlisted in March 1917 and later served under Douglas MacArthur in the Forty-second "Rainbow" Division. Spotted Tail, who was fond of MacArthur because the colonel was brave and "never says very much," fought on six different fronts and was in the Argonne Forest when the war ended. He later became a tribal councilman.[59] Fred Blythe Bauer, an Eastern Cherokee veteran who had served with the army air corps in France, became an important spokesman against the Indian New Deal of the 1930s and, along with fellow veteran Jack Jackson, agitated for suffrage rights in the postwar era.

That military service during World War I exerted a significant influence on veterans there can be little doubt. For soldiers of all races, the war years marked a defining—if not altogether pleasant—moment in their lives. Did military service "transform" Indian soldiers and hasten assimilation? The results are mixed. As government officials, reservation superintendents, and Indian veterans themselves testified, military service helped train and educate thousands of Native Americans and provided a host of other experiences that broadened their outlook on life, especially for Indians coming from isolated areas and for those who had never attended boarding schools.

For those veterans coming from urban backgrounds, for those who had graduated from boarding schools, and for college-educated Indians, the war exerted an important albeit lesser influence. Once again, the individual Indian's level of education and acculturation, the location of his home, and his prewar association with the majority culture were important filters through which wartime military service permeated. The relative thickness—or absence—of these filters either minimized or maximized the degree of change wrought by the war.

It was partly in response to the apparent transformation in Indian character that the federal government in the postwar era moved to bestow citizenship upon American Indians. Although over half of the Native American population had secured citizenship prior to World War I (as a result of previous treaties, the Dawes Act of 1887, the act of March 3, 1901, that extended citizenship to the Five Civilized Tribes of Oklahoma, forced patenting, or, in the case of Indian women, by marrying a citizen), an estimated 125,000 Native Americans in 1919 still did not possess American citizenship.[60]

The immediate cause for the postwar crusade to grant Indians citizenship was their participation in World War I. Indian reform organizations such as the Society of American Indians and the National Indian Association pointed to Native American sacrifices during World War I as proof that Indians were worthy of citizenship. At their convention at Pierre, South Dakota, in September 1918, delegates from the Society of American Indians resolved that the close of the war should lead to an improvement in the "legal status and condition" of Native Americans. "A grateful government and people," it continued, "will not withhold from the Native American race full rights as free men under the constitution." The sooner Native Americans obtained citizenship, reformers predicted, "the sooner the cloud will be raised from Indian manhood and what is left of the race in bonds of restraint will emerge into the light of progress."[61]

Two months later, Dr. Joseph Kossuth Dixon, a longtime advocate of segregated Indian units and Native American citizenship, wrote an impassioned appeal to President Woodrow Wilson, in which he pleaded for "the emancipation of the North American Indian." By declaring as citizens all Indians who served in the military during the war as well as all Indians who had reached the age of eighteen on April 6, 1917 (the day that the United States declared war), Dixon argued, Wilson could "sweep clean the national house of democracy, and put the crown on the Goddess of Victory, by issuing a

'Proclamation of Emancipation for the North American Indian,' who has shed his blood for a country and a flag that he could not call his own."[62]

At its annual meeting in New York in December 1918, the National Indian Association (NIA) had adopted resolutions that included a demand for Indian citizenship and a desire to place on record its "sincere admiration of the loyalty and patriotism of our Indians, as evidenced by their prompt . . . voluntary response to their country's call to the flag."[63] A year later, it reported the existence of "a growing public sentiment in favor of granting citizenship to the Indians, due, in large measure, to the splendid loyalty to the flag exhibited by the Indian race."[64]

Other groups also advocated extending citizenship to American Indian veterans. At the first national convention of the American Legion held in Minneapolis, Minnesota, in December 1919, veterans adopted a resolution recommending that American Indians who honorably served in the late war be granted citizenship. Westerners supported the idea for practical political reasons. The expansion of Indian rights, they hoped, promised to reduce federal interference in their local affairs.[65]

Others contended that citizenship would hasten Indian assimilation and reduce the federal government's responsibility for Indian welfare. Assimilationists had argued for decades that granting citizenship to Native Americans would advance the dissolution of tribal ties and help solve the Indian problem. They reasoned that the Constitution could protect Indian rights and liberties much more effectively than could a cumbersome bureaucracy. The traditional "guardian–ward" relationship between government and Indians, they argued, should be discontinued. By giving Native Americans the privileges and responsibilities of citizenship, one assimilationist predicted, Indians "would gladly flee" from their "worthless past" and take great pride in the fact that they were now "useful."[66]

In an article published in the 1926 edition of the *California Law Review*, Chauncey Shafter Goodrich argued that Indian citizenship legislation did not "seriously affect the status of the Indians concerned" because the federal government continued to maintain restrictions on Indian lands, and because the legislation did not guarantee suffrage rights. Goodrich concluded, therefore, that the primary motive behind Indian citizenship legislation after World War I was the "well established federal policy of unloading responsibility for the Indian on the states."[67]

One of the first Indian citizenship bills introduced during World War I was that of Arizona senator Carl Hayden. Presented to the Senate on July 26, 1917, the bill (H.R. 5526) called for the conferral of citizenship on all Native Americans, the closing of tribal rolls, and the disbursal of tribal funds.

Five months later, in January 1918, Representative Charles D. Carter of Oklahoma introduced H.R. 9253, which would, among other things, confer citizenship on Native Americans and terminate BIA supervision over "competent Indians." Carter introduced new Indian citizenship bills each year from 1918 to 1921, but like the Hayden measure, they failed to gain passage.[68]

The Hayden and Carter bills fell short of passage for several reasons. The measures called for "competency tests" and the surrender of interest in tribal property as prerequisites for Indian citizenship. These requirements, John W. Larner, Jr., has asserted, made "citizenship unattractive or unavailable to most Indians." In addition, those who advocated citizenship for Native Americans could not agree on strategy. For example, assimilationist-minded "friends of the Indian" (like the National Indian Association and the Indian Rights Association) demanded that Native Americans receive complete and unrestricted citizenship and called for the immediate abolition of the BIA. Their opponents, on the other hand, supported Indian citizenship, but insisted that it be restricted and that the BIA continue to play the role of guardian over Indian property. In June 1919, the Board of Indian Commissioners reported that many Indians were ready for citizenship, but added that "there [remained] thousands of Indians . . . who have not advanced far enough to warrant the withdrawal of the Nation's guardianship."[69]

On June 5, 1919, Representative Homer P. Snyder of New York, the chairman of the House committee on Indian affairs, introduced another Indian citizenship bill (H.R. 5007). Contrary to the Hayden and Carter bills, Snyder's measure was a scaled-down version that called on the government to confer citizenship upon "every American Indian who served in the Military or Naval Establishments of the United States during the war against the Imperial German Government" and had received an honorable discharge. In addition, his bill would not require Indian veterans to forfeit their rights to tribal annuities and property. Those who wished to take advantage of the opportunity, however, had to identify themselves before a court of competent jurisdiction.[70]

On July 21 the House committee on Indian affairs reported favorably on the measure, and two months later the Snyder bill passed the House. On September 27, 1919, Senator Charles Curtis of Kansas, who claimed affiliation with both the Kaw and Osage tribes and was a member of the Senate committee on Indian affairs (not to mention the future vice president to Herbert Hoover), called for the bill's passage, and, on October 22, the Senate passed the measure without amendment. Congress presented the bill to President Wilson on October 25, and it became law without his signature on November 6, 1919.[71] Commissioner Sells commended the new law. "I hail it," he noted in his annual report, "as a just and fitting tribute to the intelligence, patriotism, and courage of the young men of a virile and enduring race."[72]

The administration of the Indian Citizenship Act of 1919 fell to the Bureau of Naturalization, which, instead of adopting a quick, simple mechanism to implement the act, established a rather complicated procedure. Any Indian veteran desirous of citizenship had to fill out an application in triplicate, sworn to before the reservation superintendent or another qualified official. The superintendent would then mail the application to the Bureau of Naturalization. The naturalization service then advised the applicant when and where to appear in court so that a Bureau of Naturalization official could examine the person's credentials. If everything was in order, the applicant had to make a formal petition in the office of the clerk of court and obtain a certificate of citizenship.[73]

Not surprisingly, many Indian veterans, by now accustomed to the tedious workings of the federal bureaucracy, unwilling to jeopardize their claims to tribal sovereignty (they were, after all, already citizens of their respective Indian Nations), and unconvinced that citizenship would benefit them, opted to forego the hassle of obtaining certificates of citizenship. Consequently, very few of them bothered to apply for citizenship in 1919, waiting, perhaps, for an easier method of acquiring equal protection under the constitution or until someone convinced them that citizenship was in their best interests.[74]

Four and a half years later, in June 1924, Congress passed new legislation. Introduced again by Homer P. Snyder, the law conveyed blanket citizenship upon the remaining 125,000 noncitizen Indians living in the United States.[75] While most historians agree that Indian participation in World War I provided the primary impetus for the 1919 citizenship measure, the role of Native American wartime service in the passage of the 1924 law has been a matter of some debate.

Gary C. Stein has argued persuasively that the Senate committee on Indian affairs, rather than reform groups or Indian participation in World War I, provided the primary catalyst for the measure's passage. Filled with such "inveterate Progressives" as Burton Wheeler, Lynn J. Frazier, Charles McNary, and Robert LaFollette, the committee, according to Stein, pushed for passage of an Indian citizenship bill as a regulatory measure rather than as a piece of social legislation.[76]

Russel L. Barsh has also linked the passage of the Indian Citizenship Act of 1924 to the workings of Progressive-era bureaucrats. He contended that, as early as 1912, President-elect Woodrow Wilson had commissioned Arthur Ludington, a Yale-educated progressive, to formulate a long-term strategy for Indian assimilation. Ludington proceeded to develop a three-phased plan, the second phase of which called for a "period of final training" where Indians would receive a restricted form of citizenship. According to Barsh, the Indian Citizenship Act of 1924 (which was, in fact, a form of restricted citizenship because Native Americans were still subject to certain restrictions regarding their property) was roughly in keeping with Ludington's plan.[77]

Another explanation for blanket citizenship in 1924 includes simple partisan politics. Robert F. Berkhofer and Jennings C. Wise have proposed that extending citizenship to Native Americans could have potentially determined the political complexion in states with large Indian populations, such as Oklahoma, Arizona, and New Mexico. Thus, Republican Commissioner of Indian Affairs Charles H. Burke, expecting that Native Americans (out of gratitude) would cast their votes for Calvin Coolidge, encouraged the passage of Indian-citizenship legislation. Advocates of this theory assume erroneously, however, that citizenship for Indians translated into voting rights as well.[78]

A strong case, however, can also be made for the traditional assessment that Indian participation in World War I stimulated the formulation and ultimate passage of the Indian Citizenship Act of 1924.[79] Commissioner Cato Sells wrote, in May 1920, that "no one questions the war-time evidence of the Indians' Americanism or that it carries great weight in the plea for his citizenship."[80] Instead of enacting a blanket citizenship law for all American Indians, however, the measure passed in 1919 restricted citizenship to veterans and required Native Americans to go through a tedious, bureaucratic process to gain certificates of citizenship. Consequently, Congress needed to pass a new, simple, expedient mechanism that bestowed citizenship quickly and painlessly. The Indian Citizenship Act of 1924 provided just that.

The earlier law also failed to recognize the wartime contributions of thousands of Indian farmers, stockraisers, students, and women who sacrificed a great deal of time, effort, and money for the American Expeditionary Force overseas. People from across the nation marveled at the Indians' Liberty loan and war savings stamp contributions, Native American work with the Red Cross, and greatly improved agricultural production on Indian farms. As Francis Paul Prucha postulated in his two-volume work on Indian policy entitled *The Great Father*, although the federal government in 1919 gave Indian veterans the opportunity to obtain citizenship, "the patriotic fervor that persisted after the war seemed to call for a measure to complete the circle. It came in 1924."[81]

One can also look to the many politicians and reformers who continued to plead for Indian citizenship by using Native American war service as an important justification. A month after Congress enacted the Indian Citizenship Act of 1919, for example, members of the National Indian Association declared that citizenship should be extended to all Native Americans. "On the principle that half a loaf is better than none," NIA members "rejoiced" that Congress had finally decided to grant citizenship to Indian veterans. However, they continued, Indian claims to citizenship "must be pressed not alone as a favor to be granted for splendid services rendered" during the war, but as a matter of "simple justice and right" as well.[82]

In January 1920, Dr. Joseph K. Dixon addressed the House committee on military affairs concerning Indian citizenship. He testified that "the Indian has proven by his manhood and patriotism that he is capable of 100 percent citizenship. He has bought it with his blood on the battlefields of France. . . . To fail to give him citizenship," he continued, "is to prove a lack of patriotic gratitude on our part."[83]

Representative Melville Clyde Kelly of Pennsylvania (who corresponded with Dixon on the matter of Indian citizenship) insisted that Indian contributions during the war ought to result in their acquisition of full citizenship. Backed by the Indian Rights Association, the American Civil Liberties Union, and such prominent Indian policy reformers as Richard Pratt, Dr. Carlos Montezuma, and Thomas G. Bishop, Kelly in August 1921 delivered a speech before the House of Representatives, in which he demanded the immediate abolition of the Bureau of Indian Affairs and the extension of citizenship to all Native Americans. He reminded the House that Native Americans "faced the German shells," but then, when they returned home, they were met with "the Hohenzollern rule of the Indian Bureau. They took a fighting chance for freedom," Kelly continued, and "they took a fighting chance in the Great War. They helped free the world from armed brutality; we should now free them from autocratic bureaucracy." It is a strange doctrine, he concluded, that a "law-abiding race must be disenfranchised and kept in bondage in order that lawless citizens may be restrained from preying upon them."[84]

With some certainty, then, Native American service in World War I was the initial and perhaps most important catalyst for Indian citizenship in 1924. That the Senate committee on Indian affairs contained a number of progressive politicians made passage that much easier. While the better-educated and affluent Indian population rejoiced that their brethren were finally American citizens, to most Indians citizenship did little to noticeably change their lives. The federal government, by virtue of the 1916 *United States* v. *Nice* ruling, still exercised its role as "guardian" over thousands of Indian people and many BIA restrictions remained in place. Native Americans would have to wait another decade before meaningful changes took place in Indian country.

Conclusion

PERHAPS THE MOST IMPORTANT LESSON ONE CAN LEARN FROM AN examination of Indian contributions during World War I was the remarkable diversity of Native American responses. Just as there was no monolithic "Indian" experience—no "consensus" Indian history, so to speak—it would be equally erroneous to suggest that there was a unified "Sioux response" or "Cherokee response." Tribal identity, while important, provides only clues rather than completely satisfactory answers to questions like these: Why did Indians enlist in such large numbers? What factors motivated Native Americans on the homefront to sacrifice their time and talents for the war effort? How did the war affect Indian veterans in the postwar era? In order to find the solutions to such questions, one must examine how the influences of tribal cultures interacted with the individual characteristics of the participants. One's level of education, socioeconomic status, citizenship, frequency of contact with non-Indian cultures, and the location of one's home (to name just a few) must also be added to the mix. The results of such an approach, though not clear-cut or simple, at least get closer to the truth and are a good deal more reflective of Indian history in the modern era.

By nearly all accounts, Indian soldiers fought well and made positive contributions to the American effort on the Western Front. General John Pershing, writing in September 1920, commented that "the North American Indian took his place beside every other American in offering his life in the great cause, where as a splendid soldier, he fought with the courage and valor of his ancestors."[1] The widespread belief that Indians were "inherent" or "instinctive" fighters, however, exerted a considerable influence over the duties assigned to them. Many Native American soldiers tried to live up to the fantastic expectations and, for a variety of reasons, accepted dangerous assignments without complaint. It should come as little surprise, therefore, that the stereotypes persisted and that Native Americans faced similar pressures during World War II.[2]

For many Indian men, service during World War I was a defining moment in their lives and oral histories attest to the importance that Native Americans attached to their tenure as "doughboys." Even today, veterans are honored at American Legion functions on reservations and at powwows where special songs to honor veterans and show patriotism have become an important part of modern Indian celebrations.[3] Although World War I has become for many Americans a "forgotten conflict," Native Americans continue to honor and remember loved ones killed during the "Great War." A recent edition of the *Winnebago Indian News*, for instance, published, in honor of Veterans Day, a list of Winnebago veterans who had served.[4]

Military service provided thousands of Indian soldiers from across the country with opportunities to become acquainted and share common experiences. Young men from dozens of different tribes met either at training camp, aboard transport ships, or overseas, and they formed friendships that endured after the war's end. Thus, World War I fostered Pan-Indianism among veterans, and through the formation of organizations such as American Indians of the World War (AIWW), the League of Indians of Canada, and the Wigwam Club (the organization established by Indian women and designed to aid returned soldiers), veterans discussed political matters affecting their peoples and pledged themselves never to forget their disabled comrades or their fealty to each other amid the complexities of life as minorities in an Anglo-dominated society.[5] Although the overall impact of Indian veteran organizations on BIA policies and on reservations was probably minimal, such activities anticipated the establishment of important reform organizations in the postwar era that fought for Indian rights and for better living conditions on reservations. Indian veterans were frequently in the vanguard of these reform efforts.

Wartime service provided Indian soldiers with valuable lessons. In addition to instilling and reinforcing the virtues of discipline, confidence, and responsibility, the military taught many Native Americans mechanical and clerical skills, hygiene, and the English language. Military service furthermore provided Indian men with opportunities to travel abroad and to experience different lifestyles and cultures. Native Americans lived and fought beside whites, and together they shared moments of great joy and witnessed unspeakable horrors. Of even greater importance, however, by training, traveling, and going on furlough with their white comrades, Indian men were, perhaps for the first time in their lives, treated as equals. They received a firsthand look at how the majority society worked and thought. Whites, meanwhile, gained valuable insights into how Indians felt about the war, about native cultures, and about Native American hopes for the future. For both white and Indian soldiers, therefore, service in the war tended to de-villainize and de-mythologize popular misconceptions and helped foster a realistic appreciation and understanding of each other's identities. The governments claims, therefore, that Indian soldiers returned home with a "broadened outlook" on life were at least somewhat accurate, and there were numerous reports that wartime service had heightened Indian political awareness. The same assessment can apply with equal validity to thousands of other Americans in the AEF.[6]

For Native Americans on the homefront, the war's effect on their daily lives was mixed. While some Indian peoples, particularly those living in the Southwest, struggled to maintain their isolation and played little part in the war effort, others like the Plains and Oklahoma tribes played active and important roles. Indian women contributed surprisingly large amounts to Liberty bond and war savings stamp drives and thousands joined the Red Cross. Such activities may have altered long-held misconceptions of gender inequity among Indian peoples. For a small minority of Native Americans, the war provided off-reservation jobs in shipyards, auto factories, and the growing aircraft industry. Indian school students, meanwhile, gained summertime employment as agricultural laborers.

The federal government and popular media applauded Indian contributions and sacrifices at home, but wartime exigencies prompted devastating cuts in appropriations for Indian health care and education. Reservation officials, meanwhile, often in collusion with western ranchers, pressured Indian farmers and stockraisers to sell their herds and to lease their lands to non-Indians.

Thus, for many Native Americans on the homefront, the war in Europe appeared to have had either a minimal or negative influence on their daily lives. Cast off on remote reservations under the supervision of a horde of government bureaucrats, some Native Americans undoubtedly questioned why Indian boys were fighting and dying to preserve a system of government that all but excluded them and stood idly by while the Native American land base eroded. Telling evidence of Indian disillusionment with BIA policies is the story of an elderly Sioux man who, when asked what he felt ought to be done with the Kaiser, responded that the German leader should be confined to a reservation, given an allotment, and forced to farm. When the Kaiser asked for help, the old man continued, the Indian agent should say to him, "Now you lazy bad man, you farm and make your living by farming, rain or no rain; and if you do not make your own living don't come to the Agency whining when you have no food in your stomach and no money, but stay here on your farm and grow fat till you starve." The old man's response reportedly met with the approval of most of the other older Indians on hand.[7]

Indian participation in World War I presented new challenges and opportunities for the BIA, and is an important episode in the evolution of federal Indian policy in the twentieth century. The debate over segregated Indian units reflected the larger conflict between assimilationists and preservationists over the ultimate goals and direction of federal Indian policy and over what means should be used to accomplish those goals. Commissioner of Indian Affairs Cato Sells viewed the war as an unexpected but welcomed opportunity to advance the cause of assimilation, and he unhesitatingly did so through a combination of integrating Indian soldiers into white units, boosting Indian agricultural production, and forced patenting. Indian citizenship measures passed in 1919 and 1924 were also applauded by many assimilationists as necessary steps in solving the Indian problem. In some ways, therefore, the goals of Indian policymakers during World War I demonstrated an amazing degree of continuity with those of the late nineteenth century who had placed so much hope in the Dawes Act. The opponents of allotment, however, were gathering strength. The BIA's frantic wartime efforts to salvage assimilation as the solution to the "Indian problem" can be seen as the "last gasp" of a disastrous and discredited policy.

Finally, Indian military service in World War I was a catalyst for change. Few of the young men who entered stateside army training camps or stepped onto the battlefields of France returned home without having acquired new insights and attitudes. Some came home bearing deep physical and emotional scars that undermined their reintegration into society. For them, the war was a painful memory that haunted them for the rest of their lives. But others gained a sense of purpose, discipline, and pride during their brief tenure as "doughboys"—traits that often enabled them to survive and at times prosper in the postwar era. In some ways, therefore, military service accomplished many of the objectives set by assimilationists.

Contradicting BIA policies aimed at hastening assimilation and acculturation, however, military service promoted Indian cultural practices and traditions rather than diminishing them. Participation in World War I opened new channels for Native Americans to practice (if in modified fashion) their traditional values and customs, and it encouraged the resurgence of victory dances, war songs, feasts, and giveaways. Among some Indian peoples, veterans acquired the privilege of entering previously inaccessible warrior societies, and children got the opportunity to witness elaborate burial rituals for "warriors" killed in France as well as other traditional ceremonies. Although Indian cultures had exhibited resilience during the first decades of the twentieth century, the war added renewed vigor and vitality, especially to those traditions associated with warfare. Because Native Americans often performed the traditional ceremonies under the guise of American patriotism, such practices became more acceptable to BIA policymakers and the white population at large. Consequently, the cultural renascence that accompanied World War I helped to strengthen and safeguard several aspects of Indian cultures until legislation that provided legal sanction for their survival could be passed in the 1930s.

Notes

Introduction

1. Statement of Congressman George E. Foss, Committee on Public Information, *War Message and Facts behind It* (Washington, D.C.: Government Printing Office, 1917), 16.

2. John Ellis, *Eye Deep in Hell: Trench Warfare in World War I* (New York: Pantheon Books, 1976), 4, 73–79.

3. Summary of Incidents and Comments Recently Gathered Evidencing the Superior Fitness of American Indians over the Average Soldier for Scout Service, 1918, Records of the Historical Section of the General Staff, Records of the American Expeditionary Force, Record Group 120, National Archives, Washington, D.C.

4. Francis Paul Prucha, *The Great Father: The United States Government and the American Indians*, vol. 2 (Lincoln: University of Nebraska Press, 1984), 1248.

5. *Second Report of the Provost Marshal General to the Secretary of War on the Operations of the Selective Service System to December 20, 1918* (Washington, D.C.: Government Printing Office, 1919): 198.

Chapter 1

1. Gary B. Nash, *Red, White, and Black: The Peoples of Early North America* (Englewood Cliffs: Prentice Hall, 1992), 142.

2. Edward Everett Dale and Aaston Litton, *Cherokee Cavaliers* (Norman: University of Oklahoma Press, 1995), 194; Arrell Morgan Gibson, *The American Indian: Prehistory to Present* (New York: D. C. Heath Co., 1980), 371.

3. George B. Grinnell, *Two Great Scouts and Their Pawnee Battalion* (Lincoln: University of Nebraska Press, 1973), 19, 71–74; Robert M. Utley, *Frontier Regulars: The United States Army and the Indian, 1866–1891* (New York: MacMillan Publishing Co., 1973), 22.

4. *Army Reorganization Act, Statutes at Large*, 14, sec. 6, 333 (1866); Thomas W. Dunlay, *Wolves for Blue Soldiers: Indian Scouts and Auxiliaries with the United States Army, 1860–1890* (Lincoln: University of Nebraska Press, 1982), 43–59; Utley, *Frontier Regulars*, 11.

5. Dunlay, *Wolves for Blue Soldiers*, 199–205; Royal B. Hassrick, *The Sioux: Life and Customs of a Warrior Society* (Norman: University of Oklahoma Press, 1964).

6. Francis Paul Prucha, *The Great Father: The United States Government and the American Indians*, vol. 2 (Lincoln: University of Nebraska Press, 1984), 656.

7. Richard N. Ellis, "Copper-Skinned Soldiers: The Apache Scouts," *Great Plains Journal* 5 (Spring 1966): 51–65.

8. Ibid; Robert M. Utley, *The Indian Frontier of the American West, 1846–1890* (Albuquerque: University of New Mexico Press, 1984), 197–201.

9. Ellis, "Copper-Skinned Soldiers," 59–60; Dunlay, *Wolves for Blue Soldiers,* 59–68; Charles DeBenedetti, *The Peace Reform in American History* (Bloomington: Indiana University Press, 1980), 4–5.

10. Ellis, "Copper-Skinned Soldiers," 59–60; Dunlay, *Wolves for Blue Soldiers,* 59–68.

11. Dunlay, *Wolves for Blue Soldiers,* 59–68. Robert Wooster, *The Military and the United States Indian Policy, 1865–1903* (New Haven: Yale University Press, 1988), 128.

12. Francis A. Walker, "The Indian Question," *North American Review* 116 (April 1873): 343.

13. Ibid., 344.

14. William Bruce White, "The Military and the Melting Pot: The American Army and Minority Groups, 1865–1924" (Ph.D. diss., University of Wisconsin, 1968), 25; Frederick Webb Hodge, ed., *Handbook of American Indians North of Mexico,* pt. 1, Bureau of American Ethnology Bulletin 30 (Washington, D.C.: Government Printing Office, 1907), 23; Byron Price, "The Utopian Experiment: The Army and the Indian, 1890–1897," *By Valor and Arms* 3 (Spring 1977): 16–18.

15. Sally Hyer, *One House, One Voice, One Heart: Native American Education at the Santa Fe Indian School* (Santa Fe: Museum of New Mexico Press, 1990), 4–17; Margaret Szasz, *Education and the American Indian: The Road to Self-Determination, 1928–1973* (Albuquerque: University of New Mexico Press, 1974), 8–11; K. Tsianina Lomawaima, *They Called it Prairie Light: The Story of Chilocco Indian School* (Lincoln: University of Nebraska Press, 1994), xi–5; David W. Adams, "Schooling the Hopi: Federal Indian Policy Writ Small, 1887–1917," *Pacific Historical Review* 48 (August 1979): 335–56.

16. Dunlay, *Wolves for Blue Soldiers,* 187–98.

17. H. C. Cushing, "Military Colonization of the Indians," *The United Service* (September 1880): 370–75.

18. Price, "Utopian Experiment" 16–17.

19. Congress, Senate, Committee on Indian Affairs, *Bill to Establish an Indian Military Academy,* 48th Cong., 1st sess., 1884, S. Rept. 348, serial no. 2175, 1–2; Price, "Utopian Experiment," 17.

20. Francis Paul Prucha, "Thomas Jefferson Morgan, 1889–1893," in Robert M. Kvasnicka and Herman J. Viola, eds., *The Commissioners of Indian Affairs, 1824–1977* (Lincoln: University of Nebraska Press, 1979), 193; White, "Military and the Melting Pot," 28–32.

21. Michael L. Tate, "From Scout to Doughboy: The National Debate over Integrating American Indians in the Military, 1891–1918," *Western Historical Quarterly* 17 (October 1986): 419; Don Rickey, Jr., "Warrior Soldiers: The All Indian 'L' Troop, 6th U.S. Cavalry, in the Early 1890's," in Ray Brandes, ed., *Trooper West: Military and Indian Affairs on the American Frontier* (San Diego: Frontier Heritage Press, 1970), 42.

22. William H. Powell, "The Indian as Soldier," *The United Service* 3 (March 1890): 232–34.

23. Katherine M. Weist, "Ned Casey and His Cheyenne Scouts: A Noble Experiment in an Atmosphere of Tension," *Montana: The Magazine of Western History* 27 (Winter 1977): 26–34.

24. William H. Powell, "The Indian Problem," *The United Service* 5 (April 1891): 338; Powell, "Indian as Soldier," 232–34.

25. Price, "Utopian Experiment," 18–19.

26. Weist, "Ned Casey and His Cheyenne Scouts," 28–36; Richard Upton, *The Indian as Soldier at Fort Custer, Montana, 1890–1895* (El Segundo, Calif.: Upton and Sons, 1983), 17–21.

27. Homer W. Wheeler, *Buffalo Days* (Indianapolis: The Bobbs-Merrill Co., 1925), 287–312.

28. Rickey, "Warrior Soldiers," 42–43.

29. White, "Military and the Melting Pot," 34.

30. Fairfax Downey and Jacques N. Jacobsen, Jr., *The Red/Bluecoats* (Fort Collins: The Old Army Press, 1973), 13–14.

31. Price, "Utopian Experiment," 20; William Bruce White, "The American Indian as Soldier, 1890–1919," *The Canadian Review of American Studies* 7 (Spring 1976): 17. Michael L. Tate notes that the all-white Sixth, Eleventh, Fifteenth, and Nineteenth Infantry Regiments were also excluded from the experiment until February 1892. See Michael L. Tate, "Soldiers of the Line: Apache Companies in the U.S. Army, 1891–1897," *Arizona and the West* 16 (Winter 1974): 348.

32. Price, "Utopian Experiment," 20–21; Eric Feaver, "Indian Soldiers, 1891–1895: An Experiment on the Closing Frontier," *Prologue* 7 (Summer 1975): 110–11.

33. Price, "Utopian Experiment," 23.

34. Feaver, "Indian Soldiers," 111–13; Weist, "Ned Casey and His Cheyenne Scouts," 37–39; Tate, "Soldiers of the Line," 343–50; Upton, *Indian as Soldier*, 128. Frank E. Vandiver, *Black Jack: The Life and Times of John J. Pershing* (College Station: Texas A & M University Press, 1977), 99–101.

35. Feaver, "Indian Soldiers," 112–13; White, "American Indian as Soldier," 18; Ralph K. Andrist, *The Long Death: The Last Days of the Plains Indians* (New York: MacMillan Publishing Co., 1993), 338.

36. Price, "Utopian Experiment," 24–25; Feaver, "Indian Soldiers,," 111–12.

37. William T. Hagan, *Indian Police and Judges: Experiments in Acculturation and Control* (Lincoln: University of Nebraska Press, 1966), 25, 42–49.

38. Ibid; White, "Military and the Melting Pot," 52.

39. Feaver, "Indian Soldiers," 113–14; Rickey, "Warrior Soldiers," 49–54; Price, "Utopian Experiment," 24–28.

40. Feaver, "Indian Soldiers," 113–14; Rickey, "Warrior Soldiers," 50–54; Tate, "Soldiers of the Line," 363; Price, "Utopian Experiment," 25–28.

41. Charles G. Hibbard, "Fort Douglas, 1862–1916: Pivotal Link on the Western Frontier" (Ph.D. diss., University of Utah, 1980), 238–39; White, "Military and the Melting Pot," 44–45.

42. Feaver, "Indian Soldiers," 113–14; Rickey, "Warrior Soldiers," 49–54; Price, "Utopian Experiment," 24–28; Hibbard, "Fort Douglas," 238–39; White, "Military and the Melting Pot," 44–45; Tate, "Soldiers of the Line," 349.

43. Thomas H. Wilson, "The Indian as Soldier," *The Illustrated American* 18 (1895).

44. Ibid.

45. Hugh L. Scott, *Some Memories of a Soldier* (New York: The Century Company, 1928), 169–70; White, "Military and the Melting Pot," 51; White, "American Indian as Soldier," 18; Tate, "From Scout to Doughboy," 419–20.

46. White, "Military and the Melting Pot," 49, 51; Price, "Utopian Experiment," 26–28; Dunlay, *Wolves for Blue Soldiers*, 195–98.

47. Price, "Utopian Experiment," 30–31; Tate, "From Scout to Doughboy," 419–20.

48. Upton, *Indian as Soldier*, 99–100, 123; Rickey, "Warrior Soldiers," 57–58; Price, "Utopian Experiment," 28–29.

49. Dunlay, *Wolves for Blue Soldiers*, 198.

50. *Army Appropriation Act, Statutes at Large*, 28, sec. 2, 216 (1894); White, "Military and the Melting Pot," 55.

51. White, "Military and the Melting Pot," 55.

52. Clifford P. Westermeier, *Who Rush to Glory: The Cowboy Volunteers of 1898* (Caldwell: The Caxton Printers, 1958), 42–46.

53. Dale L. Walker, *Death Was the Black Horse: The Story of Rough Rider Buckey O'Neill* (Austin: Madrona Press, 1975), 127.

54. John Alley, "Oklahoma in the Spanish-American War," *Chronicles of Oklahoma* 20 (March 1942): 47; Victor M. Locke, Interview by Ameila F. Harris, October 25, 1937, interview no. 9003, transcript, Works Progress Administration Oral History Project, Indian Pioneer History Project for Oklahoma, Oklahoma Historical Society, Oklahoma City.

55. Walker, *Death Was the Black Horse*, 127–36; Alley, "Oklahoma in the Spanish-American War," 44–45; Virgil C. Jones, *Roosevelt's Rough Riders* (New York: Doubleday and Company, 1971), 127, 235.

56. Jones, *Roosevelt's Rough Riders*, 280–81.

Chapter 2

1. Brian W. Dippie, *The Vanishing American: White Attitudes and United States Indian Policy* (Middletown: Wesleyan University Press, 1982), 10–13.

2. Lee Clark Mitchell, *Witnesses to a Vanishing America: The Nineteenth Century Response* (Princeton: Princeton University Press, 1981), 34, 163, 178, 182; Dippie, *Vanishing American*, 26, 32–44; Arrell Morgan Gibson, *The American Indian: Prehistory to the Present* (Lexington: D. C. Heath and Company, 1980), 316.

3. Carl Schurz, "Present Aspects of the Indian Problem," *North American Review* 133 (July 1881): 7–9.

4. Gibson, *American Indian*, 496–97.

5. Ibid., 448, 493, 495.

6. Dippie, *Vanishing American*, 124–27, 164–70; Mitchell, *Witnesses to a Vanishing America*, 164–65.

7. Dippie, *Vanishing American*, 199.

8. William R. Draper, "The Last of the Red Race," *Cosmopolitan* 32 (January 1902): 244–46.

9. Thomas F. Millard, "The Passing of the American Indian," *The Forum* 34 (January 1903): 466–80; "The Disappearance of the American Indian," *Current Literature* 34 (May 1903): 540–46.

10. "Presentation of Aboriginal Life," *The Word Carrier of the Santee Normal Training School*, 46 (March–April 1918): 1 (located in the Center for Western Studies, Augustana College, Sioux Falls, S.D.). Ella Higginson, *The Vanishing Race and Other Poems* (Bellingham, Wash.: C. M. Sherman, 1911), 5.

11. John Upton Terrell, *American Indian Almanac*, 2d ed., (New York: Barnes and Noble, 1994), 443.

12. Edward N. Saveth, "Theodore Roosevelt: Image and Ideology," in Leonard Dinnerstein and Kenneth T. Jackson, eds., *American Vistas: 1877 to the Present* (New York: Oxford University Press, 1995), 132–33; Paula Richardson Fleming and Judith Lynn Luska, *Grand Endeavors of American Indian Photography* (Washington, D.C.: Smithsonian Institution Press, 1993), 12.

13. Fleming and Luska, *Grand Endeavors of American Indian Photography*, 29–31, 39–40, 107–8; Edward S. Curtis, *The North American Indians* (New York: Aperture, 1972), 6.

14. Susan A. Krouse, "Photographing the Vanishing Race," *Visual Anthropology* 3 (1990): 213–16.

15. *American Indian Portraits from the Wanamaker Expedition of 1913* (Brattleboro, Vt.: The Stephen Greene Press, 1971), 2–4; Krouse, "Photographing the Vanishing Race," 215–16; Louis L. Pfaller, "James McLaughlin and the Rodman Wanamaker Expedition of 1913," *North Dakota History* 44 (Spring 1977): 4; Joseph K. Dixon, *The Vanishing Race* (New York: Doubleday, Page and Co., 1913), xv.

16. *American Indian Portraits from the Wanamaker Expedition*, 2–4; Pfaller, "James McLaughlin," 4; Dixon, *Vanishing Race*, xv; Russel L. Barsh, "An American Heart of Darkness: The 1913 Expedition for American Indian Citizenship," *Great Plains Quarterly* 13 (Spring 1993): 93; Dippie, *Vanishing American*, 212–13.

17. *American Indian Portraits from the Wanamaker Expedition*, 3–4; Frederick E. Hoxie, *A Final Promise: The Campaign to Assimilate the Indians, 1880–1920* (Lincoln: University of Nebraska Press, 1984), 102; Pfaller, "James McLaughlin," 45; Barsh, "American Heart of Darkness," 94–98.

18. *American Indian Portraits from the Wanamaker Expedition*, 3–4; Pfaller, "James McLaughlin," 5; Barsh, "American Heart of Darkness," 100–103; Alan Trachtenberg, "Playing American," unpublished lecture, William Hammond Mathers Museum, Indiana University, Bloomington; Dippie, *Vanishing American*, 213–16.

19. In a letter to President Wilson in May 1913, Joseph Dixon described the approaching Wanamaker Expedition as an "expedition of patriotism." Joseph K. Dixon, to President Woodrow Wilson, May 24, 1913, Woodrow Wilson Papers, Series 4, Executive Office Files, Library of Congress, Washington, D.C.; Pfaller, "James McLaughlin," 5; Dixon, *Vanishing Race*, vii, 5.

20. Gibson, *American Indian*, 522.

21. Donald Parman, "Francis Ellington Leupp, 1905–1909," in Robert M. Kvasnicka and Herman J. Viola, eds., *The Commissioners of Indian Affairs, 1824–1977* (Lincoln: University of Nebraska Press, 1979), 231.

22. Necah Furman, "Seedtime for Indian Reform: An Evaluation of Commissioner Francis Ellington Leupp," *Red River Valley Historical Review* 2 (Winter 1975): 499, 502; Dippie, *Vanishing American*, 185–86.

23. Gibson, *American Indian*, 522.

24. Department of the Interior, *Annual Report of the Commissioner of Indian Affairs*, 59th Cong., 2d sess., 1906, H. doc. 5, 16.

25. John F. Berens, "Old Campaigners, New Realities: Indian Policy Reform in the Progressive Era, 1900–1912," *Mid-America* (January 1977): 52–57.

26. Thomas M. Holm, "Indians and Progressives: From Vanishing Policy to the Indian New Deal" (Ph.D. diss., University of Oklahoma, 1978), 128–34; David R. Lewis, "Still Native: The Significance of Native Americans in the History of the Twentieth Century American West," *Western Historical Quarterly* 24 (May 1993): 206.

27. Michael L. Tate, "From Scout to Doughboy: The National Debate over Integrating American Indians in the Military, 1891–1918," *Western Historical Quarterly* 17 (October 1986): 420–21; William Bruce White, "The American Indian as Soldier, 1890–1919," *The Canadian Review of American Studies* 7 (Spring 1976): 19.

28. William Bruce White, "The Military and the Melting Pot: The American Army and Minority Groups, 1865–1924" (Ph.D. diss., University of Wisconsin, 1968), 60.

29. Tate, "From Scout to Doughboy," 421–22; James A. Shannon, "With the Apache Scouts in Mexico," *Journal of the United States Cavalry Association* 27 (April 1917): 539–57; "White Soldiers and Red Indian Scouts in the Villa Chase," *Collier's* 57 (April 29, 1916): 8; Michael L. Tate, "Pershing's Pets: Apache Scouts in the Mexican Punitive Expedition of 1916," *New Mexico Historical Review* 66 (January 1991): 49–71.

30. Shelby Perkin, Interview by Pete W. Cole, May 20, 1937, interview no. 5911, transcript, Works Progress Administration Oral History Project, Indian Pioneer History Project for Oklahoma, Oklahoma Historical Society, Oklahoma City; Donald E. Houston, "The Oklahoma National Guard on the Mexican Border, 1916," *Chronicles of Oklahoma* 53 (Winter 1975–1976): 447–62; Tate, "From Scout to Doughboy," 422–23.

31. Robert A. Trennert, Jr., *The Phoenix Indian School: Forced Assimilation in Arizona, 1891–1935* (Norman: University of Oklahoma Press, 1988), 160–61.

32. Tate, "From Scout to Doughboy," 423–24; Donald Parman, *Indians and the American West in the Twentieth Century* (Bloomington: Indiana University Press, 1994), 60.

33. "More Segregation," *The Indian School Journal* 17 (April 1917): 431.

34. Congress, House, *Bill to Raise Ten or More Regiments of Indian Cavalry*, 65th Cong., 1st sess., H.R. 3970, *Congressional Record*, vol. 55, daily ed. (April 30, 1917); Tate, "From Scout to Doughboy," 424.

35. Congress, House, Committee on Military Affairs, *Argument by Dr. Joseph Kossuth Dixon*, 65th Cong., 1st sess., July 25, 1917, 1–5; Pfaller, "James McLaughlin," 10.

36. Ibid., 5–10.

37. Ibid., 10–15.

38. Ibid., 15–25.

39. Ibid., 16–17.

40. Ibid., 15–25.

41. Ibid., 31–32.

42. Tate, "From Scout to Doughboy," 426; Hugh L. Scott, *Some Memories of a Soldier* (New York: The Century Company, 1928), 562–63; Congress, House, Committee on Military Affairs, *Army Reorganization*, 66th Cong., 2d sess., January 28, 1920, 2176–77; Joseph Dixon to General John J. Pershing, July 30, 1918; Pershing to Dixon, September 3, 1918, John J. Pershing Correspondence, Indians in World War I, Dixon Collection, William Hammond Mathers Museum, Indiana University, Bloomington.

43. W.F. Love, Chief Clerk, to Adjutant General, North Carolina, File no. 39-680, General Files, 1917–1919, Records of the Provost Marshal General's Office, Records of the Selective Service System, 1917–1919, Record Group 163, Federal Records Center, Suitland, Md.

44. Pvt. Thomas L. Slow, to Cato Sells, Commissioner of Indian Affairs, May 16, 1920, File no. 43775, Central Correspondence Files, 1907-1939, Records of the Bureau of Indian Affairs, Record Group 75, National Archives, Washington, D.C.

45. Tate, "From Scout to Doughboy," 428; "Probably Caucasian Camouflage," *The Indian School Journal* 18 (December 1917): 188.

46. Tate, "From Scout to Doughboy," 427; John W. Chambers, *To Raise an Army: The Draft Comes to Modern America* (New York: The Free Press, 1987), 331–32; *Army Reorganization*, January 28, 1920, 2164.

47. Henry Blumenthal, "Woodrow Wilson and the Race Question," *Journal of Negro History* 48 (January 1963): 1–21; Chambers, *To Raise an Army*, 223.

48. Congress, House, Committee on Military Affairs, *Army Reorganization*, 66th Cong., 1st sess., September 3, 1919, 234–35.

49. "Cato Sells," *Who Was Who in America*, vol. 5 (Chicago: Marquis' Who's Who, 1973), 651–52; Department of the Interior, *Annual Report of the Commissioner of Indian Affairs* (hereafter cited as *ARCIA*), 65th Cong., 3d sess., 1918, H. doc. 1455, 3–4; also see "Indians Fight for Uncle Sam," *The Literary Digest* 56 (March 2, 1918): 81, for an explanation of Sells's opposition.

50. Lawrence C. Kelly, "Cato Sells, 1913–1920," in Kvasnicka and Viola, *Commissioners of Indian Affairs*, 244; *ARCIA*, 1918, 4.

51. J. W. Dady, Superintendent, Red Cliff School and Agency, to Cato Sells, Commissioner of Indian Affairs, February 13, 1918, Administrative Correspondence of the Superintendent, 1908–1922, Records of the Red Cliff School and Agency, 1901–1922, Records of the Bureau of Indian Affairs, Record Group 75, National Archives, Great Lakes Region, Chicago, Ill.

52. Hazel W. Hertzberg, *The Search for an American Indian Identity* (Syracuse: Syracuse University Press, 1971), 161–70.

53. "More Plans for Segregation," *The American Indian Magazine* 5 (July-September 1917): 203–4.

54. Herbert Welsh, President, IRA, to Warren H. Wise, April 15, 1918, Indian Citizenship: IRA, Dixon Collection, William Hammond Mathers Museum, Indiana University, Bloomington.

55. See *The Native American* 19 (March 1918): 63–64, or *The Indian School Journal* 18 (December 1917): 188.

56. "Indian Soldiers," *The Native American* 19 (June 1918): 170.

57. *Army Reorganization*, January 28, 1920, 2164.

58. Ibid., 2166.

59. Ibid., 2173–74.

60. Ibid., 2201–13; Draft of Dixon's Amendment to the Army Reorganization Bill of 1920, William Hammond Mathers Museum, Indiana University, Bloomington, 1–8.

61. Ibid.

62. Ibid.

63. Ibid.

64. Ibid., 2214–19; White, "Military and the Melting Pot," 67–68.

65. But Dixon's second defeat did not end the postwar fight to establish segregated units. The *New York Times* reported that on April 2, 1920, Senator James W. Wadsworth of New York, the chairman of the Senate committee on military affairs, introduced an amendment to the army reorganization bill providing for the enlistment of up to ten thousand American Indians as a separate unit of the army. Upon discharge the Indians would have all the rights of American citizens, in addition to their tribal rights. The army reorganization bill, already controversial for its call for universal military training, gained passage in June 1920—but without segregated Indian units or universal military training. See *New York Times*, April 3, 1920, p. 10; Congress, Senate, *Army Reorganization Act*, 66th Cong., 2d sess., *Senate Documents*, vol. 13, 474–90.

66. Lawrence C. Kelley, *The Assault on Assimilation: John Collier and the Origins of Indian Policy Reform* (Albuquerque: University of New Mexico Press, 1983), 327; Robert Ingersoll Brown, Secretary of the American Indian Defense Association, to L. Rodman Wanamaker, Esq., March 21, 1923; John Collier, Executive Secretary of the American Indian Defense Association, to Joseph K. Dixon, June 26, 1923; Collier to Rodman Wanamaker, November 15, 1923, Joseph K. Dixon Collection (hereafter cited as JKDC), William Hammond Mathers Museum (hereafter cited as WHMM), Bloomington, Ind.

67. Irving Bacheller, President of the American Indian Defense Association, to Joseph K. Dixon, November 27, 1923; Dixon to Collier, November 21, 1923; Western Union Telegram from Collier to Dixon, February 19, 1924; Western Union Telegram from Dixon to Collier, February 21, 1924, JKDC, WHMM, Bloomington, Ind.

68. Program of the Aztec Ball for the Benefit of the American Indian Defense Association; Frederick W. Hodge, Museum of the American Indian, to Joseph K. Dixon, June 24, 1925; Dixon to Collier, June 11, 1925, JKDC, WHMM, Bloomington, Ind.; "Indians in Tableaux at the Aztec Ball," *New York Times*, sec. 1. 15.

69. John Collier to Joseph K. Dixon, June 26, 1925, JKDC, WHMM, Bloomington, Ind.

70. "Miss Edith Reid Weds Dr. Joseph K. Dixon," *New York Times*, August 27, 1925, sec. 1, p. 19; "Photographs of American Indians," *New York Times*, October 18, 1925, sec. 9, p. 13.

71. See Dippie, *Vanishing American*, 211–15; Parman, *Indians and the American West*, 60–61; Pfaller, "James McLaughlin," 4–11; Barsh, "American Heart of Darkness," 107, 111.

72. Parman, *Indians and the American West*, 112–13; Alison Bernstein, *American Indians and World War II: Toward a New Era in Indian Affairs* (Norman: University of Oklahoma Press, 1991), 22–23.

Chapter 3

1. "Enoch Herbert Crowder," *Who Was Who in America*, vol. 1 (Chicago: The A. N. Marquis Co., 1942), 280; *Selective Service Act, Statutes at Large*, 40, sec. 1 (1917), 76–77; Edward M. Coffman, *The War to End All Wars: The American Military Experience in World War I* (New York: Oxford University Press, 1968), 20–53.

2. *Selective Service Act*, sec. 4, 79; *Introduction to the Index for the Records of the Selective Service System*, Record Group 163, Federal Records Center, Suitland, Md., 3; John W. Chambers, *To Raise an Army: The Draft Comes to America* (New York: The Free Press, 1987), 182.

3. Department of the Interior, *ARCIA*, 65th Cong., 2d sess., 1917, H. doc. 915, 6.

4. Memorandum from Cato Sells, Commissioner of Indian Affairs, June 5, 1918, File no. 49055, Central Correspondence Files (hereafter cited as CCF), 1907–1939, Records of the Bureau of Indian Affairs (hereafter cited as RBIA), Record Group (hereafter cited as RG) 75, National Archives (hereafter cited as NA), Washington, D.C.

5. Ibid; *Second Report of the Provost Marshal General to the Secretary of War on the Operations of the Selective Service System to December 20, 1918* (Washington, D.C.: Government Printing Office, 1918), 22.

6. Tom Ration, Interview by Terry Carroll, October 11, 1968, interview no. 358, tran-

script, Doris Duke Indian Oral History Collection, Navajo Transcripts, General Library, Special Collection MSS314BC, Box 12, Folder 358, University of New Mexico, Albuquerque.

7. Cato Sells, Commissioner of Indian Affairs, to James Hildebrande, June 4, 1917, File no. 52485, Cherokee Nation Files, RBIA, RG 75, NA, Washington, D.C.; Michael L. Tate, "From Scout to Doughboy: The National Debate over Integrating American Indians in the Military," *Western Historical Quarterly* 17 (October 1986): 429.

8. Cato Sells, Commissioner of Indian Affairs, to John E. Raker, U.S. Representative, June 13, 1918, File no. 47130, CCF, 1907–1939, RBIA, RG 75, NA, Washington, D.C.

9. Congress, House, Committee on Military Affairs, *Argument by Dr. Joseph Kossuth Dixon*, 65th Cong., 1st sess., July 25, 1917, 25.

10. The Dawes Act (General Allotment Act) of February 8, 1887, provided that at the president's direction, Indian lands could be allotted in severalty and allottees would be granted immediate citizenship, although the federal government would hold their lands in trust for twenty-five years. The Burke Act of May 8, 1906, amended the Dawes Act and provided that after the allotment of lands, citizenship would be deferred until after the twenty-five year trust period had expired. The law also provided, however, that the secretary of the interior could, at his discretion, convey fee patents and citizenship to "competent Indians" prior to the expiration of the trust period.

11. Cato Sells, Commissioner of Indian Affairs, to Reservation Superintendents, July 19, 1918, File no. 53378, CCF, 1907–1939, RBIA, RG 75, NA, Washington, D.C.

12. Sells to Reservation Superintendents, July 19, 1918; Sells to Reservation Superintendents, July 5, 1917, Circular 1305-D, as quoted in "The Indian and the Selective Service Law," *The Indian School Journal* 18 (October 1917): 72; Enoch H. Crowder, Provost Marshal General, to Cato Sells, April 29, 1918, Registration of Indians, 1918, Administrative Correspondence of the Superintendent, 1908–1922, Records of the Red Cliff School and Agency, RBIA, RG 75, NA, Great Lakes Region, Chicago, Ill.; *Second Annual Report of the Provost Marshal General*, 1918, 32–33.

13. "Indian and the Selective Service Law," 72.

14. *Report of the Provost Marshal General to the Secretary of War on the First Draft under the Selective Service Act, 1917* (Washington, D.C.: Government Printing Office, 1918), 34; *Act to Regulate the Immigration of Aliens, Statutes at Large*, 39, sec. 1 (1917), 874; Chambers, *To Raise an Army*, 191–92, 231.

15. Enoch H. Crowder, Provost Marshal General, to the Adjutant General of South Dakota, April 8, 1918, File no. 39-10, South Dakota; William W. Soule, District Board of South Dakota, to W. A. Morris, Adjutant General of South Dakota, April 15, 1918, File no. 39-10, South Dakota, States Files, 1917–1919; William W. Soule, District Board of South Dakota, to W. A. Morris, Adjutant General of South Dakota, April 15, 1918, File no. 39-680, General File, 1917–1919, Records of the Provost Marshal General's Office, 1917–1919 (hereafter cited as RPMGO), Records of the Selective Service System, 1917–1919 (hereafter cited as RSSS), RG 163, Federal Records Center (FRC), Suitland, Md.

16. Howard W. Adams, Chief Aliens Division, Memorandum for the Record, April 20, 1918, File no. 39-11; Office of the Provost Marshal General, to W. A. Morris, Adjutant General of South Dakota, April 20, 1918, File no. 39-11; Milton T. Benham, Chairman, Local Board, to W. A. Morris, Adjutant General of South Dakota, April 29, 1918, File no. 39-11, South Dakota, States Files, 1917–1919, RPMGO, RSSS, RG 163, FRC, Suitland, Md.

17. W. A. Morris, Adjutant General of South Dakota, to Crowder, May 14, 1918, File no. 39-10, South Dakota, States Files, 1917–1919, RPMGO, RSSS, RG 163, FRC, Suitland, Md.

18. S. V. Stewart, Governor of Montana, to Crowder, September 28, 1917, File no. 72-1, Montana, States Files, 1917–1919, RPMGO, RSSS, RG 163, FRC, Suitland, Md.

19. Registration card of Arthur Bear, June 5, 1917, Draft Registration Cards, 1917–1918, Legal and Legislative Records, 1917–1918, Tama Agency, 1896–1947, RBIA, RG 75, NA, Great Lakes Region, Chicago, Ill.; "Indians the Same as Whites," *The American Indian Magazine* 5 (July 1917): 198.

20. Enoch H. Crowder, Provost Marshal General, to Governors of South Carolina, North Carolina, and Florida, September 9, 1917; T. W. Bickett, Governor of North Carolina, to Crowder, September 14, 1917, and Crowder to Bickett, September 14, 1917, File no. 61-1, North Carolina, States Files, 1917–1919; Crowder to Adjutant General of the Army, October 19, 1918, File no. 68-753, General File, 1917–1919, RPMGO, RSSS, RG 163, FRC, Suitland, Md.

21. C. D. Munro, Superintendent, Fort Belknap Agency, to Cato Sells, Commissioner of Indian Affairs, March 15, 1918, File no. 13-84; E. B. Merritt, Assistant Commissioner of Indian Affairs, to the Adjutant General of the Army, March 27, 1918, File no. 13-84; Crowder to the Adjutant General of the Army, April 20, 1918, File no. 13-84, General File, 1917–1919, RPMGO, RSSS, RG 163, FRC, Suitland, Md.

22. Enoch H. Crowder, Provost Marshal General, to Cato Sells, Commissioner of Indian Affairs, May 21, 1918, File no. 43430, CCF, 1907–1939, RBIA, RG 75, NA, Washington, D.C.

23. L. C. Clark, Local Board for McIntosh County, to E. H. Gibson, the Adjutant General of Oklahoma, September 4, 1918, File no. 72-1, Oklahoma, States Files, 1917–1919, RPMGO, RSSS, RG 163, FRC, Suitland, Md.

24. Local Board for Graham County, North Carolina, to Enoch H. Crowder, Provost Marshal General, June 5, 1918, File no. 72-1, North Carolina; Crowder to the Adjutant General of North Carolina, June 10, 1918, File no. 72-1, North Carolina; Crowder to the Adjutant General of Oklahoma, September 19, 1918, File no. 72-1, Oklahoma, States Files, 1917–1919, RPMGO, RSSS, RG 163, FRC, Suitland, Md.; Henry Owl, "The Indian in the War," *The Word Carrier of the Santee Normal Training School* (hereafter cited as *The Word Carrier*) 46 (July–August–September 1918): 15.

25. Based on Dr. Joseph K. Dixon's estimate of 50,000 adult males during the army reorganization hearings in January 1920. See Congress, House, Committee on Military Affairs, *Army Reorganization*, 66th Cong., 2d sess., January 28, 1920, 2181. Commissioner Sells's annual report in 1919 estimated the number of able-bodied adult males at 44,511. See *ARCIA*, 65th Cong., 2d sess., H. doc. 409, Table 11, 122.

26. *Second Report of the Provost Marshal General*, 1918, 198; Jennings C. Wise, *The Red Man in the New World Drama* (Washington, D.C.: W. F. Roberts Co., 1931), 524–25.

27. E. B. Merritt, Assistant Commissioner of Indian Affairs, to George Lawrence, December 7, 1918, File no. 94910; Merritt to Mrs. Florence Gritts, October 16, 1917, File no. 94887, Cherokee Nation Files; Alex Cadotta, to Newton D. Baker, Secretary of War, November 25, 1919, File no. 37699, General Services, Category 125, CCF, 1907–1939, RBIA, RG 75, NA, Washington, D.C.; Assistant Secretary of the Interior Hopkins, to Robert Lansing, Secretary of State, Central Classified Files, 1907–1936, Office of the Secretary, Records of the Department of the Interior (hereafter cited as RDI), RG 48, NA, Washington, D.C.

28. But if 80 percent of all Indian soldiers had enlisted, the actual total would have

been much higher. The Provost Marshal General's office reported that prior to September 1918, 6,509 Indians were inducted. Even if 25 percent of them failed medical exams or were mustered out during basic training, that would still leave approximately 4,900 draftees who served during the war. If, as Cato Sells claimed, 80 percent of all Indian soldiers were enlistees, then some 25,000 served, which is highly unlikely. Where Sells got his inaccurate information remains unknown. A more likely ratio of draftees to enlistees would be about 50 percent each—roughly 6,500 were drafted and 6,000 enlisted, bringing the total number of Indians soldiers to around 12,500.

29. Department of the Interior, *ARCIA*, 65th Cong., 3d sess., 1918, H. doc. 1455, 5; Department of the Interior, Office of Indian Affairs, Bulletin No. 6, "Indians, North America," 1920, 2; Russel L. Barsh, "American Indians in the Great War," *Ethnohistory* 38 (Summer 1991): 277–78; Chambers, *To Raise an Army*, 231; Wise, *Red Man in the New World Drama*, 524–25.

30. Thomas Holm, "Fighting a White Man's War: The Extent and Legacy of American Indian Participation in World War II," in Peter Iverson, ed., *The Plains Indians of the Twentieth Century* (Norman: University of Oklahoma Press, 1985), 151.

31. *ARCIA*, 1918, 4.

32. Ibid.

33. "The Good Coming Out of the War," *The Word Carrier* 46 (May–June 1918): 11.

34. Barsh, "American Indians in the Great War," 288.

35. *Thirty-ninth Annual Report of the National Indian Association* (New York: 1918), 9; "Oneida Indian Walks Fifty Miles to Report for Service," *The Indian's Friend* 31 (September 1918): 1.

36. Arrell Morgan Gibson, *The American Indian: Prehistory to Present* (Lexington: D. C. Heath and Co., 1980), 526; Francis Paul Prucha, *The Great Father: The United States Government and the American Indians*, vol. 2, (Lincoln: University of Nebraska Press, 1984), 782; "Reasons Why Indians Should Join the Regular Army," *The American Indian Magazine* 5 (July–September 1917): 141–43.

37. Peter Iverson, *Carlos Montezuma and the Changing World of the American Indians* (Albuquerque: University of New Mexico Press, 1982), 112–13.

38. Carolyn T. Foreman, *Indians Abroad, 1493–1938* (Norman: University of Oklahoma Press, 1943), 211; "Indians in Europe," *The American Indian Magazine* 6 (Spring 1918): 21; Tate, "From Scout to Doughboy," 428.

39. Thomas E. Mails, *The People Called Apache* (Englewood Cliffs, N.J.: Prentice-Hall, 1974), 308. *ARCIA*, 1918, Table 10, 130; U.S. Navy Recruiting brochure, State Council of Defense, 1917, Administrative Correspondence of the Superintendent, 1908–1922, Records of the Red Cliff School and Agency, RBIA, RG 75, NA, Great Lakes Region, Chicago, Ill.; William Baldridge to Mr. Allen, October 24, 1917, as quoted in *The Indian School Journal* 18 (November 1917): 123.

40. "Indian Quits Job," *The Indian School Journal* 17 (May 1917): 466.

41. Norman B. Wiltsey, *Brave Warriors* (Caldwell: Caxton Printers, 1963), 226–27; "How Indian Chief Helped Uncle Sam," *New York Times*, January 26, 1919, Sec. 3, 3; "Indian Loyalty," *The Indian's Friend* 30 (November 1917): 6; "Indians and the War," *The Indian's Friend* 30 (May 1918): 1; "One Indian's Bit," *The Word Carrier* 48 (May–June 1919): 9.

42. Josephine Gwin Wadena, Interview by Cynthia Kelsey, August 24, 1968, interview no. 0187, transcript, Doris Duke Oral History Collection, South Dakota Oral History Center, Institute of American Indian Studies, University of South Dakota, Vermillion;

Helen C. Rountree, "The Indians of Virginia: A Third Race in a Biracial State," in Walter L. Williams, ed., *Southeastern Indians since the Removal Era* (Athens: University of Georgia Press, 1979), 39; Donald L. Parman, *Indians and the American West in the Twentieth Century* (Bloomington: Indiana University Press, 1994), 61–62.

43. Mary Austin, "A'wa Tseighe Comes Home from the War," *The Nation* 124 (April 6, 1927): 367–69.

44. Alex Cadotta, to Newton D. Baker, Secretary of War, November 25, 1919, File no. 37699, CCF, 1907–1939, RBIA, RG 75, NA, Washington, D.C.

45. Arthur C. Parker, "Why the Red Man Fights for Democracy," *The Native American* 18 (December 1917): 238–39; Peter Nabokov, ed., *Native American Testimony: A Chronicle of Indian–White Relations from Prophecy to the Present, 1492–1992* (New York: Viking Press, 1991), 279; "Indians Are a Big Factor in World War," *The Indian School Journal* 19 (October 1918), 69.

46. Francis Nelson, to Newton D. Baker, Secretary of War, February 10, 1918, File no. 39-680, General File, 1917–1919, RPMGO, RSSS, RG 163, FRC, Suitland, Md.

47. Mary B. Davis, ed., *Native America in the Twentieth Century: An Encyclopedia* (New York: Garland Publishing, 1994), 300; Parman, *Indians and the American West*, 63–64; John Thunder, "Canadian Indian Soldiers Killed in France," *The Word Carrier* 46 (May–June 1918): 1.

48. Parman, *Indians and the American West*, 64.

49. "Indians Are a Big Factor in World War," 68; "Discipline Code for the Oglala Indian Training School," *Oglala Light* (January 1919): 10–11; Sally Hyer, *One House, One Voice, One Heart: Native American Education at the Santa Fe Indian School* (Santa Fe: Museum of New Mexico Press, 1990), 3–17; K. Tsianina Lomawaima, *They Called it Prairie Light: The Story of Chilocco Indian School* (Lincoln: University of Nebraska Press, 1994), 101–5.

50. James B. Kitch, Superintendent of the Standing Rock Indian School, to Cato Sells, Commissioner of Indian Affairs, August 16, 1920; J. D. Huff, Superintendent of the Santa Fe Indian School, to Sells, August 13, 1920; F. M. Conser, Superintendent of the Sherman Institute, to Sells, August 14, 1920; Orders, Circulars, Letters, 1920–1921, Answers to Circulars, Circular 1625, RBIA, RG 75, NA, Washington, D.C.; Lomawaima, *They Called it Prairie Light*, 21; *A Brief Sketch of the Record of the American Negro and Indian in the Great War* (Boston: Boston Hampton Committee, 1919), 3.

51. Superintendent of the Shivwits School to Charles H. Burke, Commissioner of Indian Affairs, January 26, 1921; Francis A. Swayne, Superintendent of the Western Shoshone Schools, to Burke, February 21, 1921; Henry M. Carter, Superintendent of the Fallon Indian School, to Cato Sells, August 19, 1920; Superintendent of the Goshute Indian School to Sells, September 13, 1920; Orders, Circulars, Letters, 1920–1921, Answers to Circulars, Circular 1625, RBIA, RG 75, NA, Washington, D.C.

52. John R. Brown, "Our Part in the War," *The Native American* 18 (April 1917): 124–25; E. C. Finney, Acting Secretary of the Interior, to John W. Weeks, Secretary of War, January 8, 1923; Hubert Work, Secretary of the Interior, to John W. Weeks, Secretary of War, June 8, 1923; Finney to Weeks, June 30, 1923, Central Classified Files, 1907–1936, Office of the Secretary, RDI, RG 48, NA, Washington, D.C.

53. "Our Military Men," *The Native American* 18 (June 1917): 205; Phoenix Students in Army," *The Native American* 19 (June 1, 1918): 181; Robert A. Trennert, Jr., *The Phoenix Indian School: Forced Assimilation in Arizona, 1891–1935* (Norman: University of Oklahoma Press, 1988), 161; Charles Roberts, "The Cushman Indian Trades School

and World War I," *American Indian Quarterly* 11 (Summer 1987): 224; "Six Carlisle Indians Join the Navy," *The Indian School Journal* 18 (January 1918): 229.

54. "Hampton Indians Are Doing Their Bit," *The Indian's Friend* 30 (January 1918): 1; "Six Carlisle Indians Join the Navy," and "Schools Have Furnished More Than 1,200 to Navy Alone," *The Indian School Journal* 18 (January 1918): 229; "Chilocco Boys in the Army and Navy," *The American Indian Magazine* 5 (July 1917): 202.

55. *ARCIA*, 1917, 6; Warren K. Moorehead, "Indians Anxious to Enlist," *New York Times* November 2, 1917, 14; "Indian School Training," *The American Indian Magazine* 6 (Spring 1918): 22–23; Barsh, "American Indians in the Great War," 278.

56. John R. Finger, "Conscription, Citizenship, and Civilization: World War I and the Eastern Band of Cherokee," *North Carolina Historical Review* 63 (July 1986): 283–308; Finger, *Cherokee Americans: The Eastern Band of Cherokees in the Twentieth Century* (Lincoln: University of Nebraska Press, 1991), 36.

57. Richard N. Ellis, "Indians at Ibapah in Revolt: Goshutes, the Draft and the Indian Bureau, 1917–1919," *Nevada Historical Society Quarterly* 19 (Fall 1976): 163–65; David L. Wood, "Gosiute-Shoshone Draft Resistance, 1917–1918," *Utah Historical Quarterly* 49 (Spring 1981): 188.

58. Cato Sells, Commissioner of Indian Affairs, to Franklin K. Lane, Secretary of the Interior, January 31, 1918; Lane to Thomas W. Gregory, Attorney General, February 15, 1918, Central Classified Files, 1907–1936, Office of the Secretary, RDI, RG 48, NA, Washington, D.C.; Ellis, "Indians at Ibapah in Revolt," 168–69.

59. Ellis, "Indians at Ibapah in Revolt," 165–66; Wood, "Gosiute-Shoshone Draft Resistance," 178.

60. Commanding Officer, Fort Douglas, Utah, to Commanding General, West Department, March 30, 1918, File no. 17-194, General File, 1917–1919, RPMGO, RSSS, RG 163, FRC, Suitland, Md.; Wood, "Gosiute-Shoshone Draft Resistance," 180–82.

61. Finger, "Conscription, Citizenship, and Civilization," 290; Angie Debo, *A History of the Indians of the United States* (Norman: University of Oklahoma Press, 1970), 353; *Army Reorganization*, January 28, 1920, 2175; Erl A. Bates, President of the Onondaga Indian Welfare Society, to Cato Sells, Commissioner of Indian Affairs, May 13, 1918, File no. 72-1, New York, States Files, 1917–1919, RPMGO, RSSS, 1917–1919, RG 163, FRC, Suitland, M.

62. Erl A. Bates, President of the Onondaga Welfare Society, to Cato Sells, Commissioner of Indian Affairs, May 13, 1918; Enoch H. Crowder, Provost Marshal General, to Governor of New York, May 27, 1918; Crowder to Sells, May 28, 1918, File no. 72-1, New York, States Files, 1917–1919, RPMGO, RSSS, RG 163, FRC, Suitland, Md.

63. Erl A. Bates, President of the Onondaga Indian Welfare Society, to Cato Sells, Commissioner of Indian Affairs, June 5, 1918, File no. 72-1, New York, States Files, 1917–1919, RPMGO, RSSS, RG 163, FRC, Suitland, Md.

64. Chief Thunderwater, Council of Tribes, to the Adjutant General of the Army, September 27, 1918, File no. 72-1, New York, States Files, 1917–1919, RPMGO, RSSS, RG 163, FRC, Suitland, Md.

65. Enoch H. Crowder, Provost Marshal General, to Cato Sells, Commissioner of Indian Affairs, May 10, 1918, File no. 61-113; C. B. Miller, U.S. Representative, Minnesota, to the Chippewa Indians of Sucker Point, January 11, 1918, File no. 39-680, General File, 1917–1919, RPMGO, RSSS, RG 163, FRC, Suitland, Md.

66. Harry B. Seddicum, Field Clerk, to Gabe E. Parker, Superintendent for Five Tribes, August 17, 1917; Seddicum to Parker, November 5, 1917; Joe H. Strain, Acting Superin-

tendent for the Five Civilized Tribes, to Cato Sells, Commissioner of Indian Affairs, November 8, 1917, Central Classified Files, 1907–1939, Five Civilized Tribes, File no. 105466-17-125, RBIA, RG 75, NA, Washington, D.C.

67. Harry B. Seddicum, Field Agent, to Gabe E. Parker, Superintendent for the Five Civilized Tribes, June 15, 1918; Parker to Seddicum, June 19, 1918; James C. Davis, Creek National Attorney, to Cato Sells, Commissioner of Indian Affairs, December 18, 1918, Central Classified Files, 1907–1939, Five Civilized Tribes, File no. 49330-18-121, RBIA, RG 75, NA, Washington, D.C.; "Creek Indians Rise against the Draft," *New York Times*, June 6, 1918, 11.

68. S. Stopilius, Assistant Secretary of the Interior, to Thomas W. Gregory, Attorney General, September 10, 1917; Assistant Secretary of the Interior Hopkins to Thomas W. Gregory, Attorney General, December 18, 1917; Cato Sells, Commissioner of Indian Affairs, to Franklin K. Lane, Secretary of the Interior, March 9, 1918, Central Classified Files, 1907–1936, Office of the Secretary, RDI, RG 48, NA, Washington, D.C.; Stopilius to Newton D. Baker, Secretary of War, December 20, 1917, File no. 17-77; W. H. Sage, Brigadier General, U.S. Army, to Enoch H. Crowder, File no. 586, General File, 1917–1919, RPMGO, RSSS, RG 163, FRC, Suitland, Md.; Barsh, "American Indians in the Great War," 281; Ellis, "Indians at Ibapah in Revolt," 169; Ben Stonecool to Edgar B. Merritt, Assistant Commissioner of Indian Affairs, January 15, 1919, File no. 88709, CCF, 1907–1939, RBIA, RG 75, NA, Washington, D.C.; Hilda Faunce, *Desert Wife* (1928; repr., Lincoln: University of Nebraska Press, 1981), 289–94.

69. *Final Report of the Provost Marshal General to the Secretary of War on the Operation of the Selective Service System to July 15, 1919* (Washington, D.C.: Government Printing Office, 1920), 11–12.

Chapter 4

1. Edward M. Coffman, *The War to End all Wars: The American Military Experience in World War I* (New York: Oxford University Press, 1968), 62–63; John R. Finger, "Conscription, Citizenship, and Civilization: World War I and the Eastern Band of Cherokee," *North Carolina Historical Review* 63 (July 1986), 302; Guy Woodson, "From Oklahoma to Hillesheim (probably Hildesheim): A Soldier's Travels through WWI," pt.1, *The National Tribune*, December 22, 1986; Lewis E. Sears, to Edgar A. Allen, Superintendent, Chilocco Indian School, in *The Indian School Journal* 18 (April 1918): 351; Robert C. Starr, to Edgar A. Allen, letter in *The Indian School Journal* 18 (December 1917): 173.

2. Ann Anastas, *Psychological Testing*, 6th ed. (New York: MacMillan Co., 1988), 11–12.

3. Despite the tests' apparent social and cultural biases, Jennings Wise maintained they demonstrated that Native Americans were superior to white soldiers "in mental poise and the power to resist strain." See Jennings C. Wise, *The Red Man in the New World Drama* (Washington, D.C.: W. F. Roberts Co., 1931), 532. According to T. R. Garth in the December 1, 1922, issue of *Science* magazine, national intelligence tests suggested that Indians of mixed blood were more intelligent than full-bloods. See T. R. Garth, "The Intelligence of Indians," *Science* 56 (December 1, 1922): 635–36; and/or Frank Wilson Blackmar, "The Socialization of the American Indian," *The American Journal of Sociology* 34 (January 1929): 660–61. Coffman, *War to End All Wars*, 60–61; John W. Chambers, *To Raise an Army: The Draft Comes to Modern America* (New York: The Free Press, 1987), 230.

4. Robert B. Huffman, Ft. Logan, Colo., to M. Louisa I. Riggs, Santee Normal Training School, December 30, 1917; Huffman to Riggs, January 20, 1918; United Church of Christ Archives, South Dakota Conference, M. Louisa I. Riggs Papers, Correspondence, Center for Western Studies, Augustana College, Sioux Falls, S.D.

5. Coffman, *War to End all Wars*, 62–63; Finger, "Conscription, Citizenship, and Civilization," 302; Guy Woodson, "From Oklahoma to Hillesheim"; Lewis E. Sears, to Edgar A. Allen, Superintendent, Chilocco Indian School, printed in *The Indian School Journal* 18 (April 1918): 351; Robert C. Starr, to Edgar A. Allen, letter in *The Indian School Journal* 18 (December 1917): 173.

6. Robert C. Starr, to Edgar A. Allen, Superintendent of Chilocco Indian School, in *The Indian School Journal* 18 (December 1917): 173.

7. "Indian Patriotism," *Word Carrier* 46 (January-February 1918): 3; Robert A. Trennert, *The Phoenix Indian School: Forced Assimilation in Arizona, 1891–1935* (Norman: University of Oklahoma Press, 1988), 161; Congress, House, Committee on Military Affairs, *Army Reorganization*, 66th Cong., 2d sess., January 28, 1920, 2167–68; Russel L. Barsh, "American Indians in the Great War," *Ethnohistory* 38 (Summer 1991): 282; Verne De Witt Rowell, "Canadian Indians at the Front," *Current History* 6 (August 1917): 291–92; James Dempsey, "The Indians and World War One," *Alberta History* 31 (Summer 1983): 4; Michael L. Tate, "From Scout to Doughboy: The National Debate over Integrating American Indians into the Military, 1891–1918," *Western Historical Quarterly* 17 (October 1986): 425, 430; Lonnie White, "Indian Soldiers in the 36th Division," *Military History of Texas and the Southwest* 15 (1979): 8–11.

8. Fullerton L. Waldo, *America at the Front* (New York: E. P. Dutton and Co., 1918), 4–5; Carolyn T. Foreman, *Indians Abroad, 1493–1938* (Norman: University of Oklahoma Press, 1943), 200; Rita G. Napier, "Across the Big Water: American Indians' Perception of Europe and Europeans, 1887–1906," in Christian F. Feest, ed., *Indians and Europe* (Aachen: Rader Verlag, 1987), 385–86; Luther Standing Bear, *My People the Sioux*, ed. E. A. Brininstoll (Lincoln: University of Nebraska Press, 1975), 248–50.

9. Felix Renville, Interview by Gerald Wolff, August 11, 1976, interview no. 1529, transcript; Leo Shooter, Interview by Steve Plummer, June 20, 1972, interview no. 831, transcript; Doris Duke Indian Oral History Collection (hereafter cited as DDIOWC), Institute of American Indian Studies (hereafter cited as IAIS), University of South Dakota (hereafter cited as USD), Vermillion, S.D.

10. Waldo, *America at the Front*, 49–56; *Army Reorganization*, January 28, 1920, 2199; Coffman, *War to End All Wars*, 121–50; James M. Morris, *History of the U.S. Army* (New York: Bison Books, 1986), 122.

11. Morris, *History of the U.S. Army*, 122–23; Coffman, *War to End All Wars*, 155–59; Summary of Incidents and Comments Recently Gathered Evidencing the Superior Fitness of American Indians over the Average Soldiers for Scout Service, 1918, Records of the Historical Section of the General Staff (hereafter cited as RHSGS), Records of the American Expeditionary Force (hereafter cited as RAEF), RG 120, NA, Washington, D.C.; *Army Reorganization*, January 28, 1920, 2188; "Allies Widen Wedge with Reinforcements," *New York Times*, July 22, 1918, 2.

12. Department of the Interior, Office of Indian Affairs (hereafter cited as OIA), Bulletin No. 15, *American Indians in the Great War* (1922), 2; Department of the Interior, *ARCIA*, 66th Cong., 2d sess., 1919, H. doc 409, 13–14; Foreman, *Indians Abroad*, 212.

13. OIA, Bulletin No. 15, *American Indians in the Great War*, 2–3.

14. Coffman, *War to End All Wars*, 253–55; E. B. Merritt, Assistant Commissioner of

Indian Affairs, to George R. Fish, November 22, 1918, File no. 92168, General Services, Category 125, CCF, 1907–1939, RBIA, RG 75, NA, Washington, D.C.; *ARCIA*, 1919, 13–14.

15. Frederick Palmer, *America in France* (New York: Dodd, Mead and Co., 1918), 395.

16. *Army Reorganization*, January 28, 1920, 2184.

17. Summary of Incidents and Comments, RHSGS, RAEF, RG 120, NA, Washington, D.C.; *Army Reorganization*, January 28, 1920, 2183–84.

18. Coffman, *War to End All Wars*, 262–83; Morris, *History of the U.S. Army*, 123–24; Palmer, *America in France*, 418–19.

19. *Army Reorganization*, January 28, 1920, 2190–91; Summary of Incidents and Comments; Questionnaires from the 2d Division, Box 3471, RHSGS, RAEF; RG 120, NA, Washington, D.C.

20. Questionnaires from the 5th Division, Box 3472, RHSGS, RAEF, RG 120, NA, Washington, D.C.

21. Coffman, *War to End All Wars*, 299–302; Morris, *History of the U.S. Army*, 124.

22. Morris, *History of the U.S. Army*, 124; *Army Reorganization*, January 28, 1920, 2185.

23. Wendell Westover, *Suicide Battalions* (New York: The Knickerbocker Press, 1929), 245–46.

24. Coffman, *War to End all Wars*, 323–24; O'Hara Smith, "Chief Lo was with the Lost Battalion in France," *The American Indian* 1 (November 1926): 9; *Army Reorganization*, January 28, 1920, 2187–88.

25. Questionnaire of Josiah A. Powless, 308th Infantry, 77th Division, Box 3473, RHSGS, RAEF, RG 120, NA, Washington, D.C.; List of Indians Decorated in World War One, JKDC, WHMM, Indiana University, Bloomington, Ind.

26. James McCarthy, *A Papago Traveler: The Memories of James McCarthy*, ed. John G. Westover (Tucson: Sun Tracks and the University of Arizona Press, 1985), 83–87.

27. Statements of William A. Hayes, Chaplain, 321st Infantry, 81st Division and Ammons Tramper, Corporal, Company I, 321st Infantry, 81st Division, Box 3473, RHSGS, RAEF, RG 120, NA, Washington, D.C.

28. Questionnaire of George Allen Owl, Company I, 321st Infantry, 81st Division, Box 3473, RHSGS, RAEF, RG 120, NA, Washington, D.C.; Finger, "Conscription, Citizenship, and Civilization," 297–304.

29. Order No. 13910 D (Extract), Decoration of Private Joseph Oklahombi and unidentified newspaper clipping, located in Oklahombi Reference File, Oklahoma Historical Society, Oklahoma City; *ARCIA*, 1919, 14.

30. White, "Indian Soldiers in the 36th Division," 14–15.

31. OIA, Bulletin No. 15, *American Indians in the Great War*, 1–2; *ARCIA*, 1919, 13.

32. Coffman, *War to End All Wars*, 299–302; Morris, *History of the U.S. Army*, 124; James G. Harbord, *America in the World War* (New York: Houghton Mifflin Co., 1933), 95.

33. White, "Indian Soldiers in the 36th Division," 16.

34. Barsh, "American Indians in the Great War," 278, 298.

35. Summary of Incidents and Comments, RHSGS, RAEF, RG 120, NA, Washington, D.C.; O'Hara Smith, "Indian Soldier has Thrilling Experience in No Man's Land," *The American Indian* 1 (April 1927): 3; Frank Tyner, Interview by J. W. Tyner, August 28, 1969, interview T-512-3, transcript, DDIOHC, Western History Collection, University of Oklahoma, Norman.

36. Record of J. M. Gordon, Indians in World War, List of, Administrative Correspondence of the Superintendent, 1908–1922, Records of the Red Cliff School and Agency, 1901–1922, RBIA, RG 75, NA, Great Lakes Region, Chicago, Ill.; *ARCIA*, 1919, 13; Summary of Incidents and Comments; Comments of Captain Philip E. Barth, 142d Infantry, 36th Division, RHSGS, RAEF, RG 120, NA, Washington, D.C.; John Shawnego, 316th Bakery Company, to Edgar A. Allen, Superintendent, Chilocco Indian School, October 21, 1917, in *The Indian School Journal* 18 (November 1917): 123.

37. Caroline D. Appleton, "The American Indian in the War," *Outlook* 122 (May 21, 1919): 111; Barsh, "American Indians in the Great War," 280, 298.

38. The number of Native Americans who served in the navy during the war is a matter of some dispute. In a letter to Mrs. Kay L. Woodruff in October 1918 (File no. 82600, CCF, 1907–1939, RBIA, RG 75, NA, Washington, D.C.) and in his annual report in 1918, Commissioner Sells estimated that there were approximately one thousand Indians in the navy. An article in *The Indian School Journal* 18 (January 1919) suggests that Indian schools furnished more than twelve hundred recruits to the navy alone. Russel Barsh notes in his article "American Indians in the Great War," however, that the number was probably closer to three hundred (see Barsh, 298, n. 9).

39. Barsh, "American Indians in the Great War," 278; *Army Reorganization*, January 28, 1920, 2191–92.

40. "Indians Enlist in U.S. Navy," *The Indian School Journal* 17 (May 1917): 466; "Phoenix Students in Navy," *The Native American* 19 (June 1, 1918): 181.

41. *ARCIA*, 1919, 14; Wise, *Red Man in the New World Drama*, 526–27.

42. Robert H. Lowie, *Indians of the Plains* (Lincoln: University of Nebraska Press, 1982), 108–9.

43. Frank C. Sherman, "The Indians Made an Enviable Record During World War," *The American Indian* 2 (January 1928): 12; Brian W. Dippie, *The Vanishing American: White Attitudes and U.S. Indian Policy* (Middletown: Wesleyan University Press, 1982), 194.

44. McCarthy, *Papago Traveler*, 74–75.

45. Mary Austin, "A'wa Tseighe Comes Home from the War," *The Nation* 124 (April 6, 1927): 367–69.

Chapter 5

1. Jennings C. Wise, *The Red Man in the New World Drama* (Washington, D.C.: W. F. Roberts Co., 1931), 533.

2. For a discussion of other common stereotypes of Native Americans, see Robert Gessner, *Massacre: A Survey of Today's American Indian* (New York: Jonathon Cape and Harrison Smith, 1931), 63–101.

3. Caroline D. Appleton, "The American Indian in the War," *Outlook* 122 (May 21, 1919): 110.

4. "American Indians True to Tradition in the War," *The Literary Digest* 60 (February 8, 1919): 54.

5. "American Indians at the Front," *The Native American* 19 (September 1918): 210; "Frontier Tactics Practiced on Germans, Sport for Redskins," *The American Indian Magazine* 7 (Summer 1919): 104; "Indians Win Fame on Battle Front," *The Native American* 19 (March 1918): 81.

6. William Beebe, "A Red Indian Day," *The Atlantic Monthly* 122 (July 1918): 31.

7. Fullerton L. Waldo, *America at the Front* (New York: E. P. Dutton and Co., 1918), 104.

8. Edwin Corle, "One More Hero," *The Forum* 91 (April 1934): 250–52.

9. "Indian Scouts on the Marne Outwit the Huns," *The Indian's Friend* 31 (September 1918): 1.

10. "Indians Are Loyal; Ready to Fight," *The American Indian Magazine* 5 (July 1917): 201.

11. "American Indians True to Tradition in the War," 57; "Lo, the Rich Indian Is Eager to Fight the Savage Hun," *The Literary Digest* 57 (June 1918): 56–62.

12. "Indian Scouts Penetrate Rear of Foe Lines to Bomb Officer's Banquet," *The Indian School Journal* 19 (October 1918): 63. Native Americans were also reported to have hidden bear traps in enemy trenches. See "Indian Type Warfare," *American Indian Magazine* 6 (Autumn 1918): 148; "Indians Use Bear Traps to Catch Huns," *Indian School Journal* 19 (October 1918): 61.

13. "An Indian Gets A Move on Himself: A Match for Twenty Huns," *Word Carrier* 46 (October–November–December 1918): 20.

14. T. R. Garth, "The Intelligence of Indians," *Science* 56 (December 1, 1922): 635–36; Alison Bernstein, *American Indians and World War II: Toward a New Era in Indian Affairs* (Norman: University of Oklahoma Press, 1992): 46. For additional examples of Anglo–Indian racial attitudes, see Jack W. Schneider, "Patterns of Cultural Conflict in Southwestern Indian Fiction" (Ph.D. diss., Texas Tech University, 1977).

15. Part of the high casualty rate may have been due to the sociology of the army. Undereducated people (both Indian and non-Indian) tend to get assigned to combat units rather than to support units. The army I.Q. test (the Stanford-Binet test) given during basic training was designed to help military officials make the distinction. Those who scored poorly often came from economically depressed regions (like Appalachia, big-city slums, the Deep South, and some Indian reservations) and were often assigned to infantry units, while the better-educated types were more able to secure less dangerous assignments.

16. "War College Data, 1920," JKDC, WHMM, Indiana University, Bloomington.

17. Notes on Intelligence, Notes on a lecture by Major D. R. Mitchie, D.S.O., British Army, RHSGS, RAEF, 1917–1923, Boxes 3471-3473, RG 120, NA, Washington, D.C.

18. "Apaches Active Allies," *The Indian's Friend* 31 (November 1918): 5; Hugh T. Cunningham, "A History of the Cherokee Indians," *Chronicles of Oklahoma* 8 (December 1930): 437; Appleton, "The American Indian in the War," 110.

19. American Indians as Battalion Scouts, 1918, RHSGS, RAEF, RG 120, NA, Washington, D.C.

20. Summary of Incidents and Comments Recently Gathered Evidencing the Superior Fitness of American Indians over the Average Soldiers for Scout Service, 1918, RHSGS, RAEF, RG 120, NA, Washington, D.C.

21. Summary of Incidents and Comments, RHSGS, RAEF, RG 120, NA, Washington, D.C.

22. Ibid; American Indians as Battalion Scouts, RHSGS, RAEF; RG 120, NA, Washington, D.C.

23. American Indians as Battalion Scouts, RHSGS, RAEF, RG 120, NA, Washington, D.C.

24. Memorandum for Brigadier General Oliver L. Spaulding, Chief, Historical Section of the General Staff, February 15, 1919; Summary of Incidents and Comments, RHSGS, RAEF, RG 120, NA, Washington, D.C.

25. Summary of Incidents and Comments, RHSGS, RAEF, RG 120, NA, Washington, D.C.

26. Ibid.

27. American Indians as Battalion Scouts; Summary of Incidents and Comments, RHSGS, RAEF, RG 120, NA, Washington, D.C.

28. American Indians as Battalion Scouts, RHSGS, RAEF, RG 120, NA, Washington, D.C.

29. Bruce Catton, *The Civil War* (New York: Houghton-Mifflin Co., 1985), 149–51.

30. Snipers, Notes on a lecture by Major D. R. Mitchie, D.S.O., British Army; Summary of Incidents and Comments, RHSGS, RAEF, RG 120, NA, Washington, D.C.

31. Memorandum for Brigadier General Spaulding, RHSGS, RAEF, RG 120, NA, Washington, D.C.

32. Summary of Incidents and Comments, RHSGS, RAEF, RG 120, NA, Washington, D.C.

33. R. C. Craige, Superintendent of the Cheyenne River Agency, to Cato Sells, Commissioner of Indian Affairs, December 3, 1924, File no. 59342, General Services, Category 125, CCF, 1907–1939, RBIA, RG 75, NA, Washington, D.C.

34. The use of outdated or obscure languages for the purpose of outwitting an enemy in wartime did not originate during World War I. The British, for example, used Latin during the Boer War of 1899–1901 to confuse their Boer adversaries. See J. M. Marzolf, Major, Air Corps, to Chief Signal Officer, War Department, July 13, 1944, "Utilization of American Indians as Communication Linguists," Box 20, SRH 120, Records of the National Security Agency (hereafter cited as RNSA), RG 457, NA, Washington, D.C.

35. A. W Bloor, C.O., 142d Infantry, to the Commanding General, 36th Division, January 23, 1919, RHSGS, RAEF, RG 120, NA, Washington, D.C.; Wise, *The Red Man in the New World Drama*, 536–38; Peter Nabokov, *Native American Testimony: A Chronicle of Indian–White Relations from Prophecy to the Present, 1492–1992* (New York: Viking Press, 1991), 279; Lonnie White, "Indian Soldiers in the 36th Division," *Military History of Texas and the Southwest* 15 (1979): 17–18.

36. A. W, Bloor, C.O., 142d Infantry, to the Commanding General, 36th Division; Questionnaire of Lieutenant Ben Cloud, 164th Regiment, 41st Division, RHSGS, RAEF, RG 120, NA, Washington, D.C.; American Indian Languages, Utilization of American Indians as Communication Linguists, October 24, 1950, SRH 120, Box 20, RNSA, RG 457, NA, Washington, D.C.; William J. Morrisey, Lieutenant Colonel, 142d Infantry, to John R. Eddy, Lieutenant, Historical Section of the General Staff, March 2, 1919, RHSGS, RAEF, RG 120, NA, Washington, D.C.; "The Choctaws in the War," *The Native American* 19 (November 1918): 274–75.

37. Nabokov, *Native American Testimony*, 279; Henry Berry, *Make the Kaiser Dance* (New York: Doubleday and Company, 1978), 295; "Played Joke on the Huns," *The American Indian Magazine* 7 (Summer 1919): 101.

38. Paul Picotte, Interview by Joseph Cash, August 16, 1968, interview no. 0067, transcript, DDIOHC, South Dakota Oral History Center, IAIS, USD, Vermillion S.D.

39. Carolyn T. Foreman, *Indians Abroad, 1493–1938* (Norman: University of Oklahoma Press, 1943), 199–201; Rita Napier, "Across the Big Water: American Indians' Perceptions of Europe and Europeans, 1887–1906," in Christian F. Feest, ed., *Indians and Europe* (Aachen: Rader Verlag, 1987), 383–401.

40. Daniele Fiorentino, "Those Red Brick Faces: European Press Reactions to the In-

dians of Buffalo Bill's Wild West Show," in Feest, *Indians and Europe*, 408; Rudolf Conrad, "Mutual Fascination: Indians in Dresden and Leipzig," in Feest, *Indians and Europe*, 458–61; Karl May, *Winnetou*, trans. Michael Shaw (New York: Seabury Press, 1977), 192–93, 231–32, 266–68; Katja H. May, "German Stereotypes of Native Americans in Context of Karl May and Indianertümelei," in Naila Clerici, ed., *Victorian Brand Indian Brand: The White Shadow on the Native Image* (Torino, Italy: Il Segnalibro, 1993), 57–87.

41. Peter Bolz, "Life among the Hunkpapas: A Case Study in German Indian Lore," in Feest, *Indians and Europe*, 483–84.

42. Conrad, "Mutual Fascination," 459; Bolz, "Life among the Hunkpapas," 484.

43. "Now Laugh about the Sioux," *New York Times* August 16, 1918, 3.

44. Harold D. Lasswell, *Propaganda Technique in the World War* (New York: Garland Publishing, 1972; repr., New York: P. Smith, 1938), 82.

45. James Morgan Read, *Atrocity Propaganda, 1914–1919* (New Haven: Yale University Press, 1941), 132.

46. Alex Cadotta, to Newton D. Baker, Secretary of War, November 25, 1919, File no. 37699, General Services, Category 125, CCF, 1907–1939, RBIA, RG 75, NA, Washington, D.C.; Pierre Berton, *Vimy* (Toronto: McClelland and Steward, 1986), 241; American Indians as Battalion Scouts, RHSGS, RAEF, RG 120, NA, Washington, D.C; Herman J. Viola, *After Columbus: The Smithsonian Chronicle of the North American Indians* (Washington, D.C.: Smithsonian Books, 1990), 223; John H. Taber, *The Story of the 168th Infantry*, vol. 2 (Iowa City: State Historical Society of Iowa, 1925), 144–45.

47. American Indians as Battalion Scouts, RHSGS, RAEF, RG 120, NA, Washington, D.C.

48. Miscellaneous Correspondence of John R. Eddy, BIA, Letters Received, 1881–1906, RBIA, RG 75, NA, Washington, D.C.

49. Copely Amory, Second Lieutenant, to E. Bowditch, Lieutenant Colonel, December 26, 1918, File no. 21125, Adjutant General Files, Box 1200, RHSGS, RAEF, RG 120, NA, Washington, D.C. It seems likely that Eddy may have also known Joseph K. Dixon. Eddy was the superintendent of the Tongue River reservation from 1906 to 1914 and would have been in charge during all three Wanamaker expeditions. Whether or not he was aware of Dixon's similar efforts to create all-Indian units is unknown.

50. Special Orders No. 10, January 10, 1919; Oliver L. Spaulding, Jr., Brigadier General, Chief, Historical Section of the General Staff, February 1919, RHSGS, RAEF, RG 120, NA, Washington, D.C.; William Bruce White, "The American Indian as Soldier, 1890–1919," *The Canadian Review of American Studies* 7 (Spring 1976): 21–22; Wise, *Red Man in the New World Drama*, 533–34.

51. The American Indian, Evaluation of Eddy Questionnaire, RHSGS, RAEF, RG 120, NA, Washington, D.C.

52. Report of Otho W. Humphries, Captain, 167th Infantry, March 20, 1919, Box 3473, RHSGS, RAEF, RG 120, NA, Washington, D.C.

53. Questionnaires of Privates Thomas Linnley and James Thomas, 18th Infantry, Box 3471, RHSGS, RAEF, RG 120, NA, Washington, D.C.

54. Memorandum for Brigadier General Oliver L. Spaulding, February 15, 1919, Box 3471, RHSGS, RAEF, RG 120, NA, Washington, D.C.

55. Ibid.

56. Ibid.

57. John L. Morely, Captain, 142d Infantry to John R Eddy, First Lieutenant, Histori-

cal Section, G.S., April 10, 1919, Box 3473, RHSGS, RAEF, RG 120, NA, Washington, D.C.

58. Memorandum for Brigadier General Spaulding, RHSGS, RAEF, RG 120, NA, Washington, D.C.

59. Congress, House, Committee on Military Affairs, *Army Reorganization*, 66th Cong., 2d sess., January 28, 1920, 2183.

60. Questionnaire of John Elk, Company D, 139th Infantry, Box 3472, RHSGS, RAEF, RG 120, NA, Washington, D.C.

61. Questionnaire of Herman Yon, Company C, 307th Supply Train, Box 3473, RHSGS, RAEF, RG 120, NA, Washington, D.C.

62. Morely to Eddy, RHSGS, RAEF, RG 120, NA, Washington, D.C.

63. Questionnaire of Moran Lester, Company K, 39th Infantry, Box 3471, RHSGS, RAEF, RG 120, NA, Washington, D.C.

64. Questionnaire of Samuel A. Roy, Company E, 310th Infantry, Box 3473, RHSGS, RAEF, RG 120, NA, Washington, D.C.

65. Questionnaire of Joseph Esau, 7th Engineers, Box 3472, RHSGS, RAEF, RG 120, NA, Washington, D.C.

66. Evaluation by C. B. Cates, 96th Company, 6th Marines, Box 3471, RHSGS, RAEF, RG 120, NA, Washington, D.C.

67. F. B. Taylor, First Lieutenant, 64th Infantry, to Personnel Adjutant, 64th Infantry, Box 3472, RHSGS, RAEF, RG 120, NA, Washington, D.C.

68. Questionnaire of Tecumseh Anna, Battery B, 16th Field Artillery, Box 3471, RHSGS, RAEF, RG 120, NA, Washington, D.C.

69. Questionnaire of Edward Pine, Company B, 7th Infantry, Box 3471, RHSGS, RAEF, RG 120, NA, Washington, D.C.

70. Carl C. Brown, Captain, 144th Infantry, to Commanding Officer, 144th Infantry, March 4, 1919; Henry K. Cassidy, Captain, Company D, 165th Infantry, to Historical Section, G.S., March 14, 1919, RHSGS, RAEF, RG 120, NA, Washington, D.C.

71. The American Indian, Evaluation of Eddy Questionnaire; Memorandum for Brigadier General Spaulding, RHSGS, RAEF, RG 120, NA, Washington, D.C.

72. Remarks and Comments about Pvt. Ray C. Sanook, Cherokee Indian, RHSGS, RAEF, RG 120, NA, Washington, D.C.

73. Memorandum for Brigadier General Spaulding, RHSGS, RAEF, RG 120, NA, Washington, D.C.

74. "Good Common Sense," *The Indian School Journal* 19 (October 1918): 63.

75. Questionnaire of George Kaquatosh, Company B, 1st Machine-gunners Battalion, Box 3471, RHSGS, RAEF, RG 120, NA, Washington, D.C.

76. Questionnaire of Frank G. Osborne, Battery C, 17th Field Artillery, Box 3471, RHSGS, RAEF, RG 120, NA, Washington, D.C.

77. The American Indian, Evaluation of Eddy Questionnaire, RHSGS, RAEF, RG 120, NA, Washington, D.C.

78. Ranger Service: Proposed Effective Use of North American Indians Organization: Under Control of G-3, File no. 21125, Adjutant General Files, RHSGS, RAEF, RG 120, NA, Washington, D.C.

79. Ibid.

80. Ibid.

81. Wise, *Red Man in the New World Drama*, 544.

82. In 1919 Dr. Joseph K. Dixon, a member of the National American Indian Memo-

rial Association and advocate of preservation of Indian cultures and traditions, requested and received permission to use the Eddy questionnaires. They became an integral part of his argument of January 1920 for the establishment of segregated Indian units. The orders granting Dixon permission to use the questionnaires can be found in: Fox Conner, Chief of Staff, to the Adjutant General, September 23, 1919, File no. 21125, Adjutant General Files, RHSGS, RAEF, RG 120, NA, Washington, D.C.

83. Utilization of American Indians as Communication Linguists, 12, October 24, 1950, SRH 120, Box 20, RNSA, RG 457, NA, Washington, D.C.

Chapter 6

1. William Leckie, *The Buffalo Soldiers: A Narrative of the Negro Cavalry in the West* (Norman: University of Oklahoma Press, 1967); Arthur E. Barbeau and Florette Henri, *The Unknown Soldiers: Black American Troops in World War I* (Philadelphia: Temple University Press, 1974), 15–16; William Bruce White, "The Military and the Melting Pot: The American Army and Minority Groups, 1865–1924" (Ph.D. diss., University of Wisconsin, 1968), 272; Kelly Miller, *The World War for Human Rights* (New York: A. Jenkins and O. Keller, 1919), 524–26.

2. Barbeau and Henri, *Unknown Soldiers*, 16; White, "Military and the Melting Pot," 281; "Negro Conscription," *The New Republic* 12 (October 20, 1917): 317–18.

3. Barbeau and Henri, *Unknown Soldiers*, 14; White, "Military and the Melting Pot," 283; Emmett J. Scott, *Scott's Official History of the American Negro in the World War* (1919; repr., New York: Arno Press, 1969), 412, 459.

4. *Second Report of the Provost Marshal General to the Secretary of War on the Operations of the Selective Service System to December 20, 1918* (Washington, D.C.: Government Printing Office, 1919), 194–95.

5. Ibid., 193–94; John W. Chambers, *To Raise an Army: The Draft Comes to Modern America* (New York: The Free Press, 1987), 225–26; Charles H. Williams, *Negro Soldiers in World War I: The Human Side* (1923; repr., New York: AMS Press, 1970), 21–22; Jack D. Foner, *Blacks and the Military in American History* (New York: Praeger Publishers, 1974), 111.

6. One of the most unusual stories concerning African American troops in the war was that of Sylvester Clark Long. Born in Winston-Salem, North Carolina, to parents of Anglo, African, and Indian ancestry, Long attended a segregated school for black children as a youth. Partly in response to widespread discrimination against African Americans, Long successfully passed himself off as a "full-blood Blackfoot Indian" from Montana and secured enrollment at the Carlisle Indian School in Pennsylvania, where he changed his name to Long Lance. President Wilson later appointed him to West Point, but Long failed the academy's entrance exams. He enlisted in the Canadian army in 1917 and served without distinction until the war ended. He became an international celebrity as a great Indian officer and hero. Long committed suicide in 1932, however, fearing that his true identity as an African American was about to be exposed. See Donald B. Smith, *Long Lance: The True Story of an Imposter* (Lincoln: University of Nebraska Press, 1982); "Sylvester Long Lance," *The Indian's Friend* 30 (March 1918): 2–3; "Indian Officers in France," *American Indian Magazine* 5 (March 31, 1917): 45.

7. For evidence of the popularity of Indian soldiers in the United States Army, see Francis E. Leupp, *The Indian and His Problem* (New York: Charles Scribner's Sons, 1910),

167; Hugh L. Scott, *Some Memories of a Soldier* (New York: The Century Company, 1928), 563.

8. Congress, House, Committee on Military Affairs, *Argument by Dr. Joseph Kossuth Dixon*, 65th Cong., 1st sess., July 25, 1917, 32.

9. Congress, House, Committee on Military Affairs, *Army Reorganization*, 66th Cong., 2d sess., January 28, 1920, 2235.

10. "Where to Encamp the Negro Troops," *The Literary Digest* 55 (September 29, 1917): 14–15; Edwin R. Embree, "With the Negro Troops," *The Survey* 40 (August 10, 1918): 537; Scott, *Scott's Official History*, 75–81, 88–91, 92–104; Williams, *Negro Soldiers in World War I*, 36, 39, 55.

11. Leonard Dinnerstein et al., *Natives and Strangers: Ethnic Groups and the Building of America* (New York: Oxford University Press, 1979), 223; Miller, *World War for Human Rights*, 507, 552. Psychologist Thomas F. Pettigrew has pointed out that the pseudoscientific "intelligence" tests used during the period were often manipulated to suggest white superiority. Some tests, however, indicated that black recruits from such northern states as Ohio and Illinois had higher median scores than white recruits from Arkansas and Mississippi. See Thomas F. Pettigrew, *A Profile of the Negro American* (Princeton: D. Van Nostrand Co., 1964), 100–135; Brian W. Dippie, *The Vanishing American: White Attitudes and U.S. Indian Policy* (Middletown: Wesleyan University Press, 1982), 88–91.

12. The median mental age refers to the middle value in a distribution of mental ages (the age level at which a person is functioning cognitively). For example, if the mental ages of seven soldiers were 20, 17, 15, 13, 10, 9, and 8, the median mental age would be 13. See George O. Ferguson, Jr., "The Intelligence of Negroes at Camp Lee, Virginia," *School and Society* 9 (June 14, 1919): 723–726.

13. Lou B. Robison, Aurora, Illinois, to J. W. Dady, Superintendent of Red Cliff Agency, March 8, 1919, Information Re. Indian Soldiers, 1917–1919, Administrative Correspondence of the Superintendent, 1908–1922, Records of the Red Cliff School and Agency, 1901–1922, RBIA, RG 75, NA, Great Lakes Region, Chicago, Ill.

14. White, "Military and the Melting Pot," 274–76; Williams, *Negro Soldiers in World War I*, 63.

15. White, "Military and the Melting Pot," 292; Scott, *Scott's Official History*, 442; Barbeau and Henri, *Unknown Soldiers*, 155–63.

16. "Played Leapfrog wid Shells all ovah France," *The Literary Digest* 60 (January 18, 1919): 68.

17. "Croix de Guerre and Rare Praise for American Negro Troops," *The Literary Digest* 60 (January 18, 1919): 56; Osceola E. McKaine, "The Buffaloes: A First Class Fighting Regiment," *The Outlook* (May 22, 1918): 144.

18. Chambers, *To Raise an Army*, 223; Barbeau and Henri, *Unknown Soldiers*, 44; White, "Military and the Melting Pot," 286; Williams, *Negro Soldiers in World War I*, 140–46.

19. Barbeau and Henri, *Unknown Soldiers*, 111–60; Williams, *Negro Soldiers in World War I*, 156–61, 170, 185–88, 191–92, 205; "Croix de Guerre and Rare Praise for American Negro Troops," 55–60; Scott, *Scott's Official History*, 130–36; 178–89; "Bush Germans Better Watch that Chocolate Front," *The Literary Digest* 57 (June 15, 1918): 43–47. Charles Williams maintains that some black troops were awarded the Congressional Medal of Honor. See *Negro Soldiers in World War I*, 205. Jack Foner disputes this con-

tention in *Blacks and the Military in American History*, 164.

20. "Croix de Guerre and Rare Praise for American Negro Troops," 56; Scott, *Scott's Official History*, 276–77.

21. Harold D. Lasswell, *Propaganda Technique in the World War* (New York: Garland Publishing Co., 1972), 151–53; Earl Beck, "German Views of Negro Life in the United States, 1919–1933," *Journal of Negro History* 48 (January 1963): 25; Williams, *Negro Soldiers in World War I*, 70–71.

22. White, "Military and the Melting Pot," 292; Williams, *Negro Soldiers in World War I*, 164–66, 185, 191–92; Scott, *Scott's Official History*, 16; Foner, *Blacks and the Military in American History*, 123.

23. Scott, *Scott's Official History*, 459; "Croix de Guerre and Rare Praise for American Negro Troops," 60.

24. Miller, *World War for Human Rights*, 552–53.

25. Carole E. Christian, "Joining the Mainstream: Texas's Mexican Americans during World War I," *Southwestern Historical Quarterly* 92 (April 1989): 565–67; Matt S. Meier and Feliciano Rivera, *The Chicanos: A History of Mexican Americans* (New York: Hill and Wang, 1972), 132; W. Dirk Ratt, *Revoltosos: Mexico's Rebels in the United States, 1903–1923* (College Station: Texas A & M Press, 1981), 258–59, 276–77.

26. Christian, "Joining the Mainstream," 562; Pedro G. Castillo, "The Making of a Mexican Barrio: Los Angeles, 1890–1920" (Ph.D. diss., University of California, Santa Barbara, 1979), 57, 60–61; Ruth S. Lamb, *Mexican Americans: Sons of the Southwest* (Claremont: Ocelot Press, 1970), 106; Raul Morin, *Among the Valiant: Mexican-Americans in WWII and Korea* (Los Angeles: Borden Publishing Co., 1963), 19; *Mexicans in California: Report of Governor C. C. Young's Mexican Fact-Finding Commission* (San Francisco: R and E Associates, 1930), 19; Meier and Rivera, *Chicanos*, 127–28, 130.

27. Christian, "Joining the American Mainstream," 573; Chambers, *To Raise an Army*, 227–228; Meier and Rivera, *Chicanos*, 131; *Report of the Provost Marshal General to the Secretary of War on the First Draft under the Selective Service Act, 1917* (Washington, D.C.: Government Printing Office, 1918), 53; *Act Amending the Selective Service Act, Statutes at Large*, 40, sec. 1, 884–85.

28. Chambers, *To Raise an Army*, 226–29; Christian, "Joining the Mainstream," 575–76; *Report of the Provost Marshal General to the Secretary of War on the First Draft, 1917*, 88.

29. *Mexicans in California*, 73; Meier and Rivera, *Chicanos*, 131; Morin, *Among the Valiant*, 24, 113.

30. Christian, "Joining the Mainstream," 578–83.

31. Ibid., 587, 590–91.

32. Meier and Rivera, *Chicanos*, 133.

33. James W. St. G. Walker, "Race and Recruitment in World War I: Enlistment of Visible Minorities in the Canadian Expeditionary Force," *Canadian Historical Review* 70 (March 1989): 2, 5–8, 10–12; Michael L. Tate, "From Scout to Doughboy: The National Debate over Integrating American Indians into the Military, 1891–1918," *The Western Historical Quarterly* 17 (October 1986): 425–26.

34. Verne De Witt Rowell, "Canadian Indians at the Front," *Current History* 6 (August 1917): 291–92; James Dempsey, "The Indians and World War One," *Alberta History* 31 (Summer 1983): 4; Walker, "Race and Recruitment in World War I," 8–9, 14, 21, 25; Sally M. Weaver, "Six Nations of the Grand River, Ontario," in Bruce G. Trigger, ed., *Handbook of North American Indians*, vol. 15: *The Northeast* (Washington, D.C.:

Smithsonian Institute, 1978), 532; Fred Gaffen, *Forgotten Soldiers* (Penticon, B.C.: Theytus Books, 1985), 20–23.

35. Tate, "From Scout to Doughboy," 425; Dempsey, "Indians and World War One," 2–3; Walker, "Race and Recruitment in World War I," 25; Hana Samek, *The Blackfoot Confederacy, 1880–1920* (Albuquerque: University of New Mexico Press, 1987), 175; Gaffen, *Forgotten Soldiers*, 27, 28; Janice Summerby, *Native Soldiers: Forgotten Battlefields* (Ottawa: Government of Canada Veteran Affairs, 1993), 9–11.

36. Shelby D. Davis, "Reservoirs of Men: A History of the Black Troops of French West Africa" (Ph.D. diss., University of Geneva, 1934), 15, 46–47, 88, 97–98; Alice L. Conkin, "A Mission to Civilize: Ideology and Imperialism in French West Africa, 1895–1930" (Ph.D. diss., Princeton University, 1989), 189–90, 194; Robert W. July, *A History of the African People*, 3d ed. (New York: Charles Scribner's Sons, 1980), 401–6.

37. Mouhamed Moustapha Kane, "A History of Fuuta Tooro, 1890s–1920s: Senegal under Colonial Rule" (Ph.D. diss., Michigan State University, 1987), 339, 384, 396–97; Davis, "Reservoirs of Men," 138–39; Conkin, "Mission to Civilize," 190–92.

38. Davis, "Reservoirs of Men," 142–43; Byron Farwell, *The Great War in Africa, 1914–1918* (New York: W. W. Norton and Co., 1986), 28, 52, 55; Joe Harris Lunn, "Kande Kamara Speaks: An Oral History of the West African Experience in France, 1914–1918," in Melvin E. Page, ed., *Africa and the First World War* (New York: St. Martin's Press, 1987), 35–38.

39. Lunn, "Kande Kamara Speaks," 28; Conkin, "Mission to Civilize," 190–92; Davis, "Reservoirs of Men," 102, 158–59.

40. Scott, *Scott's Official History*, 277, 282–83; Lunn, "Kande Kamara Speaks," 39; Conkin, "Mission to Civilize," 191. Martin Gilbert's recent study of the war, *The First World War: A Complete History* (New York: Henry Holt and Co., 1994), suggests that Senegalese soldiers were terrified of poison-gas attacks and, at times, shot officers who ordered them to remain in their trenches. They also broke and ran in the face of machine-gun fire. See 145, 323.

41. James Morgan Read, *Atrocity Propaganda, 1914–1919* (New Haven: Yale University Press, 1941), 137–41; Davis, "Reservoirs of Men," 127.

42. Conkin, "Mission to Civilize," 200; Kane, "History of Fuuta Tooro," 415, 426–32; Davis, "Reservoirs of Men," 154; Lunn, "Kande Kamara Speaks," 29, 41, 43.

43. Sir Llewellyn Woodward, *Great Britain and the War of 1914-1918* (London: Methuen and Co., 1967), 99–100; Jeffrey Greenhut, "The Imperial Reserve: The Indian Infantry on the Western Front, 1914–1915" (Ph.D. diss., Kansas State University, 1978), 20–21; S. D. Pradhan, "Indian Army and the First World War," in Dewitt C. Ellinwood and S. D. Pradhan, eds., *India and World War I* (Columbia: South Asia Books, 1978), 51.

44. Greenhut, "Imperial Reserve," 18, 26–28; Zeres, "With the Frontier Cavalry," *Blackwood's Magazine* 201 (June 1917): 913; Pradhan, "Indian Army and the First World War," 56–57.

45. Greenhut, "Imperial Reserve," 43, 46–49.

46. Ibid.

47. James Willcocks, "The Indian Army Corps in France," *Blackwood's Magazine* 202 (July 1917): 2, 6; Greenhut, "Imperial Reserve," 19, 51; A. J. Stockwell, "The War and the British Empire," in John Turner, ed., *Britain and the First World War* (London: Unwin Hyman, 1988), 43; Pradhan, "Indian Army and the First World War," 53.

48. Greenhut, "Imperial Reserve," 26–28; Willcocks, "Indian Army Corps in France," 7; W. Kerr Connell, "Utam Singh," *The Spectator* 119 (July 28, 1917): 82; "India's Mar-

tial Enthusiasm," *The Literary Digest* 50 (January 16, 1915): 89; Read, *Atrocity Propaganda*, 137–38.

49. A. Yusef Ali, "India's Effort: Is it Sufficiently Understood?" *The Nineteenth Century* 81 (February 1917): 352; Greenhut, "Imperial Reserve," 31, 65; Gilbert, *First World War*, 94–95, 113, 140.

50. Greenhut, "Imperial Reserve," 71–72, 91; Gilbert, *First World War*, 130–31.

51. Ibid., 101–5, 151–58.

52. Greenhut, "Imperial Reserve," 65–66, 88, 94, 193–204; Stockwell, "War and the British Empire," 37; Willcocks, "Indian Army Corps in France," 12, 33; Ali, "India's Effort," 353; Dewitt C. Ellinwood, "The Indian Soldier, the Indian Army, and Change, 1914–1918," in Ellinwood and Pradhan, *India and World War I*, 183–84; Gilbert, *First World War*, 245.

53. Stockwell, "War and the British Empire," 43; Brenton Thoburn Badley, "Hindustan's Weight Against Hindenburg's Line," *World Outlook* 5 (March 1919): 9, 32.

54. Ellinwood, "Indian Soldier, the Indian Army, and Change," 179–207.

55. W. G. Tinckom-Fernandez, "India and the War," *The Nation* 100 (June 10, 1915): 647; "Indians and the War," *The Living Age* 284 (January 2, 1915): 57–58; A. J. Stockwell, "War and the British Empire," 43; Ali, "India's Effort," 365.

Chapter 7

1. Robert G. Valentine served as the commissioner of Indian affairs during the William Howard Taft administration, 1909–1913.

2. Department of the Interior, *ARCIA*, 65th Cong., 3d sess., 1918, H. doc. 1455, 6; *ARCIA*, 66th Cong., 2d sess., 1919, H. doc. 409, 14; Brian W. Dippie, *The Vanishing American: White Attitudes and U.S. Indian Policy* (Middletown: Wesleyan University Press, 1982), 194; Superintendent of the Five Civilized Tribes to Employees, Five Civilized Tribes, April 19, 1919, Circular 550, CCF, 1907–1936, Office of the Secretary, Box 1438, RDI, RG 48, NA, Washington, D.C.

3. *ARCIA*, 65th Cong., 2d sess., 1917, H. doc. 915, 8; *ARCIA*, 1918, 7; *ARCIA*, 1919, 14–15; Cato Sells, Commissioner of Indian Affairs, to Reservation Superintendents, April 5, 1918, Circular No. 1418, CCF, 1907–1936, Box 1438, Office of the Secretary, RDI, RG 48, NA, Washington D.C.

4. *ARCIA*, 1917, 7; "How Indian Chief Helped Uncle Sam," *New York Times*, January 26, 1919, sec. 3, p. 3; "Indians Work for Victory Loan," *The American Indian Magazine* 7 (Summer 1919): 104–5.

5. Frank E. Brown, "Pay Your Debts," *The Native American* 20 (February 8, 1919): 42–43; "Indians Are Aiding Uncle Sam Win War," *The Indian School Journal* 18 (April 1918): 351; "Indians Buy Liberty Loans," *The American Indian Magazine* 6 (Autumn 1918): 149.

6. Franklin K. Lane, Secretary of the Interior, to Walter W. Warwick, Comptroller of the Treasury, June 5, 1917; Warwick to Lane, June 9, 1917, CCF, 1907–1936, Box 1438, Office of the Secretary, RDI, RG 48, NA, Washington, D.C.

7. Congress, Senate, *Bill Authorizing the Secretary of the Interior to Invest Indian Funds in Government Bonds*, 65th Cong., 1st sess., S.J.R. 73, *Congressional Record*, vol. 55 (June 1, 1917), p. 3152; Congress, Senate, Committee on Indian Affairs, *Bill Authorizing the Secretary of the Interior to Invest Indian Funds in Government Bonds*, 65th

Cong., 1st sess., Srpt. 51 (June 11, 1917), serial n. 7249; Congress, House, Committee on Indian Affairs, *Bill Authorizing the Secretary of the Interior to Invest Indian Funds in Government Bonds*, 65th Cong., 1st sess., S.J.R. 73, *Congressional Record*, Vol. 55 (July 25, 1917), 5472; *Act Authorizing the Secretary of the Interior to Invest Indian Funds in Government Bonds*, Statutes at Large, 40, 591 (1917).

8. S. G. Hopkins, Assistant Secretary of the Interior, to George Whiteturkey, December 10, 1918, CCF, 1907–1936, Office of the Secretary, Box 1438, RDI, RG 48, NA, Washington, D.C.

9. S. G. Hopkins, Assistant Secretary of the Interior, to Mrs. Sallie Morrison, April 11, 1919, CCF, 1907–1936, Office of the Secretary, Box 1438, RDI, RG 48, NA, Washington, D.C.

10. Memorandum for the Assistant Secretary, January 13, 1919, CCF, 1907–1936, Records of the Secretary, Box 1438, RDI, RG 48, NA, Washington, D.C.

11. Toward the war's end, Commissioner Sells recommended that the Department of the Interior adopt an extraordinary measure dealing with Indian funds that seemed harmless at the time, but had the potential for tremendous fraud and abuse. In September 1918 Sells requested that reservation officials be allowed to endorse official checks and warrants drawn to the order of Indian soldiers who had gone abroad and who had not delegated powers of attorney to someone at home. The checks, Sells explained, "cannot in the nature of things be indorsed by [Indian soldiers], at least without very serious delay and inconvenience." Therefore, he recommended, reservation officials should be allowed to sign the checks and deposit them at local banks. Secretary Lane again asked the advice of Comptroller Warwick, who counseled that the Indian office could not authorize its agents to endorse checks without the previous consent of the Native Americans involved. See Cato Sells to Franklin Lane, September 18, 1918; Walter W. Warwick to Franklin Lane, October 7, 1918; CCF, 1907–1936, Box 1438, Office of the Secretary, RDI, RG 48, NA, Washington, D.C.

12. *ARCIA*, 1918, 7–9; Dippie, *Vanishing American*, 194; "Indians Conduct Red Cross Sale," *Word Carrier* 46 (July-August-September 1918): 16; "Indians Giving Freely to the War," *New York Times*, 11 July 1918, 6; Emma M. Larson, "On the War-work Path," *Sunset* 42 (February 1919): 42–43; Caroline D. Appleton, "The American Indian in the War," *Outlook* 122 (May 21, 1919): 111; "Cheyenne Present Peace Pipe to Red Cross," *The Indian's Friend* 31 (November 1918): 1; "Pueblos Join Red Cross," *The Indian's Friend* 31 (September 1918): 7.

13. Aaron McGaffey Beede, "The Dakota Indian Victory-Dance," *North Dakota Historical Quarterly* 9 (April 1942): 1174–76; Elwyn B. Robinson, *History of North Dakota* (Lincoln: University of Nebraska Press, 1966), 361–62.

14. Carolyn Niethammer, *Daughters of the Earth: The Lives and Legends of American Indian Women* (New York: Collier Books, 1977), 165–68.

15. *ARCIA*, 1918, 8; "Pe-retta's Gift to the Red Cross," *The Indian's Friend* 31 (November 1918): 5.

16. *ARCIA*, 1918, 7; Larson, "On the War-work Path," 42–43; "Indians at the Front," *The American Indian Magazine* 5 (March 1918): 64; "Indian Women Knit Industriously for Soldiers at the Front," *Indian School Journal* 18 (March 1918): 305; "Hampton Indians Are Doing their Bit," *The Indian's Friend* 30 (January 1918): 1.

17. "Work of Our Indians," *The Indian School Journal* 19 (October 1918), 63; Robert A. Trennert, "Educating Indian Girls at Nonreservation Boarding Schools, 1878–1920," *Western Historical Quarterly* 13 (July 1982): 287–88; *ARCIA*, 1919, 25; "Indian Girl

Nursing in France," *The Native American* 19 (December 28, 1918): 340; Charles Roberts, "The Cushman Indian Trades School and World War I," *American Indian Quarterly* 11 (Summer 1987): 224; Russel L. Barsh, "American Indians in the Great War," *Ethnohistory* 38 (Summer 1991): 280; Michael L. Tate, "From Scout to Doughboy: The National Debate over Integrating American Indians into the Military, 1891–1918," *Western Historical Quarterly* 17 (October 1986): 432–33; John R. Finger, *The Cherokee Americans: The Eastern Band of Cherokees in the Twentieth Century* (Lincoln: University of Nebraska Press, 1991), 36; Eva Chapell, "Tsianina—The Artist and Idealist, Grand-daughter of a Cherokee Chief," *Sunset* 42 (January 1919): 48; Carolyn T. Foreman, *Indians Abroad, 1493–1938* (Norman: University of Oklahoma Press, 1943), 217; Lee McCrae, "Indian Women Aid Their War Veterans," *Southern Workman* 59 (November 1930): 500–503.

18. Pamela M. White, "Restructuring the Domestic Sphere: Prairie Indian Women on Reserves: Image, Ideology, and State Policy, 1880–1930" (Ph.D. diss., McGill University, 1987), 249–50.

19. Francis Paul Prucha, *The Great Father: The United States Government and the American Indians*, vol. 2 (Lincoln: University of Nebraska Press, 1984), 704.

20. William R. Draper, "The Last of the Red Race," *Cosmopolitan* 32 (January 1902): 244–45. For an examination of popular stereotypes regarding Indian women, see Asebrit Sundquist, "Projections on a Blank Screen: Nineteenth Century Images of the American Indian Woman," in Naila Clerici, ed., *Victorian Brand Indian Brand: The White Shadow on the Native Image* (Torino, Italy: Il Segnalibro, 1993), 31–41.

21. *ARCIA*, 64th Cong., 2d sess., H. doc. 1899, 1916; Robert A. Trennert, Jr., *The Phoenix Indian School: Forced Assimilation in Arizona, 1891–1935* (Norman: University of Oklahoma Press, 1988), 133–34.

22. "Work of Our Indians," *The Indian School Journal* 19 (October 1918): 63; Clara Root, "What One Indian Girl Thinks of War," *The Indian School Journal* 18 (May 1918): 387–89; OIA, Bulletin No. 12, *The American Indian and Government Indian Administration*, 8.

23. Frederick E. Hoxie, *A Final Promise: The Campaign to Assimilate the Indians, 1880–1920* (Lincoln: University of Nebraska Press, 1984), x, xiii, 85–94.

24. John R. Finger, "Conscription, Citizenship and Civilization: World War I and the Eastern Band of Cherokee," *North Carolina Historical Review* 63 (July 1986): 284.

25. Cato Sells, "The First Americans as Loyal Citizens," *The American Review of Reviews* 57 (May 1918): 523–24.

26. Emma Matt Rush, "The Indians of Today," *Overland Monthly* 76 (July 1920): 38.

27. Rex F. Harlow, "American Indians Facing a New Era," *Current History* 23 (January 1926): 516.

28. *39th Annual Report of the Bureau of American Ethnology*, 66th Cong., 3d sess., 1918, H. doc. 1037, 9.

29. *ARCIA*, 1918, 18.

30. *ARCIA*, 1917, 6.

31. *ARCIA*, 1918, 3–4.

32. *ARCIA*, 1917, 25.

33. Ibid., 1917, 28.

34. David L. Wood, "American Indian Farmland and the Great War," *Agricultural History* 55 (July 1981): 249–50; Franklin K. Lane, "From the War-Path to the Plow," *The National Geographic Magazine* 27 (January–June 1915): 87. Janet A. McDonnell, *The Dispossession of the American Indian, 1887–1934* (Bloomington: Indiana University

Press, 1991), 29–30; Tate, "From Scout to Doughboy," 434.

35. Wood, "American Indian Farmland and the Great War," 249–50.

36. *ARCIA*, 1917, 26; Wood, "American Indian Farmland and the Great War," 250.

37. Joseph Medicine Crow, *From the Heart of the Crow Country* (New York: Orion Books, 1992), 119–20; *ARCIA*, 1917, 29–30.

38. "America Needs Men," *The American Indian Magazine* 5 (January–March 1917): 5; "Our Part in the War," *The Native American* 18 (April 14, 1917): 125; L. A. Lincoln, "Forward," *Oglala Light* (October 1917): 11–4; Clarence DuBose, "The Farmers' War Responsibility," *The Indian School Journal* 18 (January 1918): 211.

39. "A Liberal Indian Policy," *Word Carrier* 46 (July–August–September 1918): 14; Ross L. Spalsburg, "Editor's Comment," *Oglala Light* (June 1917): 20.

40. Wood, "American Indian Farmland and the Great War," 253, 261; *ARCIA*, 1917, 28; "War Activities in the Indian Bureau," June 11, 1918, General Services, Category 125, File no. 49055, CCF, 1907–1939, RBIA, RG 75, NA, Washington, D.C.; *ARCIA*, 1918, Table 11, 135.

41. *ARCIA*, 1918, Table 10, 130.

42. *ARCIA*, 1918, Tables 12 and 35, 140, 200; *ARCIA*, 1917, 32; "Lo, the Rich Indian Is Eager to Fight the Savage Hun," *Literary Digest* 57 (June 1918): 62; "War Activities in the Indian Bureau," General Services, Category 125, File no. 49055, RBIA, RG 75, NA, Washington, D.C.

43. McDonnell, *Dispossession of the American Indian*, 33; *ARCIA*, 1917, 29; Donald J. Berthrong, "Legacies of the Dawes Act: Bureaucrats and Land Thieves at the Cheyenne-Arapaho Agencies in Oklahoma," in Peter Iverson, ed., *The Plains Indians of the Twentieth Century* (Norman: University of Oklahoma Press, 1981), 42.

44. Wood, "American Indian Farmland and the Great War," 255; R. Douglas Hurt, *Indian Agriculture in America: Prehistory to the Present* (Lawrence: University of Kansas Press, 1987), 160–61.

45. Wood, "American Indian Farmland and the Great War," 255–60; "Indian Lands for Wheat Production," *The Native American* 19 (May 18, 1918): 154; Donald L. Parman, *Indians and the American West in the Twentieth Century* (Bloomington: Indiana University Press), 69.

46. Raymond J. DeMallie, "Pine Ridge Economy: Cultural and Historical Perspectives," in Sam Stanley, ed., *American Indian Economic Development* (Paris: Mouton Publishers, 1978), 257; Ernest L. Schusky, "The Evolution of Indian Leadership on the Great Plains, 1750–1950," *American Indian Quarterly* 10 (Winter 1986): 80; Lawrence C. Kelly, "Cato Sells, 1913–1921," in Robert M. Kvasnicka and Herman J. Viola eds., *The Commissioners of Indian Affairs, 1824–1977* (Lincoln: University of Nebraska Press, 1979), 246; *ARCIA*, 1918, Table 11, 135; Hurt, *Indian Agriculture in America*, 164–65.

47. Hurt, *Indian Agriculture in America*, 164–65; Hana Samek, *The Blackfoot Confederacy, 1880–1920* (Albuquerque: University of New Mexico Press, 1987), 176; Wood, "American Indian Farmland in the Great War," 254.

48. McDonnell, *Dispossession of the American Indian*, 38; Wood, "American Indian Farmland and the Great War," 262–63; *ARCIA*, 1919, 37; *ARCIA*, 1918, 41–42; *49th Annual Report of the Board of Indian Commissioners*, 65th Cong., 3d sess., 1918, H. doc. 1455, serial no. 7498, 361.

49. Kelly, "Cato Sells," 246; McDonnell, *Dispossession of the American Indian*, 36–38; DeMallie, "Pine Ridge Economy," 257; John Collier, *The Indians of the Americas* (New York: W. W. Norton and Co., 1947), 246; Gordon MacGregor, *Warriors without*

Weapons: A Study of the Society and Personality Development of the Pine Ridge Sioux (Chicago: University of Chicago Press, 1946), 37–39; Russel L. Barsh, "Plains Indian Agrarianism and Class Conflict," *Great Plains Quarterly* 7 (Spring 1987): 87; Parman, *Indians and the American West*, 70.

50. Medicine Crow, *From the Heart of the Crow Country*, 105; Loretta Fowler, *Arapahoe Politics, 1851–1978: Symbols in Crises of Authority* (Lincoln: University of Nebraska Press, 1982), 134; Schuskey, "Evolution of Indian Leadership on the Great Plains," 80.

51. Trennert, *Phoenix Indian School*, 162; *48th Annual Report of the Board of Indian Commissioners*, 65th Cong., 2d sess., H. doc. 915, 1917, serial no. 7358, 335–36; *ARCIA*, 1918, 11–12, 59; Barsh, "Plains Indian Agrarianism and Class Conflict," 86; *ARCIA*, 1919, 25.

52. Arrell Morgan Gibson, *The American Indian: Prehistory to the Present* (Lexington: D. C. Heath and Co., 1980), 522; "Indian School Boys Make Good in Ford Factory," *Manual Training Magazine* 18 (December 1916): 162–63; Barsh, "American Indians and the Great War," 284; Appleton, "American Indian in the War," 111–12; *ARCIA*, 1917, 43–44; *ARCIA*, 1918, 58–59; *ARCIA*, 1919, 25; Roberts, "Cushman Indian Trades School," 224.

53. *ARCIA*, 1917, 3.

54. Sean J. Flynn, "Western Assimilationist: Charles H. Burke and the Burke Act" (Master's thesis, Texas Tech University, 1988), 2; Prucha, *Great Father*, 2: 875–877; John F. Berens, "Old Campaigners, New Realities: Indian Policy Reform in the Progressive Era, 1900–1912," *Mid-America* 59 (January 1977): 62–63; Necah Furman, "Seedtime for Indian Reform: An Evaluation of the Administration of Commissioner Francis Ellington Leupp," *Red River Valley Historical Review* 2 (Winter 1975): 502–3.

55. During 1917 allotment work continued on the various Sioux reservations on the northern Plains, on the Gila River and Colorado River reservations in Arizona, and on the Fort Peck reservation in Montana. See *ARCIA*, 1917, 45.

56. Prucha, *Great Father*, 2: 770; Janet McDonnell, "Competency Commissions and Indian Land Policy, 1913–1920," *South Dakota History* 11 (Winter 1980): 22–25; Louis L. Pfaller, "James McLaughlin and the Rodman Wanamker Expedition of 1913," *North Dakota History* 44 (Spring 1977): 4; McDonnell, *Dispossession of the American Indian*, 30–31.

57. McDonnell, "Competency Commissions and Indian Land Policy," 28–30.

58. Berthrong, "Legacies of the Dawes Act," 43–44; Robert P. Nespor, "From War Lance to Plow Share: The Cheyenne Dog Soldiers as Farmers, 1879–1930s," *Chronicles of Oklahoma* 65 (Spring 1987): 63–64; McDonnell, "Competency Commissions and Indian Land Policy," 29–32.

59. *ARCIA*, 1917, 3–4; Hurt, *Indian Agriculture in America*, 162; *ARCIA*, 1919, Table 10, 116; Theodore W. Taylor, *The Bureau of Indian Affairs* (Boulder: Westview Press, 1984), 22; Joseph G. Jorgenson, "Political Economic Effects on American Indian Society, 1880–1980," *Journal of Ethnic Studies* 6 (1978), 14.

60. Hurt, *Indian Agriculture in America*, 162; *ARCIA*, 1919, Table 10, 116; Nespor, "From War Lance to Plow Share," 64; Barsh, "Plains Indian Agrarianism and Class Conflict," 86.

61. Thomas M. Holm, "Indians and Progressives: From Vanishing Policy to the Indian New Deal" (Ph.D. diss., University of Oklahoma, 1978), 208; *ARCIA*, 1919, 12.

62. "Indians Big Factor in War," *The Native American* 19 (September 21, 1918): 204–

5; O. R. Kopplin, "Full Blood Indians Volunteer," *The American Indian Magazine* 6 (Spring 1918): 56–57; "Red Men Are Apaches," *Word Carrier* 46 (July–August–September 1918): 16.

63. Frances Densmore, "The Songs of Indian Soldiers during the World War," *Musical Quarterly* 20 (October 1934): 421–23.

64. R. D. Theisz, "The Bad Speakers and the Long Braids: References to Foreign Enemies in Lakota Song Texts," in Christian F. Feest, ed., *Indians and Europe* (Aachen: Rader Verlag, 1987), 429–30.

65. Beede, "Dakota Indian Victory-Dance," 167–78.

66. Ibid.

67. Densmore, "Songs of Indian Soldiers," 423; Morris W. Foster, *Being Comanche: A Social History of an American Indian Community* (Tucson: University of Arizona Press, 1991), 125; William T. Hagan, *American Indians* (Chicago: University of Chicago Press, 1961), 148; "Lo, the Rich Indian, How he Blows his Coin," *The Literary Digest* 67 (November 20, 1920): 64.

68. Myrtle Lincoln, Interview by Julia A. Jordan, November 10, 1970, interview T-631, transcript, DDIOHC, Western History Collection, University of Oklahoma, Norman; "Indians Use Hun Scalps in Dance," *The American Indian Magazine* 7 (Fall 1919): 184.

69. Birdie Burns, Interview by Julia A. Jordan, May 27, 1968, interview T-260, transcript, DDIOHC, Western History Collection, University of Oklahoma, Norman.

70. Naomi W. LaDue, Interview by Cynthia Kelsey, August 14, 1968, interview no. 224, transcript, DDIOHC, South Dakota Oral History Center, IAIS, USD, Vermillion, South Dakota; "Notes from a Native Pastor's Sermon," *Word Carrier* 46 (July-August-September 1918): 14.

71. *49th Annual Report of the Board of Indian Commissioners*, 1918, 405.

72. Densmore, "Songs of Indian Soldiers," 424; Wilma G. Rhodes, "At an Indian Funeral," *New York Times* (27 October 1918), sec. 3, 1; "First Sioux to Die in the Present War," *The Indian's Friend* 30 (May 1918): 3.

73. Densmore, "Songs of Indian Soldiers," 425.

74. William K. Powers, "Plains Indian Music and Dance," in W. Raymond Wood and Margot Liberty, eds., *Anthropology of the Great Plains* (Lincoln: University of Nebraska Press, 1980), 219; Powers, *War Dance: Plains Indian Musical Performance* (Tucson: University of Arizona Press, 1990), 50–51.

75. Sharon O'Brien, *American Indian Tribal Governments* (Norman: University of Oklahoma Press, 1989), 80; Diane T. Putney, "Fighting the Scourge: American Indian Morbidity and Federal Policy, 1897–1928" (Ph.D. diss., Marquette University, 1980), 198–99.

76. Putney, "Fighting the Scourge," 198–99.

77. *ARCIA*, 1918, Table 14, 148; *ARCIA*, 1917, 16–17; Lewis Merriam et al., *The Problem of Indian Administration* (Baltimore: The John Hopkins Press, 1928), 204; *49th Annual Report of the Board of Indian Commissioners*, 1918, 357.

78. Prucha, *Great Father*, 2: 853; Department of the Interior, *ARCIA*, 1916, 4–9.

79. *ARCIA*, 1917, 17; Putney, "Fighting the Scourge," 204.

80. Putney, "Fighting the Scourge," 204–9; *Fiftieth Annual Report of the Board of Indian Commissioners*, 1919, 8; "Spanish Influenza: Three Day Fever: The Flu," *The Native American* 19 (October 19, 1918): 233–34; C. A. Anderson, "Influenza," *The Native American* 19 (November 30, 1918): 304; Jo Ann Blythe, "The Great Flu Epidemic of 1918," *Panhandle-Plains Historical Review* 66 (1993): 22–23.

81. "Stay at Home," *The Native American* 20 (February 8, 1919): 43; "Descendent of Seneca Chief, Artist, Soldier, Back from War," *The American Indian Magazine* 7 (Summer 1919): 104; Clara Winona Goodbear, Interview by David Jones, 25 June 25 1967, interview T-63, transcript, DDIOHC, Western History Collection, University of Oklahoma, Norman; Sadie Weller, interview by Kenneth Beals, 26 June 1967, interview T-59-2, transcript, DDIOHC, Western History Collection, University of Oklahoma, Norman, Oklahoma; Putney, "Fighting the Scourge," 209; "Influenza Chief Cause of Deaths in Home Camps," *New York Times*, January 26, 1919, sec. 3, 4.

82. *ARCIA*, 1918, 68–78; Kelly, "Cato Sells," 244; "Cato Sells Stops Payment of Money Due Indians," *The Indian School Journal* 18 (April 1918): 354; "No Booze Can Be Sold to Indians," *The Indian School Journal* 18 (December 1918): 172.

83. *48th Annual Report of the Board of Indian Commissioners, 1917, 349.*

84. Gibson, *American Indian*, 524–25; MacGregor, *Warriors without Weapons*, 91–101; Ray Blackbear, Interview by Julia Jordan, February 2, 1968, interview T-184, transcript, DDIOHC, Western History Collection, University of Oklahoma, Norman.

85. The Oklahoma Territory succeeded in banning peyote use in 1898, but the ban was repealed in 1918. In the early 1920s, the legislatures of North Dakota, South Dakota, Montana, Utah, Kansas, Nevada, Arizona, and Colorado all passed laws restricting the use of peyote. Gibson, *American Indian*, 524–25; Prucha, *Great Father*, 2: 785–89; *39th Annual Report of The National Indian Association* (New York: NIA, 1918), 12; "Indians Attend Peyote Pow Wow," *The Indian School Journal* 18 (April 1918): 354.

86. Evelyn C. Adams, *American Indian Education* (Morningside Heights: King's Crown Press, 1946), 65; Roberts, "Cushman Indian Trades School," 229–30; "Editor's Comment," *Oglala Light* (November–December 1917): 18; Christine Bolt, *American Indian Policy and American Reform* (London: Allen and Unwin, 1987), 227.

87. *ARCIA*, 1917, 4.

88. Prucha, *Great Father*, 2: 821–23; *ARCIA*, 1918, 15–33.

89. *ARCIA*, 1916, 9–11; Prucha, *Great Father*, 2: 826–27, 831; Frederick E. Hoxie, *A Final Promise: The Campaign to Assimilate the Indians, 1880–1920* (Lincoln: University of Nebraska Press, 1984), 204–6.

90. Margaret Szasz, *Education and the American Indian: The Road to Self-Determination, 1928–1973* (Albuquerque: University of New Mexico Press, 1974), 12; Hoxie, *Final Promise*, 196–97; "Brutal Punishment of Indian Children," *The American Indian Magazine* 5 (October–December 1917): 278–79; Prucha, *Great Father*, 2: 839–40.

Chapter 8

1. Dan Raincloud, Interview by Katherine Salter, August 1, 1968, interview no. 264, transcript, DDIOHC, South Dakota Oral History Center, IAIS, USD, Vermillion, S.D.

2. "Letter from Samuel LaPointe," *Word Carrier* 48 (March–April 1919): 5.

3. Edward M. Coffman, *The War to End All Wars* (New York: Oxford University Press, 1968), 357.

4. This was not always the case. Osage infantryman Oscar Sweeny, a veteran who served in the Philippines and in China, was beaten to death by a Bartlesville, Oklahoma, policeman, and Private David Tinker was shot and killed while at home on furlough. See Russel L. Barsh, "American Indians in the Great War," *Ethnohistory* 38 (Summer 1991): 294, 298.

5. *Second Report of the Provost Marshal General to the Secretary of War on the Operations of the Selective Service System to December 20, 1918* (Washington, D.C.: Government Printing Office, 1919), 198–99; Hugh L. Scott, *Some Memories of a Soldier* (New York: The Century Company, 1928), 563–64.

6. Norman B. Wiltsey, *Brave Warriors* (Caldwell: Caxton Printers, 1963), 226–27; John C. Ewers, "A Crow Chief's Tribute to the Unknown Soldier," *American West* 8 (November 1971): 34–35.

7. Assorted Newspaper clippings, File no. 45198-24, Special Series A, Old Box 17, New Box 72, General Records, 1907–1939, RBIA, RG 75, NA, Washington, D.C.; "War Honors for Indians," *New York Times* (29 June 1924): 14.

8. Resolution of Cherokee Indians of Robeson County, North Carolina, File no. 13-44, North Carolina; U.S. Senate Committee on Finance, to Enoch H. Crowder, Provost Marshal General, File no. 13-44, North Carolina, Box 225, States Files, 1917–1919, Records of the Provost Marshal General's Office, Records of the Selective Service System, 1917–1919, Record Group 163, Federal Records Center, Suitland, Md. Thomas Mails, *Fools Crow* (Garden City, N.Y.: Doubleday and Co., 1979), 91.

9. "Indians to Aid Harding," *New York Times* (August 4, 1920): 11; "Harding Says Start Idealism at Home," *New York Times* (August 19, 1920): 2.

10. Donald L. Parman, *Indians and the American West in the Twentieth Century* (Bloomington: Indiana University Press, 1994), 72–75; Arrell Morgan Gibson, *The American Indian: Prehistory to the Present* (Lexington: D. C. Heath and Co., 1980), 529–30.

11. Naomi W. LaDue, Interview by Cynthia Kelsey, August 14, 1968, interview no. 224, transcript. DDIOHC, South Dakota Oral History Center, IAIS, USD, Vermillion, S.D.

12. Moses Trudell, Interview by Herbert Hoover, August 11, 1970, interview no. 0545, transcript; George Jewitt, Interview by Steve Plummer, May 28, 1971, interview no. 682, transcript, DDIOHC, South Dakota Oral History Center, IAIS, USD, Vermillion, S.D.; Barsh, "American Indians in the Great War," 294.

13. Janet A. McDonnell, *The Dispossession of the American Indian, 1887–1934* (Bloomington: Indiana University Press, 1991), 36–38; David L. Wood, "American Indian Farmland and the Great War," *Agricultural History* 55 (July 1981): 262–65; R. Douglas Hurt, *Indian Agriculture in America: Prehistory to the Present* (Lawrence: University of Kansas Press, 1987), 164–65; Hana Samek, *The Blackfoot Confederacy, 1880–1920* (Albuquerque: University of New Mexico Press, 1987), 68, 82, 176; Gordon MacGregor, *Warriors without Weapons: A Study of the Society and Personality Development of the Pine Ridge Sioux* (Chicago: University of Chicago Press, 1946), 210–11.

14. Department of the Interior, OIA Bulletin No. 18, *The Progress of the Blackfeet Indians*, 1922, 4; Joseph G. Jorgensen, "Political Economic Effects on American Indian Society, 1880–1980," *Journal of Ethnic Studies* 6 (1978): 15.

15. See entries for "Guy W. Lambert" and "Chester A. Four Bears" in T. Emogene Paulson and Lloyd R. Moses, *Who's Who among the Sioux* (Vermillion: University of South Dakota Press, 1988), 79, 120–21; Andrew DeRockbrain, Interview by Steve Plummer, June 24, 1972, interview no. 833, transcript. DDIOHC, South Dakota Oral History Center, IAIS, USD, Vermillion, S.D.

16. R. R. Wadsworth, Supervisor in Charge, White Earth, Minnesota, to Cato Sells, Commissioner of Indian Affairs, January 27, 1921; H. M. Tidwell, Superintendent, Pine Ridge Reservation, to Sells, February 16, 1921; C. H. Allender, Financial Clerk in Charge,

Hoopa Valley Agency and School, to Sells, February 10, 1921; J. C. Hurt, Superintendent, Pawnee, Oklahoma, to Sells, January 25, 1921; Orders, Circulars, Circular Letters, 1920–21, Replies to Circular 1625, RBIA, RG 75, NA, Washington, D.C.; Parman, *Indians and the American West*, 64–65.

17. John R. Finger, "Conscription, Citizenship, and Civilization: World War I and the Eastern Band of Cherokee," *North Carolina Historical Review* 63 (July 1986): 304; James McCarthy, *A Papago Traveler: The Memories of James McCarthy*, ed. John G. Westover (Tucson: Sun Tracks and the University of Arizona Press, 1985), 87.

18. Josephine Gwin Wadena, Interview by Cynthia Kelsey, August 24, 1968, transcript, DDIOHC, South Dakota Oral History Center, IAIS, USD, Vermillion, S.D.; Thomas L. Slow, Private, U.S. Army, to Cato Sells, Commissioner of Indian Affairs, May 16, 1920, File no. 43775; Leroy H. Watson, Recruiting Officer, Camp Grant, Illinois, to Colonel I. J. Phillipson, Adjutant General's Office, December 17, 1919, File no. 108678, General Services, Category 125, CCF, 1907–1939, RBIA, RG 75, NA, Washington, D.C.

19. Alfrieda Garnenez, Interview by Gary Shumway, July 11, 1968, interview no. 381, transcript. DDIOHC, University of Utah Library, Western Americana Division, Salt Lake City. Mails, *Fools Crow*, 91, 150, 153.

20. Barsh, "American Indians in the Great War," 296.

21. Mails, *Fools Crow*, 110.

22. Joseph Oklahombi Reference File, Unidentified Newspaper clipping, Oklahoma Historical Society Archives, Oklahoma City.

23. Felix Renville, Interview by Gerald Wolff, August 11, 1976, interview no. 1529, transcript. DDIOHC, South Dakota Oral History Center, IAIS, USD, Vermillion, S.D.

24. "Indian Sniper is Stranded," *New York Times* (July 16, 1921): 11.

25. Anderson W. Cash, Secretary of American Indians of the World War, to Dr. Joseph Dixon, August 10, 1921, American Indians of the World War (Organization), Correspondence (1921), JKDC, WHMM, Indiana University, Bloomington; Nancy Shoemaker, "Urban Indians and Ethnic Choices: American Indian Organizations in Minneapolis, 1920–1950," *Western Historical Quarterly* 19 (November 1988): 436.

26. James Dempsey, "Problems of Western Canadian Indian War Veterans after World War I," *Native Studies Review* 5 (1988): 502–03.

27. Barsh, "American Indians in the Great War," 295; Finger, "Conscription, Citizenship, and Civilization," 307.

28. Ben Stonecool to Edgar B. Merritt, Assistant Commissioner of Indian Affairs, January 15, 1919, File no. 88709, General Services, Category 125, CCF, 1907–1939, RBIA, RG 75, NA, Washington, D.C.

29. Joseph K. Dixon to General John J. Pershing, December 10, 1921, Blackfeet Tribe, Conditions (1920–1925), JKDC, WHMM, Indiana University, Bloomington.

30. Theodore D. Breaulieu, "What of the Chippewas?," *The American Indian Magazine* 7 (Fall 1919).

31. Assorted Newspaper Clippings, File no. 66126, General Services, Category 125, CCF, 1907–1939, RBIA, RG 75, NA, Washington, D.C.

32. Ibid.

33. Charles D. Newton, Attorney General of the State of New York, to Edward H. Gohl, August 12, 1921, File no. 66204, General Services, Category 125, CCF, 1907–1939, RBIA, RG 75, NA, Washington, D.C.

34. Deborah S. Welch, "Zitkala-Sa: An American Indian Leader, 1876–1938" (Ph.D. diss., University of Wyoming, 1985), 154–55; Joelle Rostkowski, "The Redman's Appeal

for Justice: Deskaheh and the League of Nations," in Christian F. Feest, ed., *Indians and Europe* (Aachen: Rader Verlag, 1987), 435–53; Laurence M. Hauptman, *The Iroquois and the New Deal* (Syracuse: Syracuse University Press, 1981), 16; "Canadian Indians Want Case Submitted to Hague Court," *New York Times* (14 July 1922): 1; "Indians for Arbitration," *New York Times* (16 July 1922): 18; "Indians Startle Paris," *New York Times* (14 December 1923): 22.

35. Lawrence C. Kelly, *The Navajo Indians and Federal Indian Policy, 1900–1935* (Tucson: University of Arizona Press, 1968), 41–42.

36. Randolph C. Downes, "A Crusade for Indian Reform, 1922–1934," *Mississippi Valley Historical Review* 32 (December 1945): 334–36; Francis Paul Prucha, *The Great Father: The United States Government and the American Indian*, vol. 2 (Lincoln: University of Nebraska Press, 1984), 797–800; John Collier, *The Indians of the Americas* (New York: W. W. Norton and Co., 1947), 249; Robert Gessner, *Massacre: A Survey of Today's American Indian* (New York: Jonathon Cape and Harrison Smith, 1931), 289–308.

37. Gertrude Bonnin, Charles H. Fabens, and Matthew K. Sniffen, *Oklahoma's Poor Rich Indians: An Orgy of Graft and Exploitation of the Five Civilized Tribes—Legalized Robbery* (Philadelphia: Office of the Indian Rights Association, 1924), 5, 7, 13, 39; Prucha, *Great Father*, 2: 905–6.

38. Franklin K. Lane, Secretary of the Interior, "Hey, There! Do You Want a Home on a Farm?," Returned Soldiers, 1918, Administrative Correspondence of the Superintendent, 1908–1922, Records of the Red Cliff School and Agency, 1901–1922, RBIA, RG 75, NA, Great Lakes Region, Chicago, Ill.

39. Sarah Carter, *Lost Harvests: Prairie Indian Reserve Farmers and Government Policy* (Montreal: McGill-Queen's University Press, 1990), 251–52; J. W. Dady, Superintendent of the Red Cliff School and Agency, to Cato Sells, Commissioner of Indian Affairs, December 3, 1918, Returned Soldiers, 1918, Administrative Correspondence of the Superintendent, 1908–1922, Records of the Red Cliff School and Agency, 1901–1922, RBIA, RG 75, NA, Great Lakes Region, Chicago, Ill.; Dempsey, "Problems of Western Canadian Indian War Veterans," 11–12.

40. Franklin K. Lane, Secretary of the Interior, to Albert Isham, March 27, 1919, Box 1440, Central Classified Files, 1907–1936, Office of the Secretary, RDI, RG 48, NA, Washington, D.C.

41. "Work Calls Council on Indian Problems," *New York Times* (May 12, 1923): 18; "A Council on Indian Affairs," *New York Times* (May 14, 1923): 14; Gibson, *American Indian*, 535.

42. *ARCIA*, 66th Cong., 2d sess., H. doc. 409, 1919, 8–9.

43. *54th Annual Report of the Board of Indian Commissioners* (Washington, D.C.: Government Printing Office, 1923), 10; "Status of the American Indian," *The Indian's Friend* 32 (May 1920): 8; *ARCIA*, 66th Cong., 2d sess., H. doc. 409, 1919, 25; Caroline D. Appleton, "The American Indian in the War," *Outlook* 122 (May 21, 1919): 112; Barsh, "American Indians in the Great War," 292–93.

44. Department of the Interior, OIA, Bulletin 15, *American Indians in the Great War*, 1922, 2; *ARCIA*, 1919, 10–11.

45. *ARCIA*, 1919, 9–10.

46. Ibid., 10.

47. *ARCIA*, 1919, 11–12; OIA, Bulletin 15, *American Indians in the Great War*, 2–3; Cato Sells, Commissioner of Indian Affairs, to Evert Smith, July 25, 1919, File no. 61536,

General Services, Category 125, CCF, 1907–1939, RBIA, RG 75, NA, Washington, D.C.

48. "American Indians True to Tradition in War," *The Literary Digest* 60 (February 8, 1919): 54; "American Indians True to Tradition in the War," *Word Carrier* 48 (May–June 1919): 12.

49. John R. Gunn to Reuben Perry, Superintendent, Albuquerque Indian School, June 25, 1919, as quoted in Barsh, "American Indians in the Great War," 294.

50. "From Our Indian Pastor's Son," *Word Carrier* 48 (July–August 1919): 15.

51. Gertrude Bonnin, "Hope in the Returned Indian Soldier," *The American Indian Magazine* 7 (Summer 1919): 61–62.

52. Congress, House, Committee on Military Affairs, *Army Reorganization*, 66th Cong., 2d sess., January 28, 1920, 2235.

53. Henry M. Owl, "The Indian in the War," *Southern Workman* 47 (July 1918): 353.

54. "More and Better Indians, Thanks to White Help and the War," *The Literary Digest* 64 (March 13, 1920): 60; Emma Matt Rush, "The Indians of Today," *Overland Monthly* 76 (July 1920): 36.

55. William Keel, "What Training Camp has Done for the Indian," *The Indian School Journal* 19 (June 1919): 22–23.

56. Robert H. Lowie, *Indians of the Plains* (Lincoln: University of Nebraska Press, Bison Book ed., 1982), 112–13.

57. Don Rickey, Jr., "Warrior Soldiers: The All-Indian 'L' Troop, 6th U. S., Cavalry, in the Early 1890's," in Ray Brandes, ed., *Trooper West: Military and Indian Affairs on the American Frontier* (San Diego: Frontier Heritage Press, 1970), 58; Barsh, "American Indians in the Great War," 296; Victor M. Locke, Interview by Amelia F. Harris, 25 October 1937, interview no. 9003, transcript, Indian Pioneer History Project for Oklahoma, Oklahoma Historical Society, Oklahoma City; William N. Fenton, "Aboriginally Yours, Jesse J. Cornplanter: Hah-Wonh-Ish, The Snipe," in Margot Liberty, ed., *American Indian Intellectuals* (St. Paul: West Publishing Co., 1978), 184–86; Hauptman, *Iroquois and the New Deal*, 63, 146–50, 220; Garrick Bailey, "John Joseph Mathews," in Liberty, *American Indian Intellectuals*, 205–9.

58. "John Mackey, Sr.," in Paulson and Moses, *Who's Who among the Sioux*, 142–43; George Jewett, Interview by Steve Plummer.

59. Steve Spotted Tail, Interview by Joseph H. Cash, Summer 1967, interview no. 027, transcript, DDIOHC, South Dakota Oral History Center, IAIS, USD, Vermillion, S.D. John R. Finger, *Cherokee Americans: The Eastern Band of Cherokees in the Twentieth Century* (Lincoln: University of Nebraska Press, 1991), 85, 107.

60. Department of the Interior, OIA, Bulletin No. 12, *American Indians and Government Administration*, 1922, 3; *ARCIA*, 1919, 6–8.

61. "Indian Citizenship," *New York Times*, January 12, 1919, sec. 3, 1.

62. Joseph K. Dixon, Secretary, National Indian Memorial Association, to Woodrow Wilson, President of the United States, November 18, 1918, Series 4, Reel 246, Executive Office Files, 1913–1921, Woodrow Wilson Papers, Library of Congress, Washington, D.C.

63. *39th Annual Report of the National Indian Association* (New York: 1918), 33.

64. *40th Annual Report of the National Indian Association* (New York: 1919), 9.

65. E. B. Merritt, Assistant Commissioner of Indian Affairs, to Lemuel Bolles, National Adjutant, The American Legion, December 13, 1919, General Services, Category 125, File no. 105147, CCF, 1907–1939, RBIA, RG 75, NA, Washington, D.C.; Frederick E. Hoxie, *A Final Promise: The Campaign to Assimilate the Indians, 1880–1920* (Lincoln: University of Nebraska Press, 1984), 211.

66. Jorgensen, "Political Economic Effects on American Indian Society," 15; Louise Barnes LaBella, "The American Indian: His Progress and His Needs," *Education* 43 (March 1923): 421; Brian W. Dippie, *The Vanishing American: White Attitudes and U.S. Indian Policy* (Middletown: Wesleyan University Press, 1982), 196.

67. Chauncey Shafter Goodrich, "The Legal Status of the California Indian," *California Law Review* 14 (March 1926): 176–81.

68. Congress, Senate, *Bill to Confer Citizenship on Indians*, 65th Cong., 1st sess., H. R. 5526, *Congressional Record*, vol. 55, pt. 6, daily ed. (July 26, 1917), 5474; Congress, House, *Bill to Confer Citizenship on Indians*, 65th Cong., 2d sess., H. R. 9253, *Congressional Record*, vol. 56, pt. 2, daily ed. (January 1918), 1289; John W. Larner, Jr., "Braddock's Congressman M. Clyde Kelly and Indian Policy Reform, 1919–1928," *The Western Pennsylvania Historical Magazine* 66 (April 1983): 103.

69. Larner, "Braddock's Congressman M. Clyde Kelly," 103; *39th Annual Report of the National Indian Association, 1918*, 10–11; *50th Annual Report of the Board of Indian Commissioners* (Washington, D.C.: Government Printing Office, 1919), 6.

70. Congress, House, *Bill to Confer Citizenship on Certain Indians*, 66th Cong., 1st sess., H. R. 5007, *Congressional Record*, vol. 58, pt. 1, daily ed. (June 5, 1919), 720; *Indian Citizenship Act, Statutes at Large*, 41, 350 (1919).

71. Congress, House, Committee on Indian Affairs, *Bill to Confer Citizenship on Certain Indians*, 66th Cong., 1st sess., 1919, H. Rept. 140, serial no. 7592; Congress, Senate, Committee on Indian Affairs, *Bill to Confer Citizenship on Certain Indians*, 66th Cong., 1st sess., 1919, S. Rept. 222, serial no. 7590; Congress, House, *Bill to Confer Citizenship on Certain Indians*, 66th Cong., 1st sess., H. R. 5007, *Congressional Record*, vol. 58, pt. 8, daily ed. (October 25, 1919), 7505; R. Alton Lee, "Indian Citizenship and the Fourteenth Amendment," *South Dakota History* 4 (Spring 1974): 221.

72. Department of the Interior, *ARCIA*, 66th Cong., 3d sess., 1920, H. doc. 849, 10–11.

73. Robert S. Coleman, Chief Naturalization Examiner, to Mathias A. Sutton, Superintendent of Red Cliff School, August 14, 1920, List of Indians in World War, Red Cliff Agency, Administrative Correspondence of the Superintendent, 1908–1922, Records of the Red Cliff School and Agency, 1901–1922, RBIA, RG 75, NA, Great Lakes Region, Chicago, Ill.

74. Some Native Americans opposed citizenship because they feared its impact on tribal sovereignty and on government treaty obligations, or that it would result in the complete absorption of Indian peoples into Anglo society. See Angie Debo, *A History of the Indians of the United States* (Norman: University of Oklahoma Press, 1970), 353; D'Arcy McNickle, *Native American Tribalism: Indian Survivals and Renewals* (New York: Oxford University Press, 1973), 91; Laurence M. Hauptman, *The Iroquois and the New Deal* (Syracuse: Syracuse University Press, 1981), 5–6.

75. *An Act to Authorize the Secretary of the Interior to Issue Certificates of Citizenship to Indians, Statutes at Large*, 43, 253 (1924); Department of the Interior, Office of Indian Affairs, *Supplement to Bulletin No. 20 on Indian Citizenship*, 1924, 1; Lee, "Indian Citizenship and the Fourteenth Amendment," 221; Michael T. Smith, "The History of Indian Citizenship," *Great Plains Journal* 10 (Fall 1970): 34.

76. Gary C. Stein, "The Indian Citizenship Act of 1924," *New Mexico Historical Review* 47 (July 1972): 257–74; Margaret G. Szasz, "Indian Reform in a Decade of Prosperity," *Montana: The Magazine of Western History* 20 (Winter 1970): 24–26.

77. Russel L. Barsh, "Progressive-Era Bureaucrats and the Unity of Twentieth Century Indian Policy," *The American Indian Quarterly* 15 (Winter 1991): 1–17.

78. Robert F. Berkhofer, Jr., *The White Man's Indian* (New York: Alfred A. Knopf, 1978), 177; Jennings C. Wise, *The Red Man in the New World Drama* (Washington: W. F. Roberts Co., 1931), 545, 553; Stein, "The Indian Citizenship Act of 1924," 265. Stein also points out the fallacy of such beliefs. Although the Indian Citizenship Act of 1924 provided citizenship for Native Americans, it did not guarantee Indian suffrage rights.

79. See McNickle, *Native American Tribalism*, 91; Robert A. Trennert, Jr., *The Phoenix Indian School: Forced Assimilation in Arizona, 1891–1935* (Norman: University of Oklahoma Press, 1988), 161; William T. Hagan, *American Indians* (Chicago: University of Chicago Press, 1961), 148.

80. "Status of the American Indian," *The Indian's Friend* 32 (May 1920): 2.

81. Prucha, *Great Father*, 2: 793.

82. *40th Annual Report of the National Indian Association*, 1919, 10.

83. *Army Reorganization*, January 28, 1920, 2220.

84. Larner, "Braddock's Congressman M. Clyde Kelly and Indian Policy Reform," 104; also, see "Lo, the Poor Rich Indian in Industry," *Current Opinion* 72 (March 1922): 411–12, for Representative Kelly's stand on the BIA and Indian reform.

Conclusion

1. John J. Pershing, "Appreciation of the American Indian in the World War," September 18, 1920, Pershing, John J., Correspondence Relating to Indians in World War I, JKDC, WHMM, Indiana University, Bloomington.

2. Alison Bernstein, *American Indians and World War II: Toward a New Era in Indian Affairs* (Norman: University of Oklahoma Press, 1991), 44–45.

3. Duane K. Hale, "Indians in World War Two," *Chronicles of Oklahoma* 69 (Winter 1991): 422.

4. "The Winnebago Veterans Association Honors All Veterans," *Winnebago Indian News* (November 11, 1994): 6.

5. Nancy Shoemaker, "Urban Indians and Ethnic Choices: American Indian Organizations in Minneapolis, 1920–1950," *Western Historical Quarterly* 19 (November 1988): 436; Lee McCrae, "Indian Women Aid Their War Veterans," *The Southern Workman* 59 (November 1930): 502–3.

6. John R. Finger, "Conscription, Citizenship, and Civilization: World War I and the Eastern Band of Cherokee," *North Carolina Historical Review* 63 (July 1986): 307; George E. Frizzell, "The Politics of Cherokee Citizenship, 1898–1930," *North Carolina Historical Review* 61 (1984): 228–29; "Original American's First Vote," *The Literary Digest* 98 (September 22, 1928): 17; "Battling for Po Lo's Ballot," *The Literary Digest* 99 (October 6, 1928): 60–62.

7. Aaron McGaffey Beede, "The Dakota Indian Victory-Dance," *North Dakota Historical Quarterly* 9 (April 1942): 173–74.

Bibliography

Manuscripts

Joseph Oklahombi Reference File. Oklahoma Historical Society Archives, Oklahoma City, Oklahoma.

Joseph K. Dixon Collection. William Hammond Mathers Museum, Bloomington, Indiana.

M. Louisa I. Riggs Papers. United Church of Christ Archives, South Dakota Conference, Center for Western Studies, Augustana College, Sioux Falls, South Dakota.

Records of the Bureau of Indian Affairs. Record Group 75. National Archives, Washington, D.C.

———. Administrative Correspondence of the Superintendent, 1908–1922. Records of the Red Cliff School and Agency, 1901–1922. National Archives, Great Lakes Region, Chicago, Illinois.

———. Cherokee Nation Files.

———. General Services, Category 125, Central Correspondence Files, 1907–1939.

———. Legal and Legislative Records, 1917–1918. Tama Agency, 1896–1947.

———. Letters Received, 1881–1906.

———. Orders, Circulars, Circular Letters, 1920–1921.

———. Special Series A. General Records, 1907–1939.

Records of the Department of the Interior. Record Group 48, National Archives, Washington, D.C.

———. Office of the Secretary. Central Classified Files, 1907–1936.

Records of the Historical Section of the General Staff. Records of the American Expeditionary Force. Record Group 120. National Archives, Washington, D.C.

Records of the National Security Agency. Record Group 457. National Archives, Washington, D.C.

Records of the Provost Marshal Generals Office, 1917–1919. Records of the Selective Service System, 1917–1919. Record Group 163. Federal Records Center, Suitland, Maryland.

———. General Files, 1917–1919.

———. States Files, 1917–1919.

Woodrow Wilson Papers, Series 4, Executive Office Files, 1913–1921, Library of Congress, Washington, D.C.

Oral Histories

Doris Duke Indian Oral History Collection, General Library, Special Collections, Navajo Transcripts, University of New Mexico, Albuquerque, New Mexico.

Ration, Tom. Interview by Terry Carroll, October 11, 1968, Interview 358.

Doris Duke Indian Oral History Collection, South Dakota Oral History Center, Institute of American Indian Studies, University of South Dakota, Vermillion, South Dakota.

DeRockbrain, Andrew. Interview by Steve Plummer, June 24, 1972, Interview 833.

Everwind, Alec. Interview by Katherine Salter, July 23, 1968, Interview 168.

Jewett, George. Interview by Steve Plummer, May 28, 1971, Interview 682.

LaDue, Naomi W. Interview by Cynthia Kelsey, August 14 1968. Interview 224.

Picotte, Paul. Interview by Joseph Cash, August 16, 1968. Interview 0067.

Raincloud, Dan. Interview by Katherine Salter, August 1, 1968. Interview 264.

Renvielle, Felix. Interview by Gerald Wolff, August 11, 1976. Interview 1529.

Shooter, Leo. Interview by Steve Plummer, June 20, 1972. Interview 831.

Trudell, Moses. Interview by Herbert Hoover, August 11, 1970. Interview 0545.

Wadena, Josephine Gwin. Interview by Cynthia Kelsey, August 24, 1968. Interview 0187.

Doris Duke Indian Oral History Collection, University of Utah Library, Western Americana Division, Salt Lake City, Utah.

Garnenez, Alfrieda. Interview by Gary Shumway, July 11, 1968. Interview 381.

Lewis, Margaret. Interview by Floyd A. O'Neil, April 17, 1971. Interview 1257.

Doris Duke Indian Oral History Collection, Western History Collection, University of Oklahoma, Norman, Oklahoma.

Blackbear, Ray. Interview by Julia A. Jordan, February 2, 1968. Interview T-184.

Burns, Birdie. Interview by Julia A. Jordan, May 27, 1968. Interview T-260.

Goodbear, Clara Winona. Interview by David Jones, June 25, 1967. Interview T-63.

Lincoln, Myrtle. Interview by Julia A. Jordan, November 10, 1970. Interview T-631.

Tyner, Frank. Interview by J. W. Tyner, August 28, 1969. Interview T-512-3.

Weller, Sadie. Interview by Kenneth Beals, June 26, 1967. Interview T-59-2.

Works Progress Administration Oral History Project, Indian Pioneer History Project for Oklahoma, Oklahoma Historical Society, Oklahoma City, Oklahoma.

Locke, Victor M. Interview by Amelia F. Harris, October 25, 1937. Interview 9003.

Perkin, Shelby. Interview by Pete W. Cole, May 20, 1937. Interview 5911.

Government Documents

Act Amending the Selective Service Act, Statutes at Large. Vol. 40. 1918.

Act Authorizing the Secretary of the Interior to Invest Indian Funds in Government Bonds. Statutes at Large. Vol. 40. 1918.

Act to Regulate the Immigration of Aliens. Statutes at Large. Vol. 39. 1917.

An Act to Authorize the Secretary of the Interior to Issue Certificates of Citizenship to Indians. Statutes at Large. Vol. 43. 1924.

Army Reorganization Act. 66th Cong., 2d sess., Senate Documents. Vol. 13. Washington, D. C.: Government Printing Office, 1920.

Army Appropriation Act. Statutes at Large. Vol. 28. 1894.

Army Reorganization Act. Statutes at Large. Vol. 14. 1866.

Committee on Public Information. *War Message and Facts Behind It.* Washington, D.C.: Government Printing Office, 1917.

Department of the Interior. *Annual Report of the Commissioner of Indian Affairs.* 59th Cong., 2d sess., 1906. H. doc. 5.

Department of the Interior. *Annual Report of the Commissioner of Indian Affairs.* 64th Cong., 2d sess., 1916. H. doc. 1899.

Department of the Interior. *Annual Report of the Commissioner of Indian Affairs.* 65th Cong., 2d sess., 1917. H. doc. 915.

Department of the Interior. *Annual Report of the Commissioner of Indian Affairs.* 65th Cong., 3d sess., 1918. H. doc. 1455.

Department of the Interior. *Annual Report of the Commissioner of Indian Affairs.* 66th Cong., 2d sess., 1919. H. doc. 409.

Department of the Interior. *Annual Report of the Commissioner of Indian Affairs.* 66th Cong., 3d sess., 1920. H. doc. 849.

Department of the Interior. Office of Indian Affairs. Bulletin No. 6. *Indians, North America.* 1920.

Department of the Interior. Office of Indian Affairs. Bulletin No. 12. *The American Indian and Government Administration.* 1922.

Department of the Interior. Office of Indian Affairs. Bulletin No. 15. *American Indians in the Great War.* 1922.

Department of the Interior. Office of Indian Affairs. Bulletin No. 18. *The Progress of the Blackfeet Indians.* 1922.

Department of the Interior. Office of Indian Affairs. *Supplement to Bulletin No. 20 on Indian Citizenship.* 1924.

Hodge, Frederick Webb. *Handbook of Americans Indians North of Mexico.* Pt. 1, Bureau of American Ethnology Bulletin 30. Washington, D.C.: Government Printing Office, 1907.

Indian Citizenship Act. Statutes At Large. Vol. 41. 1919.

Report of the Provost Marshal General to the Secretary of War on the First Draft under the Selective Service Act, 1917. Washington, D.C.: Government Printing Office, 1918.

Second Report of the Provost Marshal General to the Secretary of War on the Operations of the Selective Service System to December 20, 1918. Washington, D.C.: Government Printing Office, 1919.

Selective Service Act. Statutes at Large. Vol. 40. 1917.

U.S. Congress. House of Representatives. *Bill to Confer Citizenship on Certain Indians.* 66th Cong., 1st sess., H. R. 5007. *Congressional Record.* Vol. 58, daily ed., June 5, 1919.

U.S. Congress. House of Representatives. *Bill to Confer Citizenship on Certain Indians.* 66th Cong., 1st sess., H. R. 5007. *Congressional Record.* Vol. 58, daily ed., October 25, 1919.

U.S. Congress. House of Representatives. *Bill to Confer Citizenship on Indians.* 65th Cong., 2d sess., H. R. 9253. *Congressional Record.* Vol. 56, daily ed., January 1918.

U.S. Congress. House of Representatives. *Bill to Raise Ten or More Regiments of Indian Cavalry.* 65th Cong., 1st sess., H. R. 3970. *Congressional Record.* Vol. 55, daily ed. April 30, 1917.

U.S. Congress. House of Representatives. Committee on Indian Affairs. *Argument by Dr. Joseph Kossuth Dixon*. 65th Cong., 1st sess., July 25, 1917.

U.S. Congress. House of Representatives. Committee on Indian Affairs. *Bill Authorizing the Secretary of the Interior to Invest Indian Funds in Government Bonds*. 65th Cong., 1st sess., S.J.R. 73. *Congressional Record*. Vol. 55, daily ed. July 25, 1917.

U.S. Congress. House of Representatives. Committee on Indian Affairs. *Bill to Confer Citizenship on Certain Indians*. 66th Cong., 1st sess., 1919. H. Rept. 140.

U.S. Congress. House of Representatives. Committee on Military Affairs. *Army Reorganization*. 66th Cong., 1st sess., September 3, 1919.

U.S. Congress. House of Representatives. Committee on Military Affairs. *Army Reorganization*. 66th Cong., 2d sess., January 28, 1920.

U.S. Congress, Senate. *Army Reorganization Act*. 66th Cong., 2d sess., Senate Documents. vol. 13, June 1920.

U.S. Congress. Senate. *Bill Authorizing the Secretary of the Interior to Invest Indian Funds in Government Bonds*. 65th Cong., 1st sess., S. J. R. 73. *Congressional Record*. Vol. 55, daily ed., June 1, 1917.

U.S. Congress. Senate. *Bill to Confer Citizenship on Indians*. 65th Cong., 1st sess., H. R. 5526. *Congressional Record*. Vol. 55, daily ed., July 26, 1917.

U.S. Congress. Senate. Committee on Indian Affairs. *Bill Authorizing the Secretary of the Interior to Invest Indian Funds in Government Bonds*. 65th Cong., 1st sess., 1917. S. Rept. 51.

U.S. Congress. Senate. Committee on Indian Affairs. *Bill to Confer Citizenship on Certain Indians*. 66th Cong., 1st sess., 1919. S. Rept. 222.

U.S. Congress. Senate. Committee on Indian Affairs. *Bill to Establish an Indian Military Academy*. 48th Cong., 1st sess., 1884. S. Rept. 348.

Newspapers and Indian Journals

"A Council on Indian Affairs." *New York Times*, May 14, 1923: 14.

"A Liberal Indian Policy." *Word Carrier of the Santee Normal Training School* 46 (July–August–September 1918): 14.

"Allies Widen Wedge with Reinforcements." *New York Times*, July 22, 1918: 2.

"America Needs Men." *The American Indian Magazine* 5 (January-March 1917): 5.

"American Indians at the Front." *The Native American* 19 (September 1918): 210.

"American Indians True to Traditions in the War." *Word Carrier of the Santee Normal Training School* 48 (May–June 1919): 12.

"The American Indian's Part in the World War." *The American Indian Magazine* 5 (July–September 1917): 151–53.

"An Indian Gets a Move on Himself: A Match for Twenty Huns." *Word Carrier of the Santee Normal Training School* 46 (October–November–December 1918): 20.

Anderson, C. A. "Influenza." *The Native American* 19 (November 30, 1918): 304.

"Apaches Active Allies." *The Indian's Friend* 31 (November 1918): 5.

"Army Bill to Come First in Senate." *New York Times*, April 3, 1920: 10.

Bonnin, Gertrude. "Hope in the Returned Indian Soldier." *The American Indian Magazine* 7 (Summer 1919): 61–62.

Breaulieu, Theodore D. "What of the Chippewas?" *The American Indian Magazine* 7 (Fall 1919): 141–42.

Brown, Frank E. "Pay Your Debts." *The Native American* 20 (February 8, 1919): 42–43.

Brown, John. "Our Part in the War." *The Native American* 18 (April 1917): 124–25.

"Brutal Punishment of Indian Children." *The American Indian Magazine* 5 (October–November 1917): 278–79.

"Canadian Indians Want Case Submitted to Hague Court." *New York Times*, July 14, 1922: 1.

"Cato Sells Stops Payment of Money Due Indians." *The Indian School Journal* 18 (April 1918): 354.

"Chairman Wadsworth." *New York Times*, April 3, 1920: 10.

"Cheyenne Present Peace Pipe to Red Cross." *The Indian's Friend* 31 (November 1918): 1.

"Chilocco Boys in the Army and Navy." *The American Indian Magazine* 5 (July 1917): 202.

"The Choctaws in the War." *The Native American* 19 (November 1918): 274–75.

"Creek Indians Rise Against the Draft." *New York Times*, June 6, 1918: 11.

"Descendent of Seneca Chief, Artist, Soldier, Back from War." *The American Indian Magazine* 7 (Summer 1919): 104.

"Discipline Code of the Oglala Indian Training School." *Oglala Light* (January 1919): 10–11.

DuBose, Clarence. "The Farmers' War Responsibility." *The Indian School Journal* 18 (January 1918): 211.

"Editor's Comments." *Oglala Light* (November–December 1917): 18.

"Farm Operations at Boarding School." *Oglala Light* (June 1917): 17.

"First Sioux to Die in the Present War." *The Indian's Friend* 30 (May 1918): 3.

"From Our Indian Pastor's Son." *Word Carrier of the Santee Normal Training School* 48 (July–August 1919): 15.

"Frontier Tactics Practiced on Germans, Sport for Redskins." *The American Indian Magazine* 7 (Summer 1919): 104.

"The Good Coming out of the War." *Word Carrier of the Santee Normal Training School* 46 (May–June 1918): 11.

"Good Common Sense." *The Indian School Journal* 19 (October 1918): 63.

"Hampton Indians Are Doing Their Bit." *The Indian's Friend* 30 (January 1918): 1.

"Harding Says Start Idealism at Home." *New York Times*, August 19, 1920: 2.

"How Indian Chief Helped Uncle Sam." *New York Times*, January 26, 1919, sec. 3: 3.

"The Indian and the Selective Service Law." *The Indian School Journal* 18 (October 1917): 72.

"Indian Citizenship." *New York Times*, January 12, 1919, sec. 3: 1.

"Indian Girl Nursing in France." *The Native American* 19 (December 28, 1918): 340.

"The Indian in the War." *Word Carrier of the Santee Normal Training School* 46 (July–August–September 1918): 15.

"Indian Lands for Wheat Production." *The Native American* 19 (May 18, 1918): 154.

"Indian Loyalty." *The Indian's Friend* 30 (November 1917): 6.

"Indian Officers in France." *The American Indian Magazine* 5 (March 1917): 45.

"Indian Patriotism." *Word Carrier of the Santee Normal Training School* 46 (January–February 1918): 3.

"Indian Quits Job." *The Indian School Journal* 17 (May 1917): 466.

"Indian School Training." *The American Indian Magazine* 6 (Spring 1918): 22–23.

"Indian Scouts on the Marne Outwit the Huns." *The Indian's Friend* 31 (September 1918): 1.

"Indian Scouts Penetrate Rear of Foe Lines to Bomb Officer's Banquet." *The Indian School Journal* 19 (October 1918): 63.

"Indian Sniper is Stranded." *New York Times*, July 16, 1921: 11.

"Indian Soldiers." *The Native American* 19 (June 1918): 170.

"Indian Type Warfare." *The American Indian Magazine* 6 (Autumn 1918): 148.

"Indian Women Knit Industriously for Soldiers at Front." *The Indian School Journal* 18 (March 1918): 305.

"Indians and the War." *The Indian's Friend* 30 (May 1918): 1.

"Indians Are Aiding Uncle Sam Win War." *The Indian School Journal* 18 (April 1918): 351.

"Indians Are Big Factor in the War." *The Indian's Friend* 8 (September 1918): 8.

"Indians Are a Big Factor in World War." *The Indian School Journal* 19 (October 1918): 68–69.

"Indians Are Loyal; Ready to Fight." *The American Indian Magazine* 5 (July 1917): 201.

"Indians at the Front." *The American Indian Magazine* 5 (March 1918): 64.

"Indians Attend Peyote Pow Wow." *The Indian School Journal* 18 (April 1918): 354.

"Indians Big Factor in War." *The Native American* 19 (September 21, 1918): 204–5.

"Indians Buy Liberty Loans." *The American Indian Magazine* 6 (Autumn 1918): 149.

"Indians Conduct Red Cross Sale." *Word Carrier of the Santee Normal Training School* 46 (July-August-September 1918): 16.

"Indians Enlist in the U.S. Navy." *The Indian School Journal* 17 (May 1917): 466.

"Indians for Arbitration." *New York Times*, July 16, 1922: 18.

"Indians Giving Freely to the War." *New York Times*, July 11, 1918: 6.

"Indians Go to the League." *New York Times*, September 1, 1923: 16.

"Indians in Europe." *The American Indian Magazine* 6 (Spring 1918): 21.

"Indians in Tableaux at the Aztec Ball." *New York Times*, February 7, 1925: 15.

"Indians Startle Paris." *New York Times*, December 14, 1923, 22.

"Indians the Same as Whites." *The American Indian Magazine* 5 (July 1917): 198.

"Indians to Aid Harding." *New York Times*, August 2, 1920: 11.

"Indians Use Bear Traps to Catch Huns." *The Indian School Journal* 19 (October 1918): 61.

"Indians Use Hun Scalps in Dance." *The American Indian Magazine* 7 (Fall 1919): 184.

"Indians Win Fame on Battle Front." *The Native American* 19 (March 1918): 18.

"Indians Work for Victory Loan." *The American Indian Magazine* 7 (Summer 1919): 104–5.

"Influenza Chief Cause of Deaths in Home Camps." *New York Times*, January 26, 1919, sec. 3: 4.

Keel, William. "What the Training Camp Has Done for the Indian." *The Indian School Journal* 19 (June 1919): 22–23.

Kopplin, O. R. "Full Blood Indians Volunteer." *The American Indian Magazine* 6 (Spring 1918): 56–57.

Letter from John Shawnego to Edgar A. Allen. *The Indian School Journal* 18 (November 1917): 123.

Letter from Lewis E. Sears to Edgar A. Allen. *The Indian School Journal* 18 (April 1918): 351.

Letter from Robert Starr to Edgar A. Allen. *The Indian School Journal* 18 (December 1917): 173.

Letter from Samuel Lapointe. *Word Carrier of the Santee Normal Training School* 48 (March–April 1919): 5.

Letter from William Baldridge to Edgar A. Allen. *The Indian School Journal* 18 (November 1917): 123.

Lincoln, L.A. "Forward." *Oglala Light* (October 1917): 11–14.

"Miss Edith Reid Weds Dr. Joseph K. Dixon." *New York Times*, August 27, 1925, 19.

Moorehead, Warren K. "Indians Anxious to Enlist." *New York Times*, November 2, 1917, 14.

"More Plans for Segregation." *The American Indian Magazine* 5 (July–September 1917): 203–4.

"More Segregation." *The Indian School Journal* 17 (April 1917): 431.

"No Booze Can Be Sold to Indians." *The Indian School Journal* 18 (December 1918): 172.

"Notes from a Native Pastor's Sermon." *Word Carrier of the Santee Normal Training School* 46 (July–August–September 1918): 14.

"Now Laugh at the Sioux." *New York Times*, August 16, 1918: 3.

"One Indian's Bit." *Word Carrier of the Santee Normal Training School* 48 (May–June 1919): 9.

"Oneida Indian Walks Fifty Miles to Report for Service." *The Indian's Friend* 31 (September 1918): 1.

"Our Indian Soldiers." *The American Indian Magazine* 7 (Summer 1919): 103.

"Our Military Men." *The Native American* 18 (June 1917): 205.

"Our Part in the War." *The Native American* 18 (April 14, 1917): 125.

Owl, Henry. "The Indian in the War." *The Word Carrier of the Santee Normal Training School* 46 (July-August-September 1918): 15.

Parker, Arthur C. "Why the Red Man Fights for Democracy." *The Native American* 18 (December 1917): 238–39.

"Pe-retta's Gift to the Red Cross." *The Indian's Friend* 31 (November 1918): 5.

"Phoenix Students in Army." *The Native American* 19 (June 1, 1918): 181.

"Phoenix Students in Navy." *The Native American* 19 (June 1, 1918): 181.

"Photographs of American Indians." *New York Times*, October 18, 1925, sec. 9: 13.

"Played Joke on the Huns." *The American Indian Magazine* 7 (Summer 1919): 101.

Pratt, Richard. "Wants No Separate Indian Regiments." *The Native American* 19 (February 1918): 49.

"Presentation of Aboriginal Life." *Word Carrier of the Santee Normal Training School* 46 (March–April 1918): 1.

"Preserving the Songs of the Red Man." *Word Carrier of the Santee Normal Training School* 50 (January–February 1921): 2.

"President Joins Indian Powwow." *New York Times*, July 5, 1923: 5.

"Probably Caucasian Camouflage." *The Indian School Journal* (December 18, 1917): 188.

"Pueblos Join Red Cross." *The Indian's Friend* 31 (September 1918): 7.

"Reasons Why Indians Should Join the Regular Army." *The American Indian Magazine* 5 (July–September 1917): 141–43.

"Red Men Are Apaches." *Word Carrier of the Santee Normal Training School* 46 (July-August–September 1918): 16.

Rhodes, Wilma G. "At an Indian Funeral." *New York Times*, October 27, 1918, sec. 3: 1.

Root, Clara. "What One Indian Girl Thinks of War." *The Indian School Journal* 18 (May 1918): 387–89.

"Schools Have Furnished More than 1,200 to Navy Alone." *The Indian School Journal* 18 (January 1918): 229.

"Six Carlisle Indians Join the Navy." *The Indian School Journal* 18 (January 1918): 229.

"Spanish Influenza: Three Day Fever: The Flu." *The Native American* 19 (October 19, 1918): 233–34.

Spalsburg, Ross L. "Editor's Comment." *Oglala Light* (June 1917): 20.

"Status of the American Indian." *The Indian's Friend* 32 (May 1920): 2, 7–8.

"Stay at Home." *The Native American* 20 (February 8, 1919): 43.

"Sylvester Long Lance." *The Indian's Friend* 30 (March 1918): 2–3.

Thunder, John. "Canadian Indian Soldiers Killed in France." *Word Carrier of the Santee Normal Training School* 46 (May–June 1918): 1.

"War Honors for Indians." *New York Times*, June 29, 1924: 14.

"The Winnebago Veteran's Association Honors All Veterans." *Winnebago Indian News*, November 11, 1994: 6–7.

Woodson, Guy. "From Oklahoma to Hillesheim (probably Hildesheim): A Soldier's Travels through WWI." *The National Tribune*, December 22, 1986: pt. 1.

"Work Calls Council on Indian Problems." *New York Times*, May 12, 1923: 18.

"Work of Our Indians." *The Indian School Journal* 19 (October 1918): 63.

Miscellaneous Reports

A Brief Sketch of the Record of the American Negro and Indian in the Great War. Report of the Committee on Information of the Boston Hampton Committee, 1919.

50th Annual Report of the Board of Indian Commissioners. Washington, D.C.: Government Printing Office, 1919.

54th Annual Report of the Board of Indian Commissioners. Washington, D.C.: Government Printing Office, 1923.

Final Report of the Provost Marshal General to the Secretary of War on the Operations of the Selective Service System to July 15, 1919. Washington, D.C.: Government Printing Office, 1920.

40th Annual Report of the National Indian Association. New York: 1919.

48th Annual Report of the Board of Indian Commissioners. Washington, D.C.: Government Printing Office, 1917.

49th Annual Report of the Board of Indian Commissioners. Washington, D.C.: Government Printing Office, 1918.

Mexicans in California: Report of Governor C. C. Young's Mexican Fact Finding Commission. San Francisco: R and E Associates, 1930.

39th Annual Report of the Bureau of American Ethnology, 66th Cong., 3d sess., 1918, H. doc. 1037.

39th Annual Report of the National Indian Association. New York, 1918.

Dissertations, Theses, Lectures

Camurat, Diane. "American Indians in the Great War: Real and Imagined." Ph.D. diss., Univerite Paris VII-Charles V, 1994.

Castillo, Pedro G. "The Making of a Mexican Barrio: Los Angeles, 1890–1920." Ph.D. diss., University of California, Santa Barbara, 1979.

Conkin, Alice L. "A Mission to Civilize: Ideology and Imperialism in French West Africa, 1895-1930." Ph. D. diss., Princeton University, 1989.

Davis, Shelby D. "Reservoirs of Men: A History of the Black Troops of French West Africa." Ph.D. diss., University of Geneva, 1934.

Flynn, Sean J. "Western Assimilationist: Charles H. Burke and the Burke Act." Masters thesis, Texas Tech University, 1988.

Greenhut, Jeffrey. "The Imperial Reserve: The Indian Infantry on the Western Front, 1914–1915." Ph.D. diss., Kansas State University, 1978.

Hibbard, Charles G. "Fort Douglas 1862–1916: Pivotal Link on the Western Frontier." Ph.D. diss., University of Utah, 1980.

Holm, Thomas M. "Indians and Progressives: From Vanishing Policy to the Indian New Deal." Ph.D. diss., University of Oklahoma, 1978.

Kane, Mouhamed Moustapha. "A History of Fuuta Tooro, 1890s–1920s: Senegal under Colonial Rule." Ph.D. diss., Michigan State University, 1987.

Putney, Diane T. "Fighting the Scourge: American Indian Morbidity and Federal Policy, 1897–1929." Ph.D. diss., Marquette University, 1980.

Schneider, Jack W. "Patterns of Cultural Conflict in Southwestern Indian Fiction." Ph.D. diss., Texas Tech University, 1977.

Trachtenberg, Alan. "Playing American." Unpublished lecture, William Hammond Mathers Museum, Indiana University, Bloomington, Indiana.

Welch, Deborah S. "Zitkala-Sa: An American Indian Leader, 1876–1938." Ph.D. diss., University of Wyoming, 1985.

White, Pamela M. "Restructuring the Domestic Sphere: Prairie Indian Women on Reserves: Image, Ideology, and State Policy, 1880–1930." Ph. D. diss., McGill University, 1987.

White, William Bruce. "The Military and the Melting Pot: The American Army and Minority Groups, 1865–1924." Ph. D. diss., University of Wisconsin, 1968.

Books

Adams, Evelyn C. *American Indian Education.* Morningside Heights: King's Crown Press, 1946.

American Indian Portraits from the Wanamaker Expedition of 1913. With an Introduction by Charles R. Reynolds, Jr. Brattleboro, Vermont: The Stephen Greene Press, 1971.

Anastasi, Anne. *Psychological Testing.* 6th ed. New York: MacMillan and Co., 1988.

Andrist, Ralph K. *The Long Death: The Last Days of the Plains Indians.* New York: MacMillan Publishing Co., 1993.

Barbeau, Arthur E., and Florette Henri. *The Unknown Soldiers: Black American Troops in World War I.* Philadelphia: Temple University Press, 1974.

Berkhofer, Robert F. *The White Man's Indian.* New York: Alfred A. Knopf, 1978.

Bernstein, Alison. *American Indians and World War II: Toward a New Era in Indian Affairs.* Norman: University of Oklahoma Press, 1992.

Berry, Henry. *Make the Kaiser Dance.* New York: Doubleday and Company, 1978.

Berton, Pierre. *Vimy.* Toronto: McClelland and Steward, 1986.

Blu, Karen I. *The Lumbee Problem: The Making of an American Indian People.* Cambridge: Cambridge University Press, 1980.

Bolt, Christine. *American Indian Policy and American Reform*. London: Allen and Unwin, 1987.

Bonnin, Gertrude, Charles H. Fabens, and Matthew K. Sniffen. *Oklahoma's Poor Rich Indians: An Orgy of Graft and Exploitation of the Five Civilized Tribes—Legalized Robbery*. Philadelphia: Office of the Indian Rights Association, 1924.

Brandes, Ray, ed. *Trooper West: Military and Indian Affairs on the American Frontier*. San Diego: Frontier Heritage Press, 1970.

Carter, Sara. *Lost Harvests: Prairie Indian Reserve Farmers and Government Policy*. Montreal: McGill-Queen's University Press, 1990.

Catton, Bruce. *The Civil War*. New York: Houghton Mifflin Co., 1985.

Chambers, John W. *To Raise an Army: The Draft Comes to Modern America*. New York: The Free Press, 1987.

Clerici, Naila, ed. *Victorian Brand Indian Brand: The White Shadow on the Native Image*. Torino, Italy: Il Segnalibro, 1993.

Coffman, Edward M. *The War to End All Wars: The American Military Experience in World War I*. New York: Oxford University Press, 1968.

Collier, John. *The Indians of the Americas*. New York: W. W. Norton and Co., 1947.

Crow, Joseph Medicine. *From the Heart of Crow Country*. New York: Orion Books, 1992.

Curtis, Edward S. *The North American Indians*. With an Introduction by John Epes Brown. New York: An Aperture Book, 1972.

Davis, Mary B., ed. *Native America in the Twentieth Century: An Encyclopedia*. New York: Garland Publishing Co., 1994.

DeBenedetti, Charles. *The Peace Reform in American History*. Bloomington: Indiana University Press, 1980.

Debo, Angie. *A History of the Indians of the United States*. Norman: University of Oklahoma Press, 1970.

Dinnerstein, Leonard, and Kenneth T. Jackson, eds. *American Vistas: 1877 to the Present*. 7th ed. New York: Oxford University Press, 1995.

Dinnerstein, Leonard, et al. *Natives and Strangers: Ethnic Groups and the Building of America*. New York: Oxford University Press, 1979.

Dippie, Brian W. *The Vanishing American: White Attitudes and U.S. Indian Policy*. Middletown: Wesleyan University Press, 1982.

Dixon, Joseph K. *The Vanishing Race*. New York: Doubleday, Page and Co., 1913.

Downey, Fairfax, and Jacques N. Jacobsen, Jr. *The Red/Bluecoats*. Fort Collins: The Old Army Press, 1973.

Dunlay, Thomas W. *Wolves for Blue Soldiers: Indian Scouts and Auxiliaries with the United States Army, 1860–1890*. Lincoln: University of Nebraska Press, 1982.

Ellinwood, Dewitt C., and S. D. Pradhan, eds. *India and World War I*. Columbia: Southeast Asia Books, 1978.

Ellis, John. *Eye-Deep in Hell: Trench Warfare in World War I*. New York: Pantheon Books, 1976.

Farwell, Byron. *The Great War in Africa, 1914–1918*. New York: W. W. Norton and Co., 1986.

Faunce, Hilda. *Desert Wife*. With an Introduction by Frank Waters. 1928. Reprint, Lincoln: University of Nebraska Press, 1981.

Feest, Christian F., ed. *Indians and Europe*. Aachen: Rader Verlag, 1987.

Finger, John R. *Cherokee Americans: The Eastern Band of Cherokees in the Twentieth Century*. Lincoln: University of Nebraska Press, 1991.

Fleming, Paula Richardson, and Judith Lynn Luska. *Grand Endeavors of American Indian Photography.* Washington, D. C.: Smithsonian Institution Press, 1993.

Foner, Jack D. *Blacks and the Military in American History.* New York: Praeger Publishers, 1974.

Foreman, Carolyn T. *Indians Abroad, 1493–1938.* Norman: University of Oklahoma Press, 1943.

Foster, Morris W. *Being Comanche: A Social History of an American Indian Community.* Tucson: University of Arizona Press, 1991.

Fowler, Loretta. *Arapahoe Politics, 1851–1978: Symbols in Crises of Authority.* Lincoln: University of Nebraska Press, 1982.

Gaffen, Fred. *Forgotten Soldiers.* Penticon, B.C.: Theytus Books, 1985.

Gessner, Robert. *Massacre: A Survey of Today's Indian.* New York: Jonathon Cape and Harrison Smith, 1931.

Gibson, Arrell Morgan. *The American Indian: Prehistory to the Present.* Lexington: D. C. Heath and Company, 1980.

Gilbert, Martin. *The First World War: A Complete History.* New York: Henry Holt and Co., 1994.

Grinnell, George B. *Two Great Scouts and Their Pawnee Battalion.* Lincoln: University of Nebraska Press, 1973.

Hagan, William T. *American Indians.* Chicago: University of Chicago Press, 1961.

———. *Indian Police and Judges: Experiments in Acculturation and Control.* Lincoln: University of Nebraska Press, 1966.

Harbord, James G. *America in the World War.* New York: Houghton Mifflin Co., 1933.

Hassrick, Royal B. *The Sioux: Life and Customs of a Warrior Society.* Norman: University of Oklahoma Press, 1964.

Hauptman, Laurence M. *The Iroquois and the New Deal.* Syracuse: Syracuse University Press, 1981.

Hertzberg, Hazel W. *The Search for an American Indian Identity.* Syracuse: Syracuse University Press, 1971.

Higginson, Ella. *The Vanishing Race and Other Poems.* Bellingham, Washington: C. M. Sherman, 1911.

Hoxie, Frederick E. *A Final Promise: The Campaign to Assimilate the Indians, 1880–1920.* Lincoln: University of Nebraska Press, 1984.

Hurt, R. Douglas. *Indian Agriculture in America: Prehistory to the Present.* Lawrence: University of Kansas Press, 1987.

Hyer, Sally. *One House, One Voice, One Heart: Native American Education at the Santa Fe Indian School.* Santa Fe: Museum of New Mexico Press, 1990.

Iverson, Peter. *Carlos Montezuma and the Changing World of the American Indians.* Albuquerque: University of New Mexico Press, 1982.

———. *The Plains Indians of the Twentieth Century.* Norman: University of Oklahoma Press, 1985.

Jones, Virgil C. *Roosevelt's Rough Riders.* New York: Doubleday and Company, 1971.

July, Robert W. *A History of the African People.* 3d ed. New York: Charles Scribner's Sons, 1980.

Kelly, Lawrence C. *The Assault on Assimilation: John Collier and the Origins of Indian Policy Reform.* Albuquerque: University of New Mexico Press, 1983.

———. *The Navajo Indians and Federal Indian Policy, 1900–1935.* Tucson: University of Arizona Press, 1968.

Kvasnicka, Robert M., and Herman J. Viola, eds. *The Commissioners of Indian Affairs, 1824–1977.* Lincoln: University of Nebraska Press, 1979.

Lamb, Ruth S. *Mexican Americans: Sons of the Southwest.* Claremont: Ocelot Press, 1970.

Lasswell, Harold D. *Propaganda Technique in the World War.* 1938. Reprint, New York: Garland Publishing Co., 1972.

Leckie, William. *The Buffalo Soldiers: A Narrative of the Negro Cavalry in the West.* Norman: University of Oklahoma Press, 1967.

Leupp, Francis L. *The Indian and His Problem.* New York: Charles Scribner's Sons, 1910.

Liberty, Margot. ed. *American Indian Intellectuals.* St. Paul: West Publishing Co., 1978.

Lomawaima, K. Tsianina. *They Called It Prairie Light: The Story of Chilocco Indian School.* Lincoln: University of Nebraska Press, 1994.

Lopez-Mena, Enrique. *A Biography of Homer P. Snyder.* New York: Van Rees Press, 1935.

Lowie, Robert H. *Indians of the Plains.* Lincoln: University of Nebraska Press, 1982.

MacGregor, Gordon. *Warriors without Weapons: A Study of the Society and Personality Development of the Pine Ridge Sioux.* Chicago: University of Chicago Press, 1946.

Mails, Thomas E. *Fools Crow.* Garden City: Doubleday and Co., 1979.

——. *The People Called Apache.* Englewood Cliffs: Prentice-Hall, 1974.

May, Karl. *Winnetou.* Translated by Michael Shaw. New York: The Seabury Press, 1977.

McCarthy, James. *A Papago Traveler: The Memories of James McCarthy.* Edited by John G. Westover. Tucson: Sun Tracks and the University of Arizona Press, 1985.

McDonnell, Janet A. *The Dispossession of the American Indian, 1887–1934.* Bloomington: Indiana University Press, 1991.

McNickle, D'Arcy. *Native American Tribalism: Indian Survivals and Renewals.* New York: Oxford University Press, 1973.

Meier, Matt S., and Feliciano Rivera. *The Chicanos: A History of the Mexican Americans.* New York: Hill and Wang, 1972.

Merriam, Lewis, et al. *The Problem of Indian Administration.* Baltimore: The Johns Hopkins Press, 1928.

Miller, Kelly. *The World War for Human Rights.* New York: A. Jenkins and O. Keller, 1919.

Mitchell, Lee Clark. *Witnesses to a Vanishing America: The Nineteenth Century Response.* Princeton: Princeton University Press, 1981.

Morin, Raul. *Among the Valiant: Mexican Americans in WWII and Korea.* Los Angeles: Borden Publishing Co., 1963.

Morris, James M. *History of the U.S. Army.* New York: Bison Books, 1986.

Moses, L. G., and Raymond Wilson, eds. *Indian Lives: Essays on Nineteenth and Twentieth Century Native American Leaders.* Albuquerque: University of New Mexico Press, 1985.

Nabokov, Peter, ed. *Native American Testimony: A Chronicle of Indian–White Relations from Prophecy to the Present, 1492–1992.* New York: Viking Press, 1991.

Nash, Gary B. *Red, White, and Black: The Peoples of Early North America.* Englewood Cliffs: Prentice Hall, 1992.

Niethammer, Carolyn. *Daughters of the Earth: The Lives and Legends of American Indian Women.* New York: Collier Books, 1977.

O'Brien, Sharon. *American Indian Tribal Governments.* Norman: University of Oklahoma Press, 1989.

Page, Melvin E., ed. *Africa and the First World War*. New York: St. Martin's Press, 1987.

Palmer, Frederick. *America in France*. New York: Dodd, Mead and Co., 1918.

Parman, Donald L. *Indians and the American West in the Twentieth Century*. Bloomington: Indiana University Press, 1994.

Paulson, T. Emogene, and Lloyd R. Moses. *Who's Who among the Sioux*. Vermillion: University of South Dakota Press, 1988.

Pettigrew, Thomas F. *A Profile of the American Negro*. Princeton: D. Van Nostrand Co., 1964.

Powers, William K. *War Dance: Plains Indian Musical Performance*. Tucson: University of Arizona Press, 1990.

Prucha, Francis Paul. *The Great Father: The United States Government and the American Indian*. Vol. 2. Lincoln: University of Nebraska Press, 1984.

Ratt, W. Dirk. *Revoltosos: Mexico's Rebels in the United States, 1903–1923*. College Station: Texas A&M Press, 1981.

Read, James Morgan. *Atrocity Propaganda, 1914–1919*. New Haven: Yale University Press, 1941.

Robinson, Elwyn B. *History of North Dakota*. Lincoln: University of Nebraska Press, 1966.

Samek, Hana. *The Blackfoot Confederacy, 1880–1920*. Albuquerque: University of New Mexico Press, 1987.

Scott, Emmett J. *Scott's Official History of the American Negro in the World War*. New York: Arno Press, 1969.

Scott, Hugh L. *Some Memories of a Soldier*. New York: The Century Co., 1928.

Smith, Donald B. *Long Lance: The True Story of an Imposter*. Lincoln: University of Nebraska Press, 1982.

Standing Bear, Luther. *My People the Sioux*. Edited by E. A. Brininstool. Lincoln: University of Nebraska Press, 1975.

Stanley, Sam, ed. *American Indian Economic Development*. Paris: Mouton Publishers, 1978.

Summerby, Janice. *Native Soldiers: Forgotten Battlefields*. Ottawa: Government of Canada Veteran Affairs, 1993.

Szasz, Margaret. *Education and the American Indian: The Road to Self-Determination, 1928–1973*. Albuquerque: University of New Mexico Press, 1974.

Tabor, John H. *The Story of the 168th Infantry*. Vol. 2. Iowa City: State Historical Society of Iowa, 1925.

Taylor, Theodore W. *The Bureau of Indian Affairs*. Boulder: Westview Press, 1984.

Terrell, John Upton. *American Indian Almanac*. 2d ed. New York: Barnes and Noble, 1994.

Trennert, Robert A., Jr. *The Phoenix Indian School: Forced Assimilation in Arizona, 1891–1935*. Norman: University of Oklahoma Press, 1988.

Trigger, Bruce G., ed. *Handbook of North American Indians*. Vol. 15: *The Northeast*. Washington, D.C.: Smithsonian Institute, 1978.

Turner, John, ed. *Britain and the First World War*. London: Unwin Hyman, 1988.

Upton, Richard. *The Indian as Soldier at Fort Custer, Montana, 1890–1895*. El Segundo, California: Upton and Sons, 1983.

Utley, Robert M. *Frontier Regulars: The United States Army and the Indian, 1866–1891*. New York: MacMillan Publishing Co., 1973.

————. *The Indian Frontier of the American West, 1846–1890.* Albuquerque: University of New Mexico Press, 1984.

Vandiver, Frank E. *Black Jack: The Life and Times of John J. Pershing.* College Station: Texas A & M University Press, 1977.

Viola, Herman J. *After Columbus: The Smithsonian Chronicle of the North American Indian.* Washington, D.C.: Smithsonian Books, 1990.

Waldo, Fullerton L. *America at the Front.* New York: E. P. Dutton and Co., 1918.

Walker, Dale L. *Death Was the Black Horse: The Story of Rough Rider Buckey O'Neill.* Austin: Madrona Press, 1975.

Westermeier, Clifford P. *Who Rush to Glory: The Cowboy Volunteers of 1898.* Caldwell: The Caxton Printers, 1958.

Westover, Wendell. *Suicide Battalions.* New York: The Knickerbocker Press, 1929.

Wheeler, Homer W. *Buffalo Days.* Indianapolis: The Bobbs-Merrill Co., 1925.

Who Was Who in America. Vol. 1. Chicago: The A. N. Marquis Co., 1942.

Who Was Who in America. Vol. 5. Chicago: Marquis' Who's Who, 1973.

Williams, Charles H. *Negro Soldiers in World War I: The Human Side.* New York: AMS Press, 1970.

Williams, Walter L., ed. *Southeastern Indians since the Removal Era.* Athens: University of Georgia Press, 1979.

Wiltsey, Norman B. *Brave Warriors.* Caldwell: Caxton Printers, 1963.

Wise, Jennings C. *The Red Man in the New World Drama.* Washington, D.C.: W. F. Roberts Co., 1931.

Wood, W. Raymond, and Margot Liberty, eds. *Anthropology of the Great Plains.* Lincoln: University of Nebraska Press, 1980.

Woodward, Llewellyn. *Great Britain and the War of 1914–1918.* London: Methuen and Co., 1967.

Wooster, Robert. *The Military and the United States Indian Policy, 1865–1903.* New Haven: Yale University Press, 1988.

Articles

Adams, David W. "Schooling the Hopi: Federal Indian Policy Writ Small, 1887–1917." *Pacific Historical Review* 48 (August 1979): 335–56.

Ali, A. Yusef. "India's Effort: Is It Sufficiently Understood?" *The Nineteenth Century* 81 (February 1917): 348–65.

Alley, John. "Oklahoma in the Spanish-American War." *Chronicles of Oklahoma* 20 (March 1942): 43–50.

"American Indians True to Tradition in War." *The Literary Digest* 60 (February 8, 1919): 54–57.

Appleton, Caroline D. "The American Indian in the War." *Outlook* 122 (May 21, 1919): 110–12.

Austin, Mary. "A'wa Tseighe Comes Home from the War." *The Nation* 124 (April 6, 1927): 367–69.

Badley, Brenton Thoburn. "Hindustan's Weight against Hindenburg's Line." *World Outlook* 5 (March 1919): 9, 32.

Barry, Richard. "The Red Man's Last Stand." *Harper's Magazine* 56 (May 25, 1912): 10.

Barsh, Russel L. "American Indians in the Great War." *Ethnohistory* 38 (Summer 1991): 276–303.

———. "An American Heart of Darkness: The 1913 Expedition for American Indian Citizenship." *Great Plains Quarterly* 13 (Spring 1993): 91–115.

———. "Plains Indian Agrarianism and Class Conflict." *Great Plains Quarterly* 7 (Spring 1987): 83–90.

———. "Progressive-Era Bureaucrats and the Unity of Twentieth Century Indian Policy." *The American Indian Quarterly* 15 (Winter 1991): 1–17.

"Battling for Po Lo's Ballot." *The Literary Digest* 99 (October 6, 1928): 60–62.

Beck, Earl. "German Views of Negro Life in the United States, 1919–1933." *Journal of Negro History* 48 (January 1963): 22–32.

Beebe, William. "A Red Indian Day." *The Atlantic Monthly* 122 (July 1918): 23–31.

Beede, Aaron McGaffey. "The Dakota Indian Victory Dance." *North Dakota Historical Quarterly* 9 (April 1942): 167–78.

Berens, John F. "Old Campaigners, New Realities: Indian Policy Reform in the Progressive Era, 1900–1912." *Mid-America* 59 (January 1977): 51–64.

Blackmar, Frank Wilson. "The Socialization of the American Indian." *The American Journal of Sociology* 34 (January 1929): 653–69.

Blumenthal, Henry. "Woodrow Wilson and the Race Question." *Journal of Negro History* 48 (January 1963): 1–21.

Blythe, Jo Ann. "The Great Flu Epidemic of 1918." *Panhandle-Plains Historical Review* 66 (1993): 1–23.

"Bush Germans Better Watch That Chocolate Front." *The Literary Digest* 57 (June 15, 1918): 43–47.

Cascino, Stephanie. "WWII Warriors." *Native Peoples* 8 (Winter 1995): 42–46.

Chappell, Eva. "Tsianina—The Artist and Idealist, Grand-daughter of a Cherokee Chief." *Sunset* 42 (January 1919): 48.

Christian, Carole E. "Joining the Mainstream: Texas's Mexican Americans during World War I." *Southwestern Historical Quarterly* 92 (April 1989): 559–95.

Connell, W. Kerr. "Utam Singh." *The Spectator* 119 (July 28, 1917): 82.

Corle, Edwin. "One More Hero." *The Forum* 91 (April 1934): 250–52.

"Croix de Guerre and Rare Praise for American Negro Troops." *The Literary Digest* 60 (January 18, 1919): 55–60.

Cunningham, Hugh T. "A History of the Cherokee Indians." *Chronicles of Oklahoma* 8 (December 1930): 406–43.

Cushing, H. C. "Military Colonization of the Indians." *The United Service* (September 1880): 370–75.

Dempsey, James. "The Indians and World War One." *Alberta History* 31 (Summer 1983): 1–18.

———. "Problems of Western Canadian Indian War Veterans after World War One." *Native Studies Review* 5 (1989): 1–18.

Densmore, Frances. "The Songs of Indian Soldiers during the World War." *Musical Quarterly* 20 (October 1934): 419–25.

"The Disappearance of the American Indian." *Current Literature* 34 (May 1903): 540–46.

Downes, Randolph C. "A Crusade for Indian Reform, 1922–1934." *Mississippi Valley Historical Review* 32 (December 1945): 331–54.

Draper, William R. "The Last of the Red Race." *Cosmopolitan* 32 (January 1902): 244–46.

Ellis, Richard N. "Indians at Ibapah in Revolt: The Goshutes, the Draft and the Indian Bureau, 1917–1919." *Nevada Historical Society Quarterly* 19 (Fall 1976): 163–69.

———. "Copper-Skinned Soldiers: The Apache Scouts." *Great Plains Journal* 5 (Spring 1966): 51–65.

Embree, Edwin R. "With the Negro Troops." *The Survey* 40 (August 10, 1918): 537–38.

Ewers, John C. "A Crow Chief's Tribute to the Unknown Soldier." *American West* 8 (November 1971): 30–35.

Feaver, Eric. "Indian Soldiers, 1891–1895: An Experiment on the Closing Frontier." *Prologue* 7 (Summer 1975): 109–18.

Ferguson, George O., Jr. "The Intelligence of Negroes at Camp Lee, Virginia." *School and Society* 9 (June 14, 1919): 723–26.

Finger, John R. "Conscription, Citizenship, and Civilization: World War I and the Eastern Band of Cherokee." *North Carolina Historical Review* 63 (July 1986): 283–308.

Frizzell, George E. "The Politics of Cherokee Citizenship, 1898–1930." *North Carolina Historical Review* (1984): 205–30.

Furman, Necah. "Seedtime for Indian Reform: An Evaluation of Commissioner Francis Ellington Leupp." *Red River Valley Historical Review* 2 (Winter 1975): 495–517.

Garth, T. R. "The Intelligence of Indians." *Science* 56 (December 1, 1922): 635–36.

Goodrich, Chauncey Shafter. "The Legal Status of the California Indian." *California Law Review* 14 (March 1926): 157–87.

Hale, Duane K. "Indians in World War Two." *Chronicles of Oklahoma* 69 (Winter 1991): 408–29.

Harlow, Rex F. "American Indians Facing a New Era." *Current History* 23 (January 1926): 512–17.

Houston, Donald E. "The Oklahoma National Guard on the Mexican Border, 1916." *Chronicles of Oklahoma* 53 (Winter 1975–1976): 447–62.

"If the Red Man Can Fight, Why Can't He Vote?" *The Literary Digest* 59 (December 21, 1918): 36–37.

"India's Martial Enthusiasm." *The Literary Digest* 50 (January 16, 1915): 89.

"Indian School Boys Make Good in Ford Factory." *Manual Training Magazine* 18 (December 1916): 162–63.

"Indian War Veterans Re-elect Barker Head." *The American Indian* 1 (October 1926): 16.

"Indians and the War." *The Living Age* 284 (January 2, 1915): 57–58.

"Indians Fight for Uncle Sam." *The Literary Digest* 56 (March 2, 1918): 81.

Jorgensen, Joseph G. "Political Economic Effects on American Indian Society, 1880–1980." *Journal of Ethnic Studies* 6 (1978): 1–82.

Krouse, Susan A. "Photographing the Vanishing Race." *Visual Anthropology* 3 (1990): 213–33.

LaBella, Louise Barnes. "The American Indian: His Progress and His Needs." *Education* 43 (March 1923): 416–21.

Lane, Franklin K. "From the War-path to the Plow." *The National Geographic Magazine* 27 (January-June 1915): 73–87.

Larner, John W., Jr. "Braddock's Congressman M. Clyde Kelly and Indian Policy Reform, 1919–1928." *The Western Pennsylvania Historical Magazine* 66 (April 1983): 97–111.

Larson, Emma M. "On the War-work Path." *Sunset* 42 (February 1919): 42–43.

Lee, R. Alton. "Indian Citizenship and the Fourteenth Amendment." *South Dakota History* 4 (Spring 1974): 198–221.

Lewis, David R. "Still Native: The Significance of Native Americans in the History of the Twentieth Century American West." *Western Historical Quarterly* 24 (May 1993): 203–27.

"Lo, the Poor Rich Indian in Industry." *Current Opinion* 72 (March 1922): 411–12.

"Lo, the Rich Indian, How He Blows His Coin." *The Literary Digest* 67 (November 20, 1920): 64.

"Lo, the Rich Indian is Eager to Fight the Savage Hun." *The Literary Digest* 57 (June 1918): 56–62.

Martin, Jill E. "Neither Fish, Flesh, Fowl nor Good Red Herring: The Citizenship of American Indians, 1830–1924." *Journal of the West* 29 (July 1990): 80–86.

McCrae, Lee. "Indian Women Aid Their Veterans." *Southern Workman* 59 (November 1930): 500–503.

McDonnell, Janet. "Competency Commissions and Indian Land Policy, 1913–1920." *South Dakota History* 11 (Winter 1980): 21–34.

McKaine, Osceola E. "The Buffaloes: A First Class Fighting Regiment." *The Outlook* (May 22, 1918): 144–47.

Millard, Thomas F. "The Passing of the American Indian." *The Forum* 34 (January 1903): 466–80.

"More and Better Indians, Thanks to White Help and the War." *The Literary Digest* 64 (March 13, 1920): 58–60.

"Negro Conscription." *The New Republic* 12 (October 12, 1917): 317–18.

Nespor, Robert P. "From War Lance to Plow Share: The Cheyenne Dog Soldiers as Farmers, 1879–1930s." *Chronicles of Oklahoma* 65 (Spring 1987): 42–75.

"Original American's First Vote." *The Literary Digest* 98 (September 22, 1928): 17.

Owl, Henry M. "The Indian in the War." *Southern Workman* 47 (July 1918): 353–55.

Paterson, Arthur E. "The Changing Indian and His Changing Problems." *Southern Workman* 48 (November 1919): 593–98.

Pfaller, Louis L. "James McLaughlin and the Rodman Wanamaker Expedition of 1913." *North Dakota History* 44 (Spring 1977): 4–11.

"Played Leapfrog wid Shells all ovah France." *The Literary Digest* 60 (January 18, 1919): 68.

Powell, William H. "The Indian as Soldier." *The United Service* 3 (March 1890): 229–38.

———. "The Indian Problem." *The United Service* 5 (April 1891): 329–38.

Price, Byron. "The Utopian Experiment: The Army and the Indian, 1890–1897." *By Valor and Arms* 3 (Spring 1977): 15–35.

Roberts, Charles. "The Cushman Indian Trades School and World War I." *American Indian Quarterly* 11 (Summer 1987): 221–39.

Rowell, Verne de Witt. "Canadian Indians at the Front." *Current History* 6 (August 1917): 290–93.

Rush, Emma Matt. "The Indians of Today." *Overland Monthly* 76 (July 1920): 35–39.

Schurz, Carl. "Present Aspects of the Indian Problem." *North American Review* 133 (July 1881): 1–24.

Schuskey, Ernest L. "The Evolution of Indian Leadership on the Great Plains, 1750–1950." *American Indian Quarterly* 10 (Winter 1986): 65–82.

Sells, Cato. "The First Americans as Loyal Citizens." *The American Review of Reviews* 57 (May 1918): 523–24.

Shannon, James A. "With the Apache Scouts in Mexico." *Journal of the United States Cavalry Association* 27 (April 1917): 539–57.

Sherman, Frank C. "The Indians Made an Enviable Record during World War." *The American Indian* 2 (January 1928): 12.

Shoemaker, Nancy. "Urban Indians and Ethnic Choices: American Indian Organizations in Minneapolis, 1920–1950." *Western Historical Quarterly* 19 (November 1988): 431–47.

Smith, Michael T. "The History of Indian Citizenship." *Great Plains Journal* 10 (Fall 1970): 25–35.

Smith, O'Hara. "Chief Lo Was with the Lost Battalion in France." *The American Indian* 1 (November 1926): 9.

———. "Indian Soldier Has Thrilling Experience in No Man's Land." *The American Indian* 1 (April 1927): 3.

Stein, Gary C. "The Indian Citizenship Act of 1924." *New Mexico Historical Review* 47 (July 1972): 257–74.

Szasz, Margaret G. "Indian Reform in a Decade of Prosperity." *Montana: The Magazine of Western History* 20 (Winter 1970): 16–27.

Tate, Michael L. "From Scout to Doughboy: The National Debate over Integrating American Indians into the Military, 1891–1918." *Western Historical Quarterly* 17 (October 1986): 417–37.

———. "Pershing's Pets: Apache Scouts in the Mexican Punitive Expedition of 1916." *New Mexico Historical Review* 66 (January 1991): 49–71.

———. "Soldiers of the Line: Apache Companies in the U.S. Army, 1891–1897." *Arizona and the West* 16 (Winter 1974): 342–64.

Tinckom-Fernandez, W. G. "India and the War." *The Nation* 100 (June 10, 1915): 646–48.

Trennert, Robert A. Jr. "Educating Indian Girls at Nonreservation Boarding Schools, 1878–1920." *Western Historical Quarterly* 17 (October 1986): 271–90.

Walker, Francis A. "The Indian Question." *North American Review* 116 (April 1873): 342–45, 365.

Walker, James W. St. G. "Race and Recruitment in World War I: Enlistment of Visible Minorities in the Canadian Expeditionary Force." *Canadian Historical Review* 70 (March 1989): 1–26.

Weist, Katherine M. "Ned Casey and his Cheyenne Scouts: A Noble Experiment in an Atmosphere of Tension." *Montana: The Magazine of Western History* 27 (Winter 1977): 26–39.

"Where to Encamp the Negro Troops." *The Literary Digest* 55 (September 29, 1917): 14–15.

White, Lonnie. "Indian Soldiers of the 36th Division." *Military History of Texas and the Southwest* 15 (1979): 8–20.

"White Soldiers and Red Indian Scouts in the Villa Chase." *Collier's* 57 (April 29, 1916): 8.

White, William Bruce. "The American Indian as Soldier, 1890–1919." *The Canadian Review of American Studies* 7 (Spring 1976): 15–25.

Willcocks, James. "The Indian Army Corps in France." *Blackwood's Magazine* 202 (July 1917): 1–33.

Wilson, Thomas H. "The Indian as Soldier." *The Illustrated American* 18 (1895).

Wood, David L. "American Indian Farmland and the Great War." *Agricultural History* 55 (July 1981): 249–65.

———. "Gosiute-Shoshone Draft Resistance, 1917–1918." *Utah Historical Quarterly* 49 (Spring 1981): 173–88.

Zeres, "With the Frontier Cavalry." *Blackwood's Magazine* 201 (June 1917): 912–23.

Index